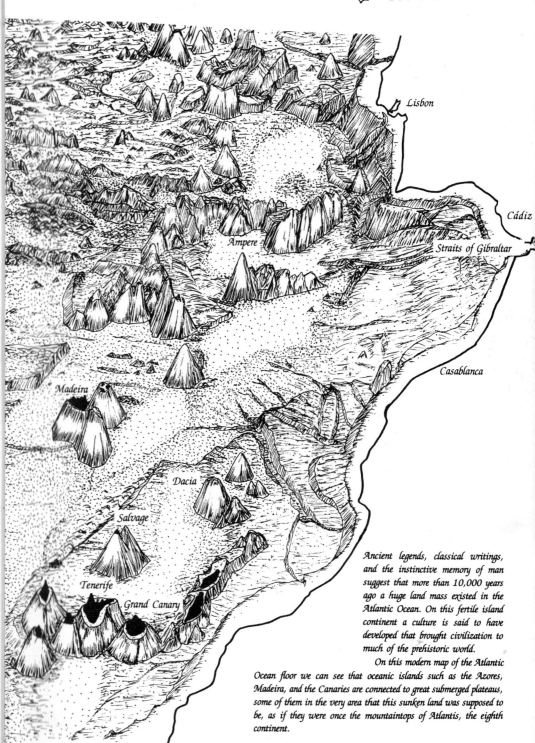

Lisbon

Cádiz

Straits of Gibraltar

Ampere

Casablanca

Madeira

Dacia

Salvage

Tenerife

Grand Canary

Ancient legends, classical writings, and the instinctive memory of man suggest that more than 10,000 years ago a huge land mass existed in the Atlantic Ocean. On this fertile island continent a culture is said to have developed that brought civilization to much of the prehistoric world.

On this modern map of the Atlantic Ocean floor we can see that oceanic islands such as the Azores, Madeira, and the Canaries are connected to great submerged plateaus, some of them in the very area that this sunken land was supposed to be, as if they were once the mountaintops of Atlantis, the eighth continent.

ATLANTIS

ATLANTIS

THE EIGHTH CONTINENT

Charles Berlitz

G. P. Putnam's Sons
New York

Library of Congress Cataloging in Publication Data

Berlitz, Charles Frambach, date.
Atlantis, the eighth continent.

Bibliography: p.
Includes index.
1. Atlantis. I. Title.
GN751.B388 1984   398.2′34   83-24606
ISBN 0-399-12892-1

Printed in the United States of America

ACKNOWLEDGMENTS

Grateful acknowledgment is made to the following four persons for their contributions to this book in research, information, photographs, maps, and field trips. Valerie Berlitz: author, researcher, editor, artist. Julius Egloff: oceanographer, marine cartographer, and geologist with many years' experience charting the ocean floor. Herbert Sawinski: archaeologist, explorer, pilot, diver, ship captain, chairman of the Fort Lauderdale Museum of Science and Archaeology; he has led recent sea and land expeditions to the ruins detailed in several chapters in this book. And J. Manson Valentine: naturalist, paleontologist, archaeologist, explorer, diver, curator honoris of the Museum of Science of Miami, research associate of the Bishop Museum of Honolulu; Dr. Valentine made the first discovery of the Bimini Wall, as described in Chapter 8.

The following persons and institutions, listed in alphabetical order, have made important contributions to this book. It is nevertheless understood that they do not necessarily share the author's opinions about the scientific and archaeological reality of Atlantis. Alexandr Bek, professor of Slavic studies, linguist. The Benincasa family, descendants of the 15th-century cartographer. José Maria Bensaúde, president of Navicor Shipping Lines, Portugal and the Azores. Gloria Cashin, mathematician, geologist. Comissão Regional de Turismo dos Açôres. Lin Berlitz Davis, diver, researcher. Adelaide de Mesnil, archaeological photographer. Sara D. Donnelly, a fifth-generation descendant of Ignatius Donnelly. Antonio Pascual Fernández, author, historian, philosopher, educator. Hamilton Forman, historian, collector of pre–Columbian artifacts. Charles Hapgood, historian, cartographer, geologist, author. The Hispanic Society of America. Government of India, Cultural Affairs Office. Ramona Kashe, chief of research for Charles Berlitz, Washington, D.C. Bob Klein, shipmaster, diver, photographer. Martin Klein, diver, inventor of Klein Side Scan Sonar. Ivan Lee, archaeologist, artist, writer, editor, publisher. Jacques Mayol, author, explorer, diver, holder of world depth record for free dive without scuba. Musée de l'Homme, Paris. Museo de Arqueología, Madrid. William A. Moore, author, lecturer. Kenneth G. Peters, historian. Dmitri Rebikoff, author, diver, inventor of underwater camera and of Pegasus underwater research vehicle. Antonio Rivera, author, lecturer. Bruno Rizatto, diver, photographer. Ivan Sanderson, author, naturalist, explorer, archaeologist. Bonnie Sawinski, illustrator, artist. John Sawinski, diver, photographer. Charlotte Schoen, chief librarian of the Cayce Foundation. Egerton Sykes, author, archaeologist, explorer, publisher, linguist. Maxime Berlitz Vollmer, philologist, mythologist. Bob Warth, researcher, president of the Society for the Investigation of the Unexplained. And appreciation to William Thompson and Nancy J. Perlman, editors of this book, for their encouragement and careful editing of *Atlantis: The Eighth Continent.*

Dedicated to all those who have believed in the ancient legend of lost Atlantis—a legend that recent discoveries are turning into a reality.

CONTENTS

ATLANTIS

1

INTRODUCTION
TO A LOST CONTINENT

Deep under the Atlantic Ocean there lie the remains of a continent. The area of this island continent, which we may call the eighth of the world's continental land divisions, can still be defined by the present Atlantic Islands, once the tops of its highest mountains. A civilization developed in these huge islands and spread, through conquest and colonization, throughout the Atlantic Basin and farther to the islands and coasts of the Mediterranean. Thousands of years before the beginnings of history in Egypt and Mesopotamia, this civilization disappeared into the Atlantic Ocean, leaving only isolated colonies on the surrounding continents which grew into the civilizations that we consider the beginnings of history. The names by which this lost land was called in most of the languages of Europe, North Africa, and the Americas, were variations of the name "Atlantis"—a memory recalled by the name of the Atlantic Ocean as well as the Atlas Mountains of North Africa. It was to the west of North Africa and Spain that legendary Atlantis was reputed to have existed.

The visionary and often mystic image evoked by the very name Atlantis has contributed to its having been generally classified as a legend, notwithstanding its wide acceptance by scholars of other ages and by the oceanic and archaeological discoveries of the last hundred years. If you look up Atlantis in the encyclopedia, you will certainly find it classified as a legend or a myth. If you look for books about Atlantis in a library catalogue in the United States you will find them listed by the Dewey Decimal System of classification (398:2) under the same category as dragons, gnomes, ghosts, and other legends. The time has perhaps arrived to establish the reality of Atlantis and the probability that its existence was a very real one to the peoples of a prehistoric world that relapsed into barbarism with its disappearance.

Although there exist a number of variants of the name Atlantis and a common memory among many tribes and ancient peoples of its one-time location and fate, the description left by Plato, the Greek philosopher who was one of the intellectual sources of western civilization, is the best known to modern and ancient scholars. Plato, in his *Critias* and *Timaeus* dialogues, left such a convincing description of Atlantis that one doubts the information he recounted could be simply imagined and was anything other than a description of a land that had once existed. According to Plato, the powerful empire of Atlantis came to a sudden end, while engaged in a war, when the central island or islands "in a terrible night and day" sank under the ocean that bears its name. Since that time, 11,500 years ago, it has lain on the bottom, drowned, lost, and almost forgotten.

But did the world ever really forget Atlantis? The world's peoples did not. All along the Atlantic Littoral—on both sides of the ocean—tribes and nations could not forget its existence or its fate, and have even remembered the name of a great land mass in the Atlantic. The name, in a variety of tongues, almost always contains the sounds A-T-L-N. Ancient nations were conscious of its location: European and African traditions placed it in the ocean to the west, while the pre–Columbian tribes of the Americas placed it in the Eastern Sea, i.e., the Atlantic Ocean.

The recollection of a far-off homeland, a final catastrophe, and the flight of survivors to other parts of the world has been kept alive for thousands of years through variants of the story of Noah's Ark, common, with different names for Noah, to all ancient peoples. And just as old beliefs have been incorporated into more recent traditions, it has been theorized that Halloween refers to an older worldwide memory; the commemoration of the mass disappearance of a large part of the world's inhabitants, who died when their world perished by earthquake, fire, and tidal waves.

Memories of a vanished continent seem to be instinctively shared even by animals. Eels swim from European and American rivers to mate in the seaweed forests of the Sargasso Sea, where a great underwater river still flows along its ancient bed through the Atlantic. Birds in their seasonal migration from Europe to South America circle over the same area in the Atlantic, perhaps looking for and not finding a place where birds once rested.

The memory of Atlantis is recalled by massive and unexplained ruins on both sides of the Atlantic. They are unexplained not only because we do not know who built them, but also because they are so huge that their construction by races *before* history seems inconceivable. And a careful re-examination of certain artifacts indicates that they represent the use of techniques and mechanical devices thousands of years before these were invented, according to the generally accepted timetable of history.

Perhaps one reason for the anti-Atlantis stance of many scientists is that even the possibility of accepting an historical Atlantis would cause a massive and onerous reassessment of history, now carefully labeled in a series of compartments.

The legend or mystique of Atlantis has been believed or discredited for centuries. Writers have argued about it since the time of Plato—2500 years ago. But, whatever its essential truth, the legend itself has developed its own reality. It has contributed greatly to the discovery of the New World, to the literature of many nations, to the study of prehistory and the exploration of the bottom of the sea.

If the golden cities and fertile plains of Atlantis once existed and suddenly were destroyed, then perhaps we are coming the full circle. In the past 6000 to 8000 years, we, the peoples of Earth, have gradually built up a world civilization that even now stands at the edge of destruction, man-made perhaps, but destruction nonetheless. Perhaps today's interest in Atlantis is motivated by an instinctive realization of this coincidence.

In modern times the search for vestiges of Atlantis has become more realistic than was ever possible in the past, encompassing as it does geology, seismology, anthropology, linguistics, and, most logically, oceanography. World-wide study of sunken coastlines, changing sea levels, and new sonar maps and exploration of the ocean floor now indicate that the ocean is considerably deeper than it was at the end of the last glaciation of 11,000 to 12,000 years ago, coincidentally within the time frame given by Plato and other sources for the destruction and drowning of Atlantis. Something happened to the world at that time that caused many of the oceanic islands and continental coastlines to be covered by the sea.

Within the last several years a number of missing parts of the Atlantean legend have fallen into place like pieces of a gigantic puzzle, a puzzle almost as old as civilized man. But an essential and completing piece would be the finding of buildings, temples, walls, and roads on the sea bottom, which would indicate that civilization had once existed on lands now under the ocean. Whether or not these ruins once formed part of the fabled cities of Atlantis, referring to them as Atlantean, as a name for the lost world before history began, has a certain appropriate quality.

And massive stone ruins have been discovered, photographed, and are now being explored off the coasts of the United States, Mexico, Cuba, Venezuela, and on the sunken banks of the Bahamas—just as underwater ruins are being investigated off the coasts of Spain and the Canary Islands, Morocco, Portugal, and the Azores and are being searched for on the coasts of other islands in the Atlantic and on the crests and slopes of underwater seamounts that once existed above sea level. These ruins not only resemble one another, but also are comparable to megalithic constructions belonging to no known culture that exists in the mountains of South America, the coasts of Europe and Asia, or the islands of the Pacific.

The ancient legend appears to be changing into fact; a fact that could be of crucial importance for the survival of our modern world and its peoples.

2

ATLANTIS, A NAME AND A LEGEND

For the past two and a half thousand years a percentage of the world's people have believed that there once existed, in the middle of the Atlantic Ocean, roughly between Spain, Africa, and the Americas, an island continent now sunk below the ocean. On this great island lived a civilized and ambitious population. There were great cities, splendid palaces, golden-roofed temples, an intricate canal system that provided irrigation for the fertile fields, and crowded harbors from which trading fleets and armies carried its commerce and culture to islands in other parts of the ocean and the shores of Europe, America, the Mediterranean Basin, and beyond. As this civilization reached its apogee, it suddenly ended in flood, earthquake, and the flames of volcanic explosions. It vanished from history and is remembered only by legends told and retold, through successive generations, by the descendants of those who escaped the disaster. The name of this island empire was Atlantis.

This word is unconsciously remembered every time one mentions the Atlantic Ocean, whose name, deriving from Atlas or Atlantis, comes down to us from a time before the existence of the Outer Ocean, as compared with the Mediterranean ("the Middle Earth") Sea, which was generally familiar to the peoples of the Mediterranean Basin.

Plato, who wrote the most detailed surviving description of Atlantis that has come down from antiquity, was insistent in locating Atlantis not in the Mediterranean but far out in the Atlantic, beyond the "pillars of Hercules" (Gibraltar on the southern coast of Spain and Mount Atlas on the northern shore of Africa). Plato specified that "the island was larger than Libya and Asia put together, and was the way to other islands, and from these islands you might pass through the whole of the opposite continent, which surrounds the true ocean; for this sea [the Mediterranean], which is within the Straits of Hercules, is only a harbor, having a narrow entrance [the Straits of Gibraltar], but that other is a real sea and the surrounding land may be most truly called a continent."

One may reflect that time has satisfactorily born out Plato's conclusion about "the opposite continent" (America), 2000 years before its discovery, or rediscovery, by Europeans. The existence of Atlantis, however, is still far from being accepted by the majority of the scientific community, which steadfastly labels it a legend or a myth, or even a hoax generated by Plato. But a series of modern discoveries now going on under the Atlantic Ocean seems to be proving that Plato essentially was correct in his account of the "legendary" Atlantis, as he was in his reference to the Americas.

Atlantis is generally referred to as a legend for several reasons, of which a principal one is that there is no recognizable bit of it to be seen on the surface of the ocean. It is true, however, that in the approximate location where it was supposed to have existed there are presently several small island groups such as the Azores, the Canaries, Madeira and, in the western Atlantic, the Bahamas. It is therefore possible that these small islands may be the mountain peaks of a greater land mass, high enough to have maintained their position above sea level when the greater part of the island, or islands, at the time of a global catastrophe, sank or was engulfed by the rising ocean.

Another understandable reason for Atlantis' status as a myth or legend is that its memory, although well preserved in racial and tribal traditions around the circle of the Atlantic and elsewhere, has come down through spoken and then transcribed legends from a very distant past. Legends become transformed in the retelling; kings and leaders become gods and demigods (and occasionally devils), endowed with divine powers. Incidents of racial or tribal history are enlarged to cosmic proportions. Geographical locations become uncertain and, in the case of Atlantis, indistinctly perceived through the mists of the sea. Those such as Plato and his approximate contemporaries, who have compiled what today we might classify as travel reports about Atlantis, have been accused of using accounts of Atlantis as a literary vehicle in order to popularize their own political or social theories of how the people of cities and nations of their own time continuum should conduct themselves.

Aristotle, one of Plato's students and founder of his own school of philosophy, was responsible for a critical thrust against Plato's report of Atlantis which has lasted through the ages and is still a favorite among members of the scientific establishment, which considers Atlantis to be a myth. Aristotle, in referring to a sudden break-off (not resumed) in Plato's account, observed, "He who invented it destroyed it." But Aristotle, having succeeded to his own satisfaction in demolishing the concept of Atlantis, unwittingly made his own contribution to the legend when he added that Phoenician and Carthaginian seafarers *did* know of a great island in the western Atlantic which they called Antilla. Perhaps he did not realize the close resemblance of the names Atlantis and Antilla, both of which since have respectively achieved a certain immortality as names for the ocean itself and its western islands.

The very sound of the name of the lost continent may serve as a test to establish what is pure legend and what is based on reality. If we make a great circle of the lands surrounding the North Atlantic Ocean and compare the names given by ancient peoples to an island continent formerly situated in the middle, we find names that strongly resemble one another but are still just enough linguistically dissimilar to offer convincing proof of a shared memory.

We owe the name *Atlantis* to the Greco-Roman world, whose writers were familiar with the idea and location of the lost continent. The tribes of northwestern Africa near the Atlantic coast were even referred to by ancient writers as Atalantes, Atarantes, and Atlantioi by classical writers as remnants of Atlantean colonists or colonial populations. The Berber tribes of North Africa retain their own legends of *Attala,* a warlike kingdom off the African coast with rich mines of gold, silver, and tin, which sent not only these metals but conquering armies to Africa. *Attala* is now under the ocean but according to prophecy will one day reappear.

The ancient Gauls, as well as the Irish, Welsh, and British Celts, believed that their ancestors came from a continent that sank into the Western Sea, the latter two naming this lost paradise Avalon.

The Basques, a racial and linguistic island in southwestern France and northern Spain, believe they are the descendants of Atlantis, which they call Atlaintika. It is current belief among the Portuguese that Atlantis (Atlantida) once existed near Portugal and that parts of it, the Azores Islands, are still pushing up their peaks from under the sea. The Iberian peoples of southern Spain trace a direct kinship to Atlantis and are increasingly aware that Spain still owns what may have been a part of the Atlantean empire—the Canary Islands. Here, curiously, the name *Atalaya* is still current as a place name, and the original inhabitants, when discovered, claimed to be the only survivors of a world-wide disaster.

The Vikings believed that *Atli* was a wondrous land in the west, and it was there also that the Teutonic races placed Valhalla, a mystic land of self-renewing fighting, drinking, and feasting. Phoenician and Carthaginian seafarers were reportedly familiar with a thriving western island that they called *Antilla,* but tended to keep secret their knowledge for reasons of commerce and colonization.

Ancient Egyptian hieroglyphic texts mention *Amenti,* the paradise of the west, abode of the dead and part of the divine sunboat. The Babylonians called their western paradise *Arallu,* and to the Arabians of antiquity the first civilization was the land of *Ad,* located in the Western Ocean. (One wonders in passing whether the Biblical Pentateuch or the Torah, in the account of Adam, may perhaps be an echo of the tradition of Ad. Did Adam represent an allegory of the first man or was Ad-Am the first civilized race?)

There are surprising references in the ancient classics of India, the *Puranas* and the *Mahabharata,* to *Attala*—"the White Island"— a continent located in the Western Ocean, half a world away from India. The approximate location given to *Attala* in the Western Ocean, when converted according to the ancient Hindu divisions of the world, was, according to latitude, on a horizontal line running through the Canary Islands and the Bahamas. (This line also passes through the site of the legendary Atlantis.) In these same and other texts the word *Atyantika* is used in relation to a final catastrophic destruction.

When the Spanish conquerors of Central and South America reached Mexico, they learned that the Aztecs believed they originally came from *Aztlán,* an island in the Eastern (to them) Ocean. The word *Aztec* may be derived from Aztlán, a concept that the Spaniards were prepared to accept since many of them believed that the inhabitants of the New World might be descendants of Atlantis and for this very reason were logical candidates for the rule of Spain through ancient Spain's former close Atlantean connection.

Throughout Mexico and then down the coast of Central America and the northern part of South America we continue to find remnants of Atlantis' haunting name; in Mexico, *Tlapallan, Tollan, Azatlán,* and *Aztlán.* Further south, in Venezuela, the conquista-

Figure 1

Figure 2

Aztec glyph drawing of Aztlán, the mountainous island in the Eastern
Sea from which the Aztecs reputedly came. This drawing was made in
the old style with Latin alphabet added. *(Figure 1)*

Columns still standing at Tula, Mexico, ascribed to the pre–Aztec
Toltec civilization. These columns once held up stone crossbeams of the
temple roof for which they formed the support. Such human-figure
support columns are called atlantes, a reference to Atlas holding up the
world. The myth of Atlas supporting the world has a counterpart in
Mexico, where one of the functions of Quetzalcoatl is to support the
sky, a concept of tremendous power, perhaps an ancient legendary
allusion to the power of the former continent of Atlantis. *(Figure 2)*

dores found a settlement called *Atlán* peopled by what they referred
to as "white Indians." Indian tribes of North America also remembered traditions that their ancestors came from an island in the
Atlantic, often giving it a name resembling Atlantis. Early explorers
in Wisconsin found a fortified village near Lake Michigan which its
inhabitants called *Azatlán.*

All of these similar names for an island continent or lost homeland do not constitute a determining proof that it once existed. They do, however, strongly indicate that Atlantis was not a literary device of Plato. These legends are of great antiquity and come from widely separated parts of the world that were not in communication with one another within the time we count as history. Even legends from the Pacific Islands, although they do not mention Atlantis by name, tell of the sinking of great land masses in the Pacific at a time when the Earth shook, islands disappeared into the ocean, and large islands became smaller ones.

It is just this question of land "disappearing" that has become a mainstay of critics of the Atlantis theory. Although an increasing number of scientists are tending to admit the possibility of important Earth changes during the existence of "modern" man on Earth, by far the majority stand fast in their opinion that there have been no important world catastrophes (except for volcanic explosions and disappearances of a few islands) for several million years.

The spread of scientific research and the input of scientific data would seem to place a barrier and destroy the logic of future Atlantean investigation. In addition, the theory of continental drift, now generally accepted as a fact, seems to leave no place for Atlantis to have existed in the middle of the ocean.

In like manner any supposition of the one-time existence of previous world empires would have to be based on actual finding and dating of artifacts. But within the Atlantis time frame of more than 11,000 years before the present time, no Atlantean artifacts have so far been identified, dated, and classified to the satisfaction of the archaeological establishment.

However, the very expertise of modern science frequently offers a variety of solutions. The same investigational techniques used by researchers certainly not preoccupied with the actuality of Atlantis have, in recent years, through underwater mapping, exploration, satellite photographs of the Earth, cultural, linguistic, and dating breakthroughs, inadvertently reopened the Atlantis controversy. The most recent tools of modern science have led us back in time to the consideration of a powerful civilization that existed thousands of years before Babylon.

3

THE RECEDING HORIZON OF HISTORY

When did history start? The presently accepted beginnings of history usually follow datable artifacts or records written on papyrus, carved on stones, or inscribed on clay, among which the oldest have been found in Egypt, Mesopotamia (Iraq), Crete, Iran, and western India, although the script of the Indus Valley is still undeciphered. In general, civilization with written history does not extend beyond 4000 years B.C.

The generally accepted archaeological opinion of 4000 B.C. (i.e., 6000 B.P.—Before Present in archaeological parlance) finds an oddly coincidental echo in the calculation of Dr. James Ussher, Archbishop of Armagh, Ireland. Dr. Ussher, a 17th-century churchman and thinker, by adding and cross-checking the ascribed life years and relationships of persons mentioned in the Bible, established a date for the world's creation as October 22, 4004 B.C., at 8 P.M., later modified by an independent calculation by the Vice- Chancellor of Cambridge University, Dr. John Lightfoot, also a 17th-century educator, who gave a specific date for the creation of Adam: October 23, 4004 B.C., at 9 A.M. Greenwich Time. (It has been suggested that Dr. Lightfoot was influenced in his choice by the beginning date of the autumn semester at Cambridge University, although it would have perhaps been preferable from the point of view of the work ethic for man to have been created on a Monday morning, at 7:30 A.M.) As late as 1900 a Dr. Seyffarth, a Leipzig theologian, also basing his calculations on Biblical reckoning of years, published a book in which he stated with pedantic certainty that it was "uncontestibly proved that on September 7, 3446 B.C., the Deluge ended and the alphabets of the races of the world were invented."

Today a strong "Creationist" movement from California has somewhat modified the above, pushing back the beginning of the world to 10,000 B.C. A number of other persons have viewed historical ages with some indifference. Henry Ford, industrialist, inventor, and father of the Model T, has been widely quoted as saying that he did not believe in history anyway or that it ever really happened.

In the last fifty years the period for the emergence of developed, if not civilized, man has been pushed back to more than two *million* years (and with new discoveries the Rift Valley of Africa, in Kenya, and in the Afar region of Ethiopia this date may be extended even further back in time). The positive development of advanced group cultures is now estimated to have occurred from fifty to a hundred thousand years ago. One of a number of examples is especially intriguing: a combination of dating techniques has established the working of an iron mine in Ngwenya, Swaziland, as having occurred 43,000 years ago. (We must assume that these ancient miners were mining for a reason and that they possessed sufficient technology to put to some specific use the material they were mining, tens of thousands of years before iron appeared in the Middle East.)

If the date of 4000 B.C. marks the boundary of historic time, this still leaves a 6000-year period before we get back to the time zone of Atlantis, a period in which history turns into legend. But with new dating techniques and new discoveries it has been established that certain very ancient cities and population centers, among which are Jericho in Israel, Çatal Hüyük in Turkey, Tiahuanaco in Bolivia, and other communities in France, Spain, Yugoslavia, Armenia, and central Asia, existed within this presumed Atlantean time zone.

Written references to this uncertain period exist in the records of subsequent nations. The Chaldean king-list went back tens of thousands of years: King Asshur-bani-pal of Assyria has left to posterity on tablets of baked clay a statement that he understood and caused to be translated writings in the dead languages of what to him was already very ancient history—the books written *before* the Flood.

Travelers returning to the eastern Mediterranean from Spain 2600 years ago told of a rich and powerful city, Tartessos, a great seaport on the southwestern coast of Spain, whose written records, as reported by the Greek historian Strabo, went back 7000 years before their time, long before the conventionally accepted invention of writing. The Egyptian year count reached far beyond the First Dy-

All of the Earth's older races share the tradition of a great flood during which a civilization was destroyed by a catastrophe: a combination of flood, earthquake, and volcanic eruptions. This Mayan bas-relief shows a Mayan "Noah" escaping from a sinking island. The Maya recorded that the lost land from which they came was once in the Eastern Sea— the Atlantic Ocean.

nasty, back to the time of the kings who reigned before the Flood, and the Hindu year count goes so far into the past that a number of other cultures do not even have numbers sufficiently large to express the concept.

Even more convincing are the discoveries of unidentified ruins under the Atlantic Ocean and the Caribbean Sea, where great stone roads or platforms were fitted into place before the glaciers melted and raised the levels of the oceans. And, as investigations continue to push back the curtain of time to include the remains of mysterious ruins and city complexes that have not yet been dated, we find within our own investigative reach a number of cities throughout the world from the time before history.

It has not yet been generally realized by the world of science that Plato's date for the end of Atlantis, long considered to be a fantasy, has already been reached by recent discoveries of civilized and city life at that period. But if we have no written records from populations of 12,000 years ago, we have no way of establishing their history according to a traditional pattern.

Even Atlantis, however widespread its tradition throughout the world, has left us no records that we can examine or translate. The report of Plato is presently the closest description we have of what the prehistoric island empire was actually like. While Plato wrote that the information came from Egyptian temple records, it is also possible that it incorporated reports from ancient Carthaginian and Phoenician seafarers whose cities and libraries were subsequently destroyed and their records burned or scattered.

By examining parts of Plato's existing two dialogues on Atlantis and comparing his information with what we now know, we get a convincing impression that Plato based his narration on fact and that he was telling, as he himself expressed it, ". . . a strange tale which is, however, certainly true."

4

THE ISLAND EMPIRE
BEFORE HISTORY BEGAN

It has frequently been observed that Plato's description of Atlantis
is too detailed for him to have been able to invent it. The report of
what Atlantis was like, the great ports and mighty fleets, the intricate
canal system, the immense temples, the prodigal use of gold and
another unidentified metal, possibly a gold alloy, called orichalcum,
the description of land allotment, agriculture and irrigation, domestic and wild animals, military levees and equipment, government
and commerce, persuade us that prior to Plato's time a number of
persons brought back eyewitness accounts of the island continent
in the Atlantic. And Plato, renowned as the greatest thinker of
antiquity by the very fact that he wrote the report, caused the account to be studied, discussed, and argued for the 2500-year period
that has elapsed since he wrote it.

Plato presented his description of Atlantis in the form of two
dialogues, *Timaeus* and *Critias,* in a discussion with several friends,
including Socrates. The dialogues, originally projected to be three
in number, appear to abruptly break off toward the end of the
second, unless the rest of it was lost in the general burning and other
destruction of ancient documents since classical times. On the other
hand it may be that Plato simply interrupted the writing because his
patron for this project, Dionysius I, Tyrant of Syracuse, who wished
to present it for reading at a prose and poetry festival in his city,
died before Plato finished the manuscript, which was subsequently
published by Crantor of Athens.

Plato attributed his information about Atlantis to that given to
Solon, the Athenian lawgiver, during a journey Solon made to Egypt.
According to Plato the original text had been passed down through

a friend of Solon's, Dropides, to Critias, the one mentioned in the dialogue. Solon had originally received this information from Egyptian priests at Saïs. The priests had translated into Greek and commented on the hieroglyphics inscribed on temple columns. (There was a school for interpreters at Saïs, established by Psammetik, one of the later Pharaohs.)

The *Timaeus* dialogue opens with an indirect allusion to Atlantis, only as concerned with "great and marvelous actions of the [prehistoric] ancestors of the Athenians, which had passed into oblivion through time and the destruction of the human race," and which had been generally forgotten by their descendants, although the Egyptians still had documentary evidence of these deeds.

It is fairly obvious that approaching the question of Atlantis through the heroism of the Athenians in opposing Atlantean dominion was both a literary ploy to gain the attention of the Athenian populace and also an attempt to inspire them to a reawakened sense of mission and greatness, then at a low point in Athens' history because of disastrous wars.

The following excerpt serves as a means of dramatically establishing the extreme age of the Egyptian records as compared with those of the Athenians:

> . . . one of the priests, who was of very great age, said, "O Solon, Solon, you Hellenes are but children, and there is never an old man who is an Hellene." Solon, hearing this, said, "What do you mean?" "I mean to say," he replied, "that in mind you are all young; there is no old opinion handed down among you by ancient tradition, nor any science which is hoary with age. And I will tell you the reason of this; there have been, and there will be again, many destructions of mankind arising out of many causes . . .

In speaking of periodic catastrophes, the Egyptian priests stressed the point that they had at hand records of important events that had happened thousands of years before Solon's visit to Saïs:

> All that has been written down of old . . . is preserved in our temples . . . when the stream from heaven descends like a pestilence and leaves only those of you who are destitute of letters and education . . . you have to begin all over again as children

and know nothing about what happened in ancient times, either among us or among yourselves.

The Egyptians, according to their ancient historian, Manetho, kept records extending back thousands of years before their first historic dynasties, well into the prehistoric period of rule called the "Reign of the Gods." Also, as the climate of Egypt has preserved tomb paintings, buildings, and even papyrus records for thousands of years, it may be expected that future discoveries of still buried tombs and temples will contribute additional references or records about the "Lost Continent."

Leading up to the description and later destruction of Atlantis, the Egyptian priests spoke of

. . . a great conflagration of things upon the Earth recurring at long intervals of time: when this happens, those who live upon the mountains and in dry and lofty places are more liable to destruction than those who dwell by rivers or on the sea shore. . . . When, on the other hand, the gods purge the Earth with a deluge of water, among you herdsmen and shepherds on the mountains are the survivors, whereas those of you who live in cities are carried by the rivers into the sea.

Plato and other scholars of his time were aware that many land-sea changes had previously occurred in various parts of the world. Herodotus had observed seashells in the Egyptian desert and a high salt concentration in Egyptian soil and rocks. Remains of sea life had been found in the desert and at the foot of the Great Pyramid in ancient times, while some modern investigators have detected evidences of a salt layer in the Queen's Chamber within the pyramid. A land bridge between Sicily and Italy was recorded in ancient documents to have submerged into the Mediterranean. Volcanic eruptions had destroyed cities, great floods had occurred, and islands had sunk and often had ·not risen again. During Plato's lifetime the Greek port city of Heliké on the Saronic Gulf fell into the sea with all its people and buildings so suddenly that it took down with it twelve Spartan warships then in the harbor.

A detailed description of Atlantis begins with homage to Athenian heroism in opposing the ocean empire and then establishes the location of Atlantis in the Atlantic Ocean:

> Many great and wonderful deeds are recorded of your state in our histories; but one of them exceeds all the rest in greatness and valor; for these histories tell of a mighty power which was aggressing wantonly against the whole of Europe and Asia, and to which your city put an end. This power came forth out of the Atlantic Ocean, for in those days the Atlantic was navigable; and there was an island situated in front of the straits which you call the Columns of Hercules: the island was larger than Libya and Asia put together, and was the way to other islands and from the islands you might pass through the whole of the opposite continent which surrounded the true ocean; for this sea which is within the Straits of Hercules is only a harbor, having a narrow entrance, but that other is a real sea, and the surrounding land may be most truly called a continent. Now, in the island of Atlantis there was a great and wonderful empire, which had rule over the whole island and several others, as well as over part of the continent; and, besides these, they subjected the parts of Libya within the Columns of Hercules as far as Egypt and of Europe as far as Tyrrhenia. The vast power of this gathered into one, endeavored to subdue at one blow our country and yours, and the whole of the land which was within the straits . . .

> *The reference to the "opposite continent," of which seafaring races such as the Phoenicians and the Cretans were probably already aware, is one of the most widely quoted excerpts of the dialogues. But what is equally curious is Plato's mention of the "other islands" as stepping-stones to the continent across the Atlantic. Plato could not have known what we now know about the depths of the Atlantic Ocean. If the water level of the Atlantic were lowered 600 to 1000 feet, as it effectively was before the last glaciation melted, the Azores, Madeira, Cape Verde, Bermuda, and the Bahamas would be vastly greater in land area, the continental shelves, presently under water, would extend far out into the sea, and other islands, now only underwater plateaus rising from the ocean floor, would have existed on the surface. Plato,*

*in making a statement about a series of islands, made an accurate
guess about the formation of the ocean bottom.*

*When Plato said "Asia," he probably meant only Asia Minor
and parts of the Middle East, while "Libya" stood for North
Africa. The combined dimensions of these areas might roughly
be equal to the size of a former Atlantean continent or series of
great islands.*

. . . and then, Solon, your country shone forth, in the excellence of her virtue and strength . . . and preserved from slavery
those who were not yet subjected, and freely liberated all the
others. . . .

*In addition to Plato's mention of invasions of Europe and
Africa from the west, ancient races in the area preserved legends,
writings, and what may be even ruins resulting from such invasions. Egyptian records tell of forays of a mysterious "people
of the sea"; Irish legends tell of invasions by the equally mysterious Firborgs, also from the Atlantic, and ruins of Irish stone
forts thousands of years old show evidence of calcination from
extreme heat; the Atlantic coasts of Spain and France as well as
the islands of the Mediterranean also retain legends and ruins
traced to invasions from the west at a point far back in time.*

Shortly after the repulsed invasion, Atlantis with its cities and
people sank into the sea.

But afterward there occurred violent earthquakes and floods,
and in a single day and night of rain all your warlike men in a
body sank into the earth, and the island of Atlantis in like
manner disappeared, and was sunk beneath the sea. And that
is the reason why the sea in those parts is impassable and im-
penetrable, because there is such a quantity of shallow mud in
the way; and this was caused by the subsidence of the island. . . .

Other references in the dialogues allude to this deluge as "the
greatest deluge of all" and reiterate that

Map of the North Atlantic area showing, at the center, the elevation
along the Mid-Atlantic Ridge. The Azores are the surviving portions of
this great mountain range still above sea level and they rest on a
plateau-like feature defined by the 2000-meter water-depth contour line.
Continental shelves around the ocean indicate sections of North
America, Europe, Africa, and Atlantic islands other than the Azores
formerly above sea level.

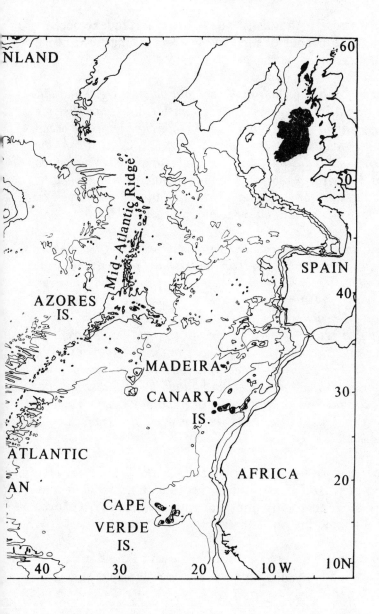

... the islands of Atlantis ... sunk by an earthquake became an impassable barrier of mud to voyagers sailing from hence [the Mediterranean world] to the ocean. ...

A sea of mud and shallow shoals, and other navigational difficulties, would have persisted for a considerable time after the engulfment of an island continent and made changes in the ocean bottom, especially near the Gibraltar–Mt. Atlas exit from the Mediterranean to the open sea. Carthaginian and Phoenician sea captains perpetrated reports that the Atlantic was unnavigable, probably to keep any Atlantic or colonial trade for themselves, a subterfuge they continued for centuries with considerable profit.

An indication of the suddenness of Atlantis' reported sinking are expanses of beach sand on underwater plateaus near the Azores at a depth of 5000 feet. The fact that sandy beaches normally form at approximately sea level suggests a sudden precipitation of beaches and coastal areas deep within the ocean. The late Professor Maurice Ewing, an eminent oceanographer, although one extremely unsympathetic to the theory of Atlantis, expressed the opinion, after an expedition had found geologically recent lava spreading on the ocean bottom, that "Either the land must have sunk two or three miles or the ocean must once have been two or three miles lower than now. Either conclusion is startling."

The greater part of the second dialogue, called *Critias,* or, more appropriately, *The Atlantic,* describes in considerable detail the natural features, architecture, customs, government, religion, and even the plant and animal life on Atlantis.

The royal dynasty, it is recounted, began with Poseidon, god of the sea, who fell in love with a mortal, Cleito, who lived on a great mountain in Atlantis.

Poseidon fell in love with her and had intercourse with her; and, breaking the ground, enclosed the hill on which she dwelt all round, making alternate zones of sea and land, larger and smaller, encircling one another; there were two of land and three of water. ... He himself, as he was a god, found no difficulty in making special arrangements for the center island, bringing two streams of water under the earth, one of warm water and the other of cold, and making every variety of food to spring up abundantly in the earth. . . .

These references to gods were often used in antiquity for illustrations and to fix events in the listener's memory rather than for religion or mystification. Plato himself has the Egyptian priest explain to Solon:

There is a story . . . that once upon a time Phaëthon, the son of Helios, having yoked the steeds in his father's chariot, because he was not able to drive them in the path of his father, burnt up all there was upon the Earth, and was himself destroyed by a thunderbolt. Now, this has the form of a myth, but really signifies a declination of the bodies moving around the earth and in the heavens. . . .

This is one more evidence of the custom of linking well-known names to historic and heroic actions, a custom not limited to ancient times. Ignatius Donnelly, congressman, lieutenant governor of Minnesota, and candidate for vice-president of the United States, who, in 1882, published a comprehensive study of Atlantis as a factual entity—Atlantis: Myths of the Antediluvian World— may have stated a partial truth in his declaration that ". . . the gods and goddesses of the ancient Greeks, the Phoenicians, the Hindus, and the Scandinavians were simply the kings, queens, and heroes of Atlantis; and the acts attributed to them in mythology are a confused recollection of real historical events."

Atlas was the firstborn son of Poseidon and Cleito. Poseidon had five pairs of twin sons, and he

. . . divided the island of Atlantis into ten portions: he gave to the firstborn of the eldest pair his mother's dwelling and the surrounding allotment, which was the largest and best, and made him king over the rest; and the others he made princes, and gave them rule over many men and a large territory. . . .

When the Canary Islands were rediscovered and explored during the late Middle Ages, the native Guanches still maintained the tradition of ten kings. So did the Maya people of southern

Mexico, on the other side of the ocean. Plato could not have known about this coincidence. In the Bible there is also an echo of ten lifespans—the ten generations before Noah.

The eldest, who was king, he named Atlas and from him the whole island and the ocean received the name of Atlantic. To his twin brother, who was born after him, and obtained as his lot the extremity of the island toward the Pillars of Hercules, as far as the country which is still called the region of Gades in that part of the world. . . .

Gades is still a city in Spain, under the modified name of Cádiz, on the ocean side of the Straits of Gibraltar. It still looks to the west, from where Atlantis, according to tradition, ruled its colonies. Cádiz may have been one of these, along with the now vanished Tartessos, which is thought to have existed on the delta of the Guadalquivir River. In this part of Spain there are enormous ruins, especially at Niebla and Huelva, which appear to have once been parts of ports, docks, or seawalls.

The terms "Atlantic" and "Atlantis" were also used by the Greek historian and traveler Herodotus to designate the ocean and a great city on an island in the ocean. He referred to several North African peoples living near the Atlas Mountains by the names "Atlantes" and "Atarantes." Herodotus' accounts preceded Plato's report and presumably came from a source other than Egypt.

Atlas and his descendants had

. . . such an amount of wealth as was never before possessed by kings and potentates, and is not likely ever to be again, and they were furnished with everything which they could have, both in city and country. For, because of the greatness of their empire, many things were brought to them from foreign countries, and the island itself provided much of what was required by them for the uses of life. In the first place, they dug out of the earth whatever was to be found there, mineral as well as metal, and that which is now only a name—orichalcum—was dug out of the earth in many parts of the island, and with the exception of gold, was esteemed the most precious of metals among the men of those days. . . .

Orichalcum may have been an amalgam whose composition is no longer known. Gold and precious metals figure prominently in all ancient accounts of Atlantis, its treasures and its mines— a memory that encouraged some European commentators to believe that Plato's Atlantis really meant the Americas, whose enormous treasures of gold and silver were quickly appropriated by the Spanish conquerors. Mining of metals was developed at a very early date; horizontal and vertical tunnels and smelting facilities and slag heaps have been found by divers in the Mediterranean off Marseilles at a depth of eighty feet, indicating a time before the Mediterranean was flooded.

There was an abundance of wood for carpenter's work, and sufficient maintenance for tame and wild animals. Moreover, there were a great number of elephants on the island, and there was provision for animals of every kind, both for those which live in lakes and marshes and rivers, and also for those which live on mountains and on plains, and therefore for the animal which is the largest and most voracious of them. . . .

Copy of an elephant headdress from an Aztec sculpture. Elephants or legends of elephants were current in ancient America. Elephant masks, architectural motifs, and giant mounds representing what appear to be elephants exist in Wisconsin and have been found in various parts of Mexico and Central America.

We now know that elephants and mastodons existed in ancient America, where the Amerindians drew pictures of them, carved them in stone, made elephant masks and great mounds in elephant form. Mammoths existed in Europe in glacial times and elephants were plentiful in North Africa. As the distance between

Africa and the Atlantic islands would have been shorter when the ocean level was lower, with perhaps a connection by a land bridge at an earlier period, this curious reference to elephants and other "voracious" animals would not seem an impossibility.

. . . whatever fragrant things there are in the earth, whether roots, or herbage, or woods . . . grew and thrived in that land; and again, the cultivated fruit of the earth, both the dry edible fruit and other species of food, which we call by the general name of legumes, and the fruit having a hard rind, affording drinks, and meats, and ointments, . . . all these that sacred island lying beneath the sun brought forth fair and wondrous in infinite abundance. . . .

The "fruit having a hard rind" and threefold usage probably refers to a coconut, unknown to Solon or Plato but described by Plato as he understood it. This "footnote" on Atlantean fruit either represents a fact or a very good guess, since it is probable that Atlantis, if it existed as a large land mass as described by Plato, would have received the warm-weather benefits of the Gulf Stream, which would have given it a climate favorable to the growth of tropical and subtropical fruit such as coconuts, pineapples, and bananas. The warm waters of the Gulf Stream would also have been cut off from Europe by the existence of a great Atlantic island, and most of Europe, in turn, would be cold and glacial. As we now know, this was exactly the case during the period of the last glaciation, at the end of which Atlantis supposedly sank into the sea and freed the Gulf Stream to furnish a warmer climate to Europe.

All these things they received from the earth, and they employed themselves in constructing their temples, and palaces, and harbors and docks . . . they bridged over the zones of sea which surrounded the ancient metropolis, and made a passage into and out of the royal palace; and then they began to build the palace in the habitation of the god and of their ancestors. This they continued to ornament in successive generations, every king surpassing the one who came before him to the utmost of his power, until they made the building a marvel to behold for size and for beauty. And, beginning from the sea, they dug a canal three hundred feet in width and one hundred feet in depth, and fifty stadia in length, which they carried through to the uttermost zone, making a passage from the sea up to this, which became a harbor, and leaving an opening sufficient to enable the largest vessels to find ingress. Moreover, they divided the zones of land which parted the zones of sea, constructing bridges of such a width as would leave a passage from a single trireme to pass out of one into another, and roofed them over; and there was a way underneath for the ships, for the banks of the zones were raised considerably above the water. Now the largest of the zones into which a passage was cut from the sea was three stadia in breadth, and the zone of land which came next of equal breadth; but the next two, as well the zone of water as of land, were two stadia, and the one which surrounded the central island was a stadium only in width. The island on which the palace was situated had a diameter of five stadia. This, and the zones and the bridge, which was the sixth part of a stadium in width, they surrounded by a stone wall, on either side placing towers, and gates on the bridges where the sea passed in. . . .

The Greek measure "stadium" was approximately 610 feet; the measurements of the canals, buildings, and land areas given by Plato have long been considered as fantasy, exaggerated to keep the attention of his readers. However, one recalls that the Venetians had the same opinion of Marco Polo's accounts of China. But Marco Polo's stories later proved to be true. And, while Plato's description of buildings and canals now under the ocean cannot be measured, proof of the presence of huge, unidentified buildings or seaports under the ocean and perhaps under the ocean bottom is now at hand.

The stone which was used in the work they quarried from underneath the center island and from underneath the zones, on the outer as well as the inner side. One kind of stone was white, another black, and the third red; and, as they quarried, they at the same time hollowed out rocks double within, having roofs formed out of the native rock. Some of their buildings were simple, but in others they put together different stones, which they intermingled for the sake of ornament, to be a natural source of delight. . . .

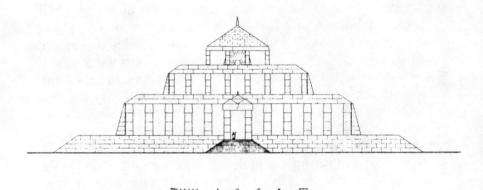

Sketch of Atlantean building as reconstructed by a Danish architect.
Measurements in meters. *Drawing courtesy of Jan Turlin.*

This particular mention of the colors of the building stones of Atlantis receives an unexpected confirmation in the prevailing color of rocks present in the Azores Islands. They are also white, black, and red.

The entire circuit of the wall which went round the outermost one they covered with a coating of brass, and the circuit of the next wall they coated with tin, and the third, which encompassed the citadel, flashed with the red light of orichalcum. The palaces in the interior of the citadel were constructed in this wise: In the center was a holy temple dedicated to Cleito and Poseidon, which remained inaccessible, and was surrounded by an enclosure of gold; this was the spot in which they originally begat the race of the ten princes, and thither they annually brought the fruits of the earth in their season from all the ten portions and performed sacrifices to each of them. Here, too, was Poseidon's own temple, of a stadium in length and half a stadium in width, and of a proportionate height, having a sort of barbaric splendor. All the outside of the temple, with the exception of the pinnacles, they covered with silver, and the pinnacles with gold. In the interior of the temple the roof was of ivory, adorned everywhere with gold and silver and orichalcum; all the other parts of the walls and pillars and floor they lined with orichalcum. In the temple they placed statues of gold; there was the god himself standing in a chariot—the charioteer of six winged horses—and of such a size that he touched the roof of the building with his head; around him there were a hundred Nereids riding on dolphins, for such were thought to be the number of them in that day. There were also in the interior of the temple other images which had been dedicated by private individuals. And around the temple on the outside were placed statues of gold of all the ten kings and of their wives; and there were many other great offerings, both of kings and of private individuals, coming both from the city itself and the foreign cities over which they held sway. . . .

The fabled treasures of Atlantis and the description of towers covered with silver and gold lying on the seafloor have fascinated readers—and treasure hunters—for thousands of years. Some of the very ancient cultures such as those of Egypt, Babylonia, Assyria, Persia, and the Incan empire of western South America collected great quantities of gold for their temples, royal palaces, and dynastic treasuries and therefore it is quite likely that a maritime power such as Atlantis would have amassed even greater treasures. Spanish records indicate that the Incas faced interior and exterior walls with thin sheets of gold. There is an interesting Greek reference to the treasures of Tartessos, the legendary city on the western coast of Spain thought to have been a colony or trading partner of Atlantis, which reported that Tartessos was so rich in precious metals that its ships were reputedly equipped with silver anchors.

[The Atlanteans had] fountains both of cold and hot springs; these were very abundant, and both kinds wonderfully adapted to use by reason of the sweetness and excellence of their waters. They constructed buildings about them, and planted suitable trees; also cisterns, some open to the heaven, others which they roofed over, to be used in winter as warm baths. There were the king's baths, and the baths of private persons, which were kept apart; also separate baths for women, and others again for horses and cattle, and to them they gave as much adornment as was suitable for them. The water which ran off they carried, some to the grove of Poseidon, where were growing all manner of trees of wonderful height and beauty, owing to the excellence of the soil; the remainder was carried by aqueducts which passed over the bridges to the outer circles; and there were many temples built and dedicated to many gods; also gardens and places of exercise, some for men and some set apart for horses, in both of the two islands formed by the zones; and in the center of the larger of the two there was a race course of a stadium in width, and in length allowed to extend all round the island, for horses to race in. . . .

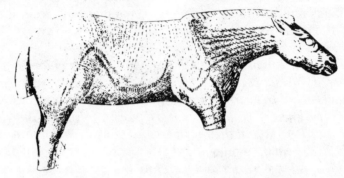

Carved stone horse from cave in Glozel, France. This horse, while carved in great detail, does not have indications of a bridle as do the other two horses represented on page 43. The horse may nevertheless have been domesticated to enable the artist to portray it in such detail.

The Atlantic Ocean still contains freshwater springs in the vicinity of the Azores Islands. Azorian fishermen apparently know where to find fresh water even in the open sea. They fill their pails from the ocean itself at a place where their memory tells them that fresh water exists, bubbling up from springs in the bottom that once, perhaps, supplied the needs of their prehistoric predecessors. Hot-water springs also are common in the Atlantic Islands. Hot water in Iceland is not only piped from springs into the cities and towns but exists in such quantity that it is used for heating buildings as well.

The reference to horses is understandable in Greek writing of Plato's period, as the horse, and horses of the sea, were associated with Poseidon, Ruler of the Sea—and of Atlantis. But Plato's mention of Atlantean horses has been frequently criticized since he refers to horses being used domestically at a time thousands of years before their appearance in drawings and sculpture as the pullers of light chariots in Egypt and as cavalry mounts in Assyria and the Middle East. However, the horse may have been domesticated by early man, either for transportation or for food, thousands of years prior to 4000 B.C. While horses in cave paintings frequently appear wild and in herds, some carved horse statuettes have been found in caves that are comparable in artistic quality to those of ancient Greece. Cave drawings of horses found in northern Europe clearly show bridles properly in place on the horse's head. Horses, once extant in the New World, may have been brought across the Atlantic by ship or by migration via the Bering Strait. However, the horse had disappeared by the time the Spanish conquerors arrived and brought the horse back to America. While there is no present indication whether or not the original American horse was domesticated, horse and human bones have been discovered together at Palo Aike, Argentina, and some other sites in South America.

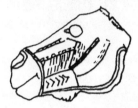 

Cro-Magnon carved representations on bone and in stone, found respectively in caves at San Michel d'Arudy and Lamarche, France, showing horses apparently wearing a form of bridle, which would indicate that horses were domesticated 20,000 to 25,000 years ago, a time period which would encompass the reported use of horses in Atlantis.

The docks were full of triremes and naval stores. . . . Crossing the outer harbors, which were three in number, you would come to a wall which began at the sea and went all round: this was everywhere distant fifty stadia from the largest zone and harbor, and enclosed the whole, meeting at the mouth of the channel toward the sea. The entire area was densely crowded with habitations; and the canal and the largest of the harbors were full of vessels and merchants coming from all parts, who, from their numbers, kept up a multitudinous sound of human voices and din of all sorts day and night. . . .

There are grounds for supposing that ancient navigation was much more advanced than was previously believed. Some Egyptian vessels were 250 feet in length, and one recorded Egyptian expedition circumnavigated Africa. Phoenician and Carthaginian vessels went even farther, leaving hundreds of Phoenician inscriptions cut in stone tablets along the banks of rivers in the jungles of Brazil and on the eastern coast of South America.

Large-scale oceanic navigation as suggested by Plato at a period thousands of years previous to the present would not only depend on organization, which Atlantis reputedly had, but also on a precise knowledge of navigation of the ocean, based on a means of calculating ship position. Although it has generally been assumed that ancient ships did not customarily sail out of sight of land, an underwater artifact found in the Mediterranean and neglected for years after its discovery was recently recognized as a Greek star computer operated by gears. Without knowing how general the use of such an instrument was, it is an indication that the ancient Greeks, Cretans, and other early seafarers would have been able to calculate their position on long sea voyages, enabling them to leave the Mediterranean and explore the Atlantic. Some sailed even farther. Copies of original maps made by such voyagers, maps that have survived the destruction of the ancient library centers where they were kept, show the coastline of the Americas at least 15,000 years before America was discovered. Other explorers plotted the coastline of Antarctica, showing coastal rivers, bays, and interior mountain ranges now thousands of feet under the ice. But the Antarctic coastline, according to bottom cores taken by research ships from the bottom of the Ross Sea and other coastal points, was ice free 8000 to 10,000 years ago, when the maps were presumably made. Examples of these maps (see page 133), now at the Library of Congress, constitute a direct testimony to the nautical and sci-

*entific progress achieved in an era prior to known history as well
as to Plato's reference to early world-wide sea travel.*

The whole country was described as being very lofty and
precipitous on the side of the sea, but the country immediately
above and surrounding the city was a level plain, itself surrounded by mountains which descended toward the sea; it was
smooth and even, but of an oblong shape, extending in one
direction three thousand stadia, and going up the country from
the sea through the center of the island two thousand stadia;
the whole region of the island lies toward the south, and is
sheltered from the north. The surrounding mountains . . . celebrated for their number and size and their beauty, in which
they exceeded all that are now to be seen anywhere; having in
them also many wealthy inhabited villages, and rivers and lakes,
and meadows supplying food enough for every animal, wild or
tame, and wood of various sorts, abundant for every kind of
work. . . . The plain . . . had been cultivated during many ages
by many generations of kings. It was rectangular, and for the
most part, straight and oblong, . . . when it followed the curve
of the circular ditch. The depth and width and length of this
ditch were incredible, and gave the impression that such a work,
in addition to so many other works, could hardly have been
wrought by the hand of man. . . . It was excavated to the depth
of a hundred feet, and its breadth was a stadium everywhere;
it was carried round the whole of the plain, and was ten thousand stadia in length. It received the streams which came down
from the mountains, and winding round the plain, and touching
the city at various points, was there let off into the sea. Likewise,
straight canals of a hundred feet in width were cut in the plain,
and again let off into the ditch, toward the sea; these canals
were at intervals of a hundred stadia, and by them they brought
down the wood from the mountains to the city, and conveyed
the fruits of the earth in ships, cutting transverse passages from
one canal into another, and to the city. . . .

*When he described the northern mountains of Atlantis and the
great plain extending to the south, Plato was making a more or
less accurate statement about the ocean bottom in the presumed
vicinity of Atlantis. Current oceanic soundings, although accom-*

plished almost 2500 years after the time of Plato, draw essentially the same picture, with high mountaintops such as Pico in the Azores and Teide in the Canaries continuing on under the water to join undersea mountain ranges. With due allowances made for further depth changes in the ocean floor and slipping of extensive areas of the ocean bottom between the grinding continental plates, Plato's description of the geography of Atlantis would resemble the way the sea bottom of the east central Atlantic would look if, in some future convulsion of the Earth, it rose again to the surface. An extensive irrigation system such as that

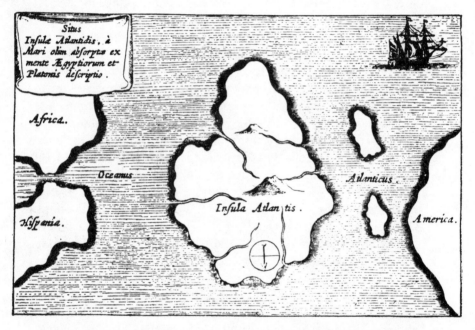

Father Athanasius Kircher, a Jesuit priest, drew a fairly detailed map of Atlantis in 1665, showing Atlantis as he thought it once was, since ocean crossings after Columbus had indicated that it no longer existed. Part of Father Kircher's inscription at left top of map reads, "Site of the island of Atlantis, in the past swallowed by the sea, in the belief of the Egyptians and Plato's description." The map, to our eyes, is upside down, since it points north. If the map is inverted, however, it suggests the true shape of the Mid-Atlantic Plateau, north and south of the Azores Islands, an unusual coincidence considering the lack of knowledge of oceanographic depths extant at that time.

described by Plato was not unusual in very ancient times. A number of civilizations such as the Incan empire of Peru and Bolivia, the Mayas of Yucatán, the empires of the Middle East, North Africa, and central Asia constructed enormous irrigation systems, of which some are still visible, but only from the air. When they were destroyed by war and climate changes, the once teeming populations vanished, and even today the areas have not regained their former population density.

. . . each of the lots in the plain had an appointed chief of men who were fit for military service, and the size of the lot was to be a square of ten stadia each way, and the total number of all the lots was sixty thousand.

And of the inhabitants of the mountains and of the rest of the country there was also a vast multitude having leaders, to whom they were assigned according to their dwellings and villages. The leader was required to furnish for war the sixth portion of a war-chariot so as to make up a total of ten thousand chariots; also two horses and riders upon them, and a light chariot without a seat, accompanied by a fighting man on foot carrying a small shield, and having a charioteer mounted to guide the horses; also, he was bound to furnish two heavy-armed men, two archers, three stone-shooters, and three javelin men, who were skirmishers, and four sailors to make up a complement of twelve hundred ships. Such was the order of war in the royal city—that of the other nine governments was different in each of them. . . .

Plato's preoccupation with the numbers of the Atlantean army and fleet probably reflects a common Greek memory of the huge Persian armies which had invaded Greece not long before Plato's period. These formidable hordes, consisting of moving masses of close to a million warriors and camp followers, were not a memory easily forgotten. In any case, considering the size of the area and the density of settlement, the size of the potential Atlantean forces would not be out of proportion with other ancient hosts.

The last part of the *Critias* dialogue deals especially with the government of Atlantis and with the decline of public probity and

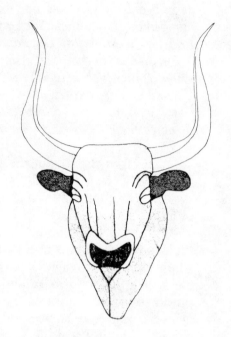

Representation of bull's head excavated in Crete, possibly one of the sacred bulls used in a ritual ceremony of considerable danger in which teams of young male and female contestants competed in vaulting over the bull's back through his sharp horns. This ritual competition may have been the basis for the Greek legend of the sacrifice of youths to the Minotaur—a monstrous half-human bull.

virtue. If Plato was using the Atlantis dialogues to make his own recommendations about good government, the observation that "Each of the ten kings, in his own division and in his own city, had the absolute control of the citizens, and in many cases of the laws, punishing and slaying whomsoever he would . . ." seems to indicate that Plato was a strong believer in "law and order."

The laws of Atlantis were inscribed on a pillar of the mysterious metal orichalcum:

> Now on the column, besides the law, there was inscribed an oath invoking mighty curses on the disobedient. . . .

When the ten hereditary kings of Atlantis met in council on public affairs alternately every five and six years they first performed sacrifices in what was a sort of royal bullfight.

> There were bulls who had the range of the temple of Poseidon; and the ten who were left alone in the temple, after they

had offered prayers to the gods that they might take the sacrifices that were acceptable to them, hunted the bulls without weapons, but with staves and nooses; and the bull which they caught they led up to the column; the victim was then struck on the head by them, and slain over the sacred inscription. . . .

Bull worship and bull sacrifice were widespread in the ancient Mediterranean civilizations of Crete, Egypt, North Africa, and Iberia and, according to Plato, a royal prerogative of Atlantis. The mystique of the ritual death of the bull, still practiced in Spain and a number of Spanish-American countries, may form a direct link with the customs of ancient Atlantis.

Finally Plato writes of a change in the nature of the Atlanteans:

For many generations, as long as the divine nature lasted in them, they were obedient to the laws, and well-affectioned toward the gods, who were their kinsmen: for they possessed true and in every way great spirits, practicing gentleness and wisdom in the various chances of life, and in their intercourse with one another. They despised everything but virtue, not caring for their present state of life, and thinking lightly on the possession of gold and other property, which seemed only a burden to them; neither were they intoxicated by luxury; nor did wealth deprive them of their self-control; . . . but when this divine portion began to fade away in them, and became diluted too often, and with too much of the mortal admixture, and the human nature got the upper hand, then, they being unable to bear their fortune, became unseemly, and to him who had an eye to see, they began to appear base, and had lost the fairest of their precious gifts; but to those who had no eye to see the true happiness, they still appeared glorious and blessed at the very time when they were filled with unrighteous avarice and power. Zeus, the god of gods, who rules with law, and is able to see into such things, perceiving that an honorable race was in a most wretched state, and wanting to inflict punishment on them, that they might be chastened and improved, collected all the gods into his most holy habitation, which, being placed in the center of the world, sees all things that partake of generation. And when he had called them together he spoke as follows: . . .

Plato's narrative breaks off just as he seems to be leading into a story of catastrophe caused by the anger of the gods over the decline of morals and the power madness of the Atlanteans. It is uncertain whether or not he wrote a third section, now lost, or interrupted his work on the death of his patron, Dionysius I, who originally commissioned it. Certain of his critics, ancient and modern, have suggested that, having established Atlantis and described it in more detail than was customary in that period in writers' accounts of foreign lands, he simply dropped it and went on to something else.

Other commentators have claimed that Plato invented the entire account, and one modern critic has observed, in an effort to dismiss the mystery of Atlantis in a single sentence, "Atlantis has been mentioned only by Plato and those who have read him."

However, as ethnological and linguistic research extends into the misty beginnings of prehistory, it is now possible to reply to this observation that, however much classical and medieval scholars may have been influenced in their beliefs by Plato, the fact remains that earlier cultures throughout the world independently preserved in their legends the memory of a great island empire that sank into the sea as a result of a world-wide disaster which shook the foundations of the Earth and inverted great areas of the land and sea. These legends, which include even the sounds of the name of the lost island, extend back far beyond the time of Athens or even the much older Babylon and the great centers of Egypt, and are shared by the Indian nations and tribes of the Americas, the inhabitants of northwestern Africa and Europe, the populations of the Pacific islands, and the earliest Hindus. Plato knew nothing of these peoples, nor they of him, but all shared a common memory of the power and destruction of the world that preceded theirs.

5

THE FORCE OF COLLECTIVE MEMORY

The British historian H. G. Wells, himself neutral on the subject of Atlantis' existence, once observed, "There is magic in names and the mightiest among these words of magic is Atlantis . . . it is as if this vision of a lost culture touched the most hidden thought of our soul." This assessment can be applied as effectively to the psyche of today's world as it was to the populations that survived the Flood and kept the legends of the world prior to theirs. The difference in the two outlooks consists of the easy acceptance of legend in very ancient times, when there was no printing, and limited or selective knowledge of geography, contrasted with our modern world, where there is certainly no shortage of books, communications, or, in general, of geographic awareness of one's surroundings. But it is the computerized knowledge and scientific expertise of the modern world, focusing indirectly and almost by chance on Atlantis, which has given within the last fifteen years more substance to the age-old legend than all of the theories, explanations, and discoveries since the island continent disappeared.

The memory of an Atlantean continent varies in form among the peoples of the lands surrounding the Atlantic Ocean. It was generally present as a myth of a western homeland or paradise among the inhabitants of present-day Ireland, Britain, Scandinavia, Spain, Portugal, and North Africa. On the opposite side, the Indian tribes of northeastern and Central America also considered it their homeland and source of civilization. Its form became more precise where written records existed, as in the case of Egypt, Phoenicia, Carthage, Greece (and through Greece, Rome), the Mayan kingdoms of Yucatán, and even India.

Heinrich Schliemann, the German amateur archaeologist who made such important contributions to archaeology, was considered a visionary or a fool until he proved that the hitherto legendary city of Troy was an actuality simply by digging for it deeply enough at the very spot where it was located by tradition, stated that during his mid-19th-century stay in St. Petersburg he personally examined two Egyptian papyri in the Hermitage Museum, one of which contained the following: "Pharaoh sent out an expedition to the west in search of traces of the land of Atlantis from whence, 3350 years before, the ancestors of the Egyptians arrived carrying with themselves all of the wisdom of their native land." According to Schliemann the search took five years, but the expedition found no trace of the vanished land.

Another Egyptian reference to what may have been the fate of Atlantis appears in one of the Harris papyri at the British Museum in London. It describes a tremendous cataclysm that had taken place thousands of years previously. We do not know, since the destruction of the ancient records was so complete, how many references to Atlantis were contained in the archives of Carthage and its parent Phoenician cities of Lebanon, or if there were Carthaginian expeditions that sailed past the Pillars of Hercules looking for vestiges of former Atlantic lands. We do know, however, that the Carthaginians habitually sailed the Atlantic in quest of new markets for trade and conquest. Ancient and medieval maps indicate that a number of islands, including the legendary Fortunate Islands and the much larger, far-off Antilla, were known to the Carthaginians and subsequently to the Romans after they obliterated their Carthaginian rivals.

Until their conquest by the Romans, however, the Carthaginians kept the Atlantic Ocean a Carthaginian secret, attacking, sinking, and killing the crews of all other vessels they encountered in the outer sea. Carthaginian security was so strict that sea captains were ordered, when in danger of capture, to scuttle their ships and kill themselves, an ending considered preferable to disgrace and death by torture if they were returned to Carthage. The dangers of the Atlantic were exaggerated by rumors spread by the Carthaginians; how great Atlantic fogs would engulf galleys and cause them to be lost until they were washed up on the coast with only skeletons at the oars, or that great masses of seaweed existed that caught ships in the middle of the ocean, through which winds could not carry nor oars propel them—in the words of a Carthaginian admiral, Himilco, "It holds back the ship like bushes." As a further discouragement to Atlantic voyagers (who would also have interfered with the Carthaginian monopoly) Himilco ominously warned of sea monsters that "moved continuously to and fro, fierce monsters swimming among the sluggish and slowly creeping ships."

In the 8th century, seven bishops with their followers allegedly escaped the Arab invasion of Portugal by sailing to islands of refuge thought to be remnants of Atlantis, far out in the Atlantic. There is a record of Arab mariners subsequently venturing out into the Atlantic in search of the pleasant island of legend, and perhaps of the escaped bishops and their flocks as well. They returned and reported their foray as unsuccessful.

Farther north along the European coast, French, British, and Irish legends mixed with the older tales of a lost island. The Irish legend of Tir-nan-n'oge concerns a great city now sunk beneath the waves, and other Celtic legends refer specifically to the City of the Golden Gates, presently under the Atlantic, reminiscent of the prodigal use of gold attributed by Plato to the Atlantean capital. Cloud formations on the horizon, seen from Atlantic beaches, tended then as now to transform themselves into castles and soaring towers. One could easily invent tales of sunken cities and drowned cathedrals whose bells could still be heard chiming on certain nights, and even days, when the thick fog covered the sea. In this manner memories of the distant past joined with distinctly local legends. Ancient Avalon became associated with the final destination of King Arthur and the rising of the ocean. The sinking of the continental shelf off Brittany was linked to the local legend of King Gradlon, whose city of Ys was drowned by the ocean because his daughter, the disobedient princess Mahu, gave to her lover the key to the dike against the sea. Such medieval legends obscure but do not change the previous traditions that the tribes of western Gaul came from Atlantis, as recollected by the long lines of huge stone menhirs and dolmens that still lead down to the western shores of Brittany and continue out under the ocean.

When the age of discovery began for Europe, the memory of Atlantis still stirred the imagination of the first navigators to explore the ocean sea. Much that had once been known had been forgotten. Although Jean de Béthencourt, a French nobleman in the service

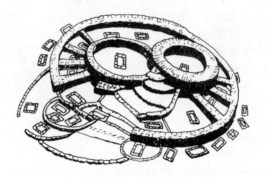

Remains of stone buildings on Canary Islands resembling circular ruins in other prehistoric sites throughout the world.

of Spain, officially "discovered" the Canary Islands in 1395, their existence had previously been noted in a Catalonian atlas published twenty years earlier, based on information copied from ancient maps. The Spanish conquerors of the Canary Islands received a vivid reminder of Atlantis when they found that the native Guanches (their word for "men") were surprised to learn that other people had survived the disaster that had flooded their world and had left them isolated on islands that were once the tops of the high mountains of their former homeland (cf. Plato's report: "When the gods purge the Earth with a deluge of water . . . you herdsmen and shepherds on the mountains are the survivors").

The Guanches, when they were discovered, presented an example of cultural disintegration, an effect often noticed among survivors of interrupted cultures. They had stone inscriptions that they could no longer read, ancient stone houses that they no longer took the trouble to repair or rebuild, and, most surprisingly of all for islanders, they had no boats, owing to their understandable fear of the sea that had swallowed the much larger lands of their ancestors.

If the Guanches had not been so quickly exterminated in subsequent warfare against the Spanish occupiers, more information concerning their legends and racial origin would be available today. They were said to be white-skinned, often with blond hair, very tall, and of a type now catalogued as the Cro-Magnon race, which first appeared in Western Europe 35,000 years ago.

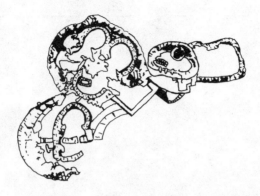

Aerial view of ruins of prehistoric stone temple or tomb at Mnajdra, on the island of Malta, showing resemblance in shape and design to unidentified ruins on the Canary Islands. Constructions of similar plan, estimated as being 10,000 years old, have been unearthed at Jericho, in Jordan. Underwater ruins with outlines similar to these circular patterns have been seen and photographed in the Atlantic Ocean by pilots flying over areas where submarine plateaus and continental shelves rise to approximately 100 feet of the surface.

When the Portuguese first arrived at the Azores, no people were living there, although someone had evidently been there before. For example, on the island of Corvo a statue was still standing of a mounted warrior pointing westward. Unfortunately, while being taken down to be sent to the King of Portugal, the statue was broken and the pieces, subsequently sent to the king, eventually disappeared. An unusual legend concerned with this statue recounts that it was called Caté or Catés. This word resembles a word in a language not of Europe but of the New World, Quechua, the language of the Inca empire of South America. In Quechua *catí* means "that way"— in other words, toward the American continents.

Christopher Columbus, who received from the Spanish crown the title of Admiral of the Ocean Sea (as opposed to the Mediterranean), may be said to have accumulated considerable "Atlantean" indoctrination prior to his first voyage. While studying all available information concerning his proposed route, he came upon an increasing number of references to Atlantis as more and more Greek documents and more accurate maps of the ocean spread across western

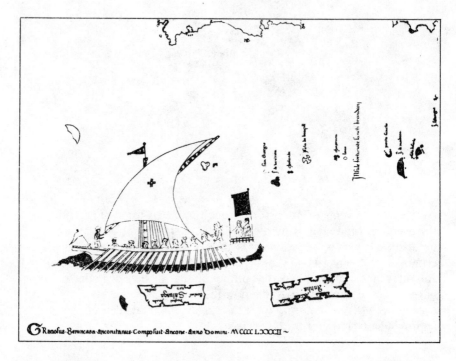

Benincasa map of 1482, said to have been carried on board the *Santa María* by Columbus. Under the ship are three islands which may indicate presumed vestiges of Atlantis: one named Antilia, another the Savage Island, and the third unidentified.

Europe after the fall of Constantinople to the Turks in 1453. Among these were the Benincasa map of 1482 showing Antilla at the approximate position of legendary Atlantis, close to another large "savage island." Columbus also perused a number of other maps showing Antilla or Atlantis spelled in various ways, and located in the western part of the Atlantic. He is thought to have had at his disposal an early copy of the Piri Re'is map (see photo section following page 80), itself recopied a number of times from early Greek sources which, among other geographic "previews," clearly showed the eastern coast of South America (as yet undiscovered) in relation to and at the correct distance from Spain and Africa.

Columbus' son, Fernando, observed that his father was exceptionally interested in reports of sunken lands under the ocean and

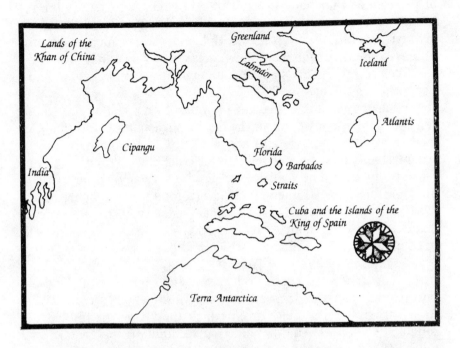

Outline of land areas across the Atlantic as copied from map given by a pilot to King Henry VII in 1500. The New World on this map is still considered to be connected to China, and Atlantis is indicated in the upper right section of the chart.

especially intrigued by the following excerpt from the play *Medea* by Seneca, the Roman playwright, philosopher, and tutor to Nero:

> *There will come a time in the late age of the world*
> > *When the ocean will relax its bonds over what it holds,*
> > *And land will appear in its glory.*
> *Thetis* will uncover new continents*
> > *And Thule† will no longer be the end of the world.*

Columbus, who had written to numerous authorities about the mysterious ocean in preparation for his voyage, was advised by a

---

*Thetis = the ocean.
†Thule = the legendary northern edge of the world.

correspondent living in Holland that he could probably stop at some of the islands that had survived the drowning of Atlantis for revictualment of his small fleet. As the island where Columbus made his first landfall, Watling, in the Bahamas, was a high point of a former submerged land mass, he may fairly be said to have followed his Dutch correspondent's advice, although he never did get to Plato's "opposite continent."

An imaginative link between Columbus' own racial origins (there is a widespread conviction in the Spanish-speaking world that Columbus was of Jewish origin) and ancient Old World memories of Atlantis has been suggested by Ignatius Donnelly: "When Columbus sailed to discover a new world, or to rediscover an old one, he took his departure from a Phoenician seaport, founded by that great race 2500 years previously. This Atlantean sailor, with his Phoenician features, sailing from an Atlantean port, simply reopened the path of commerce and colonization which had been closed when Plato's island sank into the sea."

As they continued their exploration and conquest of the New World, the Spaniards learned that the various names used by the Indian tribes for the place from which they came resembled the sound of the word Atlantis and that in addition the Indians had other legends resembling stories with which the Spaniards were already familiar from the Bible. These concerned a great flood, selected individuals who survived it on vessels with their animals, the erection of a huge tower to escape the next flood, an elaborate system of sacrifice (somewhat exaggerated among the Aztecs, who sacrificed thousands of victims every year), penance, and redemption. At first it was suggested that these new races were the ten lost tribes of Israel. Others said they were more probably surviving Atlanteans, principally because of the former Atlantean connection with Spain through the lost port city of Tartessos and the prehistoric settlements of Andalusia. Cádiz, for example, is named for Gadeiros, one of the twin sons of Poseidon, who, in Plato's account, "obtained as his lot the extremity of the island toward the Pillars of Hercules . . . which is still called the region of Gades . . . in the language of the country which is named after him," surely an easily interpreted legacy from the past to justify Spain in annexing any surviving parts of Atlantis.

Although the Spaniards were not sure who the Indians were, the Indians on their part were sure that the white strangers were the ancient white gods who many centuries before had brought them civilization. These were gods such as Quetzalcoatl for the Aztecs, Toltecs, and Maya; Kulkulkan and Votan for other Maya; Bochica for the Chibchas; and Viracocha for the Incas. All these expected gods had promised to return, bringing other white gods to continue their work of civilization. By a fatal coincidence (for the Aztecs) Cortez and his army appeared in Mexico in A.D. 1519, *ce atl* ("one reed"), the very year prophesied for Quetzalcoatl's return. Considering that Atlantis, the Eastern Island in the ocean for the Indians, and the Western Island for the Europeans, was the ancient link between the opposing continents around the ocean, it is one of the most curious coincidences in history that the Spanish conquerors were half expecting to find Atlantis, while the Amerindian races on their part were firmly expecting the return of their respective gods from this same land in the ocean. It was mainly because of the latter assumption, fostered by the Spaniards when they realized what was happening, that warlike and well-organized Indian nations that firmly believed their own legends became confused and finally were unable to successfully resist the Spaniards, whom they outnumbered thousands to one.

There were, of course, military advantages held by the conquistadores: steel swords and armor, cannons and gunpowder, giant mastiffs trained for battle, and frightening horses (the Aztecs at first thought that the horse and rider was a single animal). But these advantages would not have been sufficient for the victory of the small number of the Spaniards if their opponents had not first welcomed them in the belief that their former gods and benefactors from the Eastern Sea had returned. The power of legend and memory contributed both to the fulfillment of Seneca's prophecy and also that of Quetzalcoatl, although certainly not in the way the Aztecs expected.

After Columbus' first voyage, as European navigators became increasingly familiar with the Atlantic and its islands and found no tangible evidence of Atlantis, a number of writers, philosophers, and scientists began to look for other locations for the Lost Continent—a process that has continued to this day.

ATLANTIS IN AMERICA

Francis Bacon was one of the first English writers to assume that the missing continent was North or South America, or both of them together, and that the Indians of the Americas (Amerindians) were Atlanteans.

This supposition, while supported in part by Plato's account, which spoke of the "opposite continent" across the "real sea," would seem to neglect the existence of Atlantis as an island and not to consider the Amerindians as refugees from a sunken island, as many of the tribal legends suggest even to an approximation of the sound of its name.

Along the eastern coasts and inland regions of the Americas, unusual similarities exist between Amerindian words and words long existing in European, Asian, and African languages. These similarities were noted by the Spanish colonizers, who were astonished by the apparent fact that the Indians were using words from the ancient languages of the Old World.

Some striking examples include the Aztec (Nahuatl) word *teocalli* ("house of the gods," which resembles the Greek *theou kalia* "God's house"), the similarity between the Greek word for "river" (*potamós*) and the Indian *Potomac* and a number of rivers in eastern South America starting with *poti*. The word *tepec,* meaning "hill" in Nahuatl (Chapultepec = Grasshopper Hill), also means "hill" (*tepe*) in the Turkic languages of central Asia. Other transatlantic linguistic similarities and their associated meanings seem too close to be coincidental.

AMERINDIAN LANGUAGE	EURO-ASIAN-AFRICAN COUNTERPART
Aimara: *malku* - - "king"	Arabic: *melek* - -"king"
	Hebrew: *melekh* - - "king"
Maya: *balaam* - - "priest"	Hebrew: *bileam* - - "magician"
Guarani: *oko* - - "home"	Greek: *oika* - - "home"
Nahuatl: *papalo-tl* - - "butterfly"	Latin: *papilio* - - "butterfly"
Nahuatl: *mixtli* - - "cloud"	Greek: *omichtli* - - "cloud"
Klamath: *pniw* - - "to blow"	Greek: *pneu* - - (root) "to blow"
Quechua: *andi* - - "high mountain"	Ancient Egyptian: *andi* - - "high valley"
Quechua: *llake llake* - - "heron"	Sumerian: *lak lak* - - "heron"
Quechua: *llu llu* - - "lie"	Sumerian: *lul* - - "lie"
Araucanian: *anta* - - "sun"	Ancient Egyptian: *anta* - - "sun"
Araucanian: *bal* - - "ax"	Sumerian: *bal* - - "ax"

An unusual example of a word that sounds and means the same in a number of languages scattered throughout the Old and the New

World is the word for "father"—*aht, tata, ata*, with slight modifications. It is especially interesting in that this is not a natural sound comparable to the variants of *ma, mama, mu, um*, etc. for "mother". One is led to wonder whether these recognizable variants of what is essentially the same word for "father" represent an echo of one of the world's first languages.

AMERINDIAN & POLYNESIAN	EURO-ASIAN-AFRICAN COUNTERPART
Quechua: *taita*	Basque: *aita*
Dakotah: *atey*	Hungarian: *atya*
Zuni: *tatchu*	Tagalog: *tatay*
Seminole: *tatí*	Russian: *aht-yets*
Eskimo: *atatak*	Ancient Egyptian: *aht*
Náhuatl (Aztec) *tatli*	Turkish & Turkic languages: *ata*
Central Mexican Indian	Old Gothic (variant): *atta*
dialects: *tata*	Latin (colloquial): *tata*
Fijian: *tata*	Rumanian: *tata*
Samoan: *tata*	Slovak: *tata*
	Maltese: *tata*
	Sinhalese: *tata*
	Yiddish: *tatale*
	Cymric: *tad*

One of the more suggestive word similarities occurs in the word *atl*, which in the Nahuatl language of ancient Mexico and the Berber language of North Africa has the same meaning—"water." The doubling of this sound—*atl-atl*—was the word used for a spear-throwing device used by the Aztecs, a long flat wood contraption with a hook, enabling the user to throw his spear farther and with greater accuracy and force. This ancient word, which the Aztecs took from former peoples of Mexico who may themselves have learned it from the legendary teachers who came from the Eastern Ocean, has been adopted into English as an anthropological term to designate spear throwers still used by some jungle tribes in different parts of the world.

The presence of words from the Old World languages in the languages of the Americas for thousands of years before the rediscovery is especially interesting in view of references in the ancient Mayan book, the *Popul Vuh*, which seems like an echo of the Biblical confusion of tongues: "Those who gaze at the rising of the sun . . . had but one language before going west. Here the language of the tribes was changed. Their speech became different. All that they had heard and understood when departing from Tulan had become incomprehensible to them. . . . Alas, we have abandoned our speech. Our language was one when we departed from Tulan, one in the country where we were born."

Besides the connection of words and language there were other common memories. They included art forms, pyramids, legends of a great flood, calendar calculations, and feast days. (The Day of the Dead, our Halloween, was celebrated in pre–Columbian Mexico and Peru as well as by the Celtic Druids of the British Isles and Western Europe.) Even games were almost the same—Parcheesi was played in ancient Mexico under the name of *patolli* (see photo section following page 112). And the Basques, often presumed to be descendants of the Atlanteans, shared with the Aztecs and Maya an obsession with ball games with the startling difference that in America the loser was apt to forfeit his life along with the lost game. The Basques, the Maya, and the Ossets of the Caucasus were also united by the prevalence of the rare blood factor RH negative. While these many similarities could be the result of transatlantic visits or past integrations, it also seems logical to suppose that these coincidental similarities could have traveled east or west from a central point in the Atlantic, just as the common legends suggest.

The theory that Atlantis was really America is of course in opposition to the concept of a lost land under the ocean. It is only recently that deep-sea probes have been able to plot the true shape of the sea bottom (an obvious place to look for Atlantis!).

Numerous archaeologists and explorers over the last hundred years have searched for Atlantis in a variety of locations. Almost any extensive archaeological find that does not fit within a recognized cultural pattern is liable to elicit the rhetorical question, "Was this Atlantis?" in the ensuing headlines.

Many of the places advanced as being the basis for Plato's commentary are either sites of unusual or unexplained cultures or are cultures that more or less seem to conform with the details of Plato's description of Atlantis, except for the key reference to its position in the Atlantic Ocean.

Minoan (Cretan) figure of a goddess. The Minoan civilization (named for its famous king, Minos) was surprisingly modern in its creature comforts, plumbing facilities, and other luxuries. Minoan women apparently had equal status with men, enjoyed attractive clothing of considerable freedom, and even participated in the dangerous games with the bulls.

THERA (Santorini)

The theory that Atlantis has been found on Thera, an island of the Greek Cyclades north of Crete in the Aegean, is principally based on the opinions of Dr. Spiridon Marinatos, an archaeologist, and Dr. Angelos Galanopoulos, an archaeologist and seismologist. They believe that a tremendous volcanic explosion which took place on Thera about 1500 B.C. destroyed a cultural center and caused the Cretan maritime empire to begin its decline. Thera is now a crescent-shaped instead of a circular island, the missing part of the circle having exploded and vanished under the Aegean, leaving only an abyss in the sea hundreds of feet deep.

The fact that Thera, even with its missing part, is so much smaller than the dimensions given for Atlantis by Plato is explained by the supposition that the Egyptian priests made a mistake in the translation of the Egyptian sign for one hundred, translating the word for "hundred" as "thousand" when they interpreted the writings of Saïs to Solon, Crantor, and others. This epic error would conveniently fit in Thera to the Atlantis story since every reference to a number over a thousand would be divided by ten whereas all numbers under a thousand would be left alone. This "devaluation" would leave a larger Thera and/or Crete with the approximate measurements given by Plato for Atlantis, the canal system, and the central plain, but would cut down the number of inhabitants to a number that might have lived there, reduce the figures given for the army, and limit the fabled fleet to comparatively few vessels. It would even bring one time element into a more comprehensive focus, as Plato's figure of Atlantis existing 9000 years before *his* time (i.e., 9500 B.C.) would translate to 950 B.C., considerably closer to the scientifically calculated time of the Thera volcanic explosion of 1500 B.C. Extensive digging on Thera has revealed an advanced culture with strikingly beautiful art forms and sophisticated housing under 130 feet of volcanic ash.

An advantage of this facile solution to the question of Atlantis is that Thera and Crete are available to visitors and sightseers, with Thera experiencing a sort of tourist boom with hotels and shops relating to Atlantis and the sale of Atlantean reproductions. A supremely modern touch to the venerable legend is offered by the existence on the island of an Atlantis Rentacar company.

But Thera, despite its archaeological and Atlantean renown, is not a new discovery. Donnelly, a leading proponent of Atlantis in the Atlantic, discussed it one hundred years ago as a proof of lands sinking in volcanic eruptions and floods, together with a series of other examples in Mexico, the Caribbean, Iceland, the Atlantic Islands, Java, and India. Quite apart from the alleged mistake in the Egyptian-to-Greek translation and the fact that it was destroyed by a volcano (like Pompeii, Herculaneum, and the city of Heliké, which fell into the Gulf of Corinth), Thera is probably simply one more victim of natural disasters in the Mediterranean and is not in name or description connected with the Atlantis of Plato and other commentators. (The possibilities of traveling to "Atlantis" have not been lost on other national groups with legendary connections with Atlantis. Iberia, the Spanish airline, undertook fairly recently an advertising campaign with a dramatic photograph of the sea and mountains of the Canary Islands and a caption reading: "Only Iberia can fly your clients to the lost continent of Atlantis").

TUNISIA

The theory of Albert Hermann, a German historian and geographer, proposes that a dried-up marsh section of Tunisia—the Shott el Djerid—once a bay of the Mediterranean that later became the inland Lake Tritonia, with a citadel island in the middle, is where the real Atlantis was located. In checking the measurements of Atlantis as given by Plato, he deduced that the translation error was not of ten but of thirty, and that all of Plato's figures of dimension could and should be divided by this number. When this is done, the central plain of Tunisia, once supposedly an island, would have the dimensions attributed to Atlantis by Plato. But by this calculation the great canals and lofty cities would be downgraded to small villages with a system of ten-foot-wide irrigation ditches—hardly worthy of the grandiose aspect one expects of Atlantis.

A local tradition tells that under the waters north of Sousse, Tunisia, a powerful kingdom disappeared into the sea, perhaps a memory of vanished islands or land bridges in the Mediterranean. It is probable that most of the prehistoric sites in Tunisia were modified by the Carthaginian empire centered in Tunisia. Carthage itself, with its enormous port facilities, great temples, trading centers, and its use of elephants, has itself been frequently suggested as the model for Atlantis.

HELIGOLAND IN THE NORTH SEA

One of the first "discoveries" of Atlantis by undersea divers was accomplished in 1953 by an expedition under a German pastor, Jurgen Spanuth. Spanuth believed that the true Atlantis was once a northern civilization, now sunk under the North Sea. This, according to Spanuth, was the same tribal group that had sent the expedition which invaded Egypt during its historical periods and was depicted on the temple walls of Medinet Habu as the invasion of "the people of the sea." Spanuth's divers found parallel rock walls near Heligoland at a depth of forty-five feet, and later divers brought up worked flint implements of presumably Stone Age manufacture. The divers reported by telephone communication during the dive that the walls were made of black, white, and red rocks, the colors mentioned by Plato as the colors of the rocks of Atlantis and also used by the Aztecs and other Amerindians in describing Aztlán as "the red and black land."

Considering that parts of the North Sea were above sea level in fairly recent times, it is probable that a number of other ancient constructions will be found there in the future, in addition to the stone axes and mastodon bones that have already been brought up to the surface.

YUCATÁN AND CENTRAL AMERICA

The early French *américanistes*, the specialists in the prehistory of the Americas, such as the Abbé Brasseur de Bourbourg and

Auguste Le Plongeon, saw in the Maya art forms, culture, and science enough similarities to ancient Egypt to establish a direct link to Atlantis. Both of these remarkable researchers taught themselves the Maya language and lived among the Maya Indians, learning their legends. However, they weakened their case by excessive belief in information that is still uncertain and by making intuitive translations of texts that still have not yet been translated. The Maya written hieroglyphics can be read still only partially, except for names and dates. Although only four manuscripts escaped being burned by overenthusiastic early missionaries, it may be that the future information about Atlantis (as *Aztlán, Atitlán,* or *Atlán*) will become known if more documents or an effective key to the hieroglyphs are discovered. The extension of Maya roads and building complexes into the sea indicates flooding of extensive coastal lands, and it may be that the Mayan custom of abandoning cities and building new ones farther inland was caused by an instinctive memory of an oceanic cataclysm. Even in central Mexico the great pyramid of Cholula was built, according to tradition, to serve as a refuge from the "next" flood.

TIAHUANACO, BOLIVIA

According to a theory developed by Arthur Poznansky and seconded by others, the cyclopean stone city of Tiahuanaco was originally a seaport that was thrust two miles upward to become part of the Andes plateau eleven to twelve thousand years ago by a cataclysm which affected the whole world. This concept is seemingly supported by the presence of calcified saltwater maritime plants that make a watermark on hundreds of miles of surrounding mountains. The size of the constructions of Tiahuanaco, the use of silver tenons to hold the giant blocks together, the stone bas-reliefs that indicate a knowledge of astronomy, and prehistoric animals depicted on pottery contribute to the opinion of some researchers that this may have been the world's first civilization or part of it; in other words—Atlantis.

TARTESSOS, SOUTHERN SPAIN–NORTHERN MOROCCO

Greeks and Carthaginians had frequent contacts with Tartessos, the ancient seaport, shipbuilding and commercial entrepôt of south-

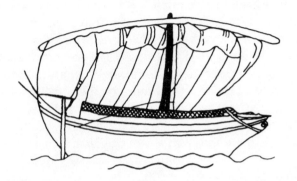

Greek sailing ship. Greek, Phoenician, and Carthaginian traders maintained a long contact with the misty city of Tartessos, on the west coast of Spain, a city so rich in metals that ship captains, in order to carry more silver, substituted silver anchors on their way back to home ports.

ern Spain. Tartessos is mentioned in the Bible as Tharshish, possessor of a great navy that brought valuable and somewhat exotic cargo to King Solomon: "... once in three years came the navy of Tharshish, bringing gold, and silver, ivory, apes, and peacocks. So King Solomon exceeded all the kings of the earth for riches. ..." (1 Kings 10:22, 23)

The Greek historian Herodotus (fifth century B.C.) also referred to a city in or on the Atlantic Ocean considered an Atlantean colony or part of Atlantis itself. He wrote of "a city called Tartessos . . . beyond the Pillars of Hercules," and, stressing the profit motive inspiring shipowners then as now, added that the Greek shipmasters ". . . made by the return voyage a profit more than any Greeks before."

Ten-thousand-year-old mines of precious metals in southern Spain have been linked with this Tartessos culture, as well as a series of enormous cut-stone constructions in Andalusia and extensive hydraulic works and walls along the Rio Tinto and Guadalquivir rivers. Archaeologists such as Adolf Schulten, O. Jensen, and R. Hennig suggest that Tartessos was Atlantis itself and extended through southern Spain over to Morocco with other large islands which are now covered by the Mediterranean. Schulten worked on this theory for fifty years without finding Tartessos, which, he concluded, had sunk under the marshes near the rivers. Helen Whishaw of the

Anglo-Hispanic School of Archaeology in Seville was of the opinion that parts of Tartessos-Atlantis may be found through the exploration of ancient passageways that exist *underneath* the present city of Seville. While there is no doubt that Tartessos disappeared, the reason for its disappearance may not have been a natural catastrophe but the sudden conquest and annihilation by the Carthaginians, who had strong feelings of antipathy toward commercial rivals. It is also possible that Tartessos and its empire were simply a vestigial colony of Atlantis, not strong enough to survive against new and powerful enemies.

WEST AFRICA—NIGERIA

Example of ancient West Africa bronze casting of the type known as the Benin bronzes, indicating both artistic and metallurgic expertise.

Leo Frobenius, a German archaeologist, bases his claim that Yorubaland and other sites along the African coast near Nigeria were the advanced cultures that gave rise to stories brought back by Phoenician navigators about mysterious civilizations in the ocean. The remarkable statues of cast bronze manufactured in Benin, and other cultural patterns, represent an African civilization of considerable development. The Yoruba god of the ocean, Olokun, shares a number of attributes with Poseidon, god of the sea and legendary founder of Atlantis.

EAST AFRICA OR ARABIA

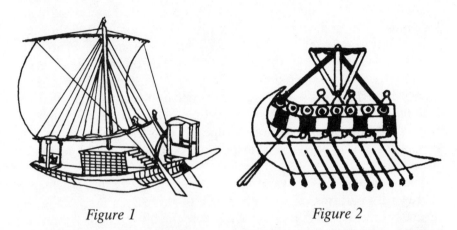

| Figure 1 | Figure 2 |

Egyptian ship used for navigation on the Nile and beyond. Some larger cargo-bearing ships measured 250 to 300 feet in length and were capable of making long journeys down the African coast. There existed a former "Suez" canal cut through the desert and connecting the Nile with the Red Sea. *(Figure 1)*

Contemporary representation of Middle Eastern galley. Galleys of Phoenicia and Israel explored the African coasts of the Red Sea and beyond in search of trading goods and treasure. *(Figure 2)*

Somewhere along the coast of the Red Sea and inland lay the locations of the legendary lands of Punt and Ophir. Punt, according to Egyptian records, was a far land well down the east coast of Africa to which the Egyptians sent well-organized fleets on expeditions of exploration and for the gathering of treasures, dwarfs, animals, and slaves.

Both the Hebrews and the Phoenicians sent fleets to Ophir in search of gold and precious stones as well as *almud* (sandalwood?) trees, which, according to the Bible, were used for the construction of the Temple at Jerusalem. These treasure-filled places may have been situated in Somalia, Eritrea, Ethiopia, or even farther south in Zimbabwe and perhaps in southern Arabia. Like many other fabled and unidentified lands, they have been suggested as prototypes for Atlantis.

BRAZIL

Large stone cities thousands of years old, with avenues paved with stone blocks, and huge pyramids now covered with trees, supposedly located in the Brazilian jungle, have been reported and described by a number of explorers who allegedly visited them during the last several centuries. Many explorers searching for them have been lost in the jungle, including an entire military expedition. These mysterious cities were considered by Colonel P. H. Fawcett (who disappeared in 1925 while on one of his repeated searches) as having a direct contact with Atlantis or even being Atlantis itself, when the climate in Amazonia was more temperate and the Amazon and its tributaries flowed through a fertile area before the land became a jungle.

The very name *Brazil* contains a strange memory or knowledge shared with cultures on the other side of the ocean. According to legends current in Western Europe before the discovery of America, Brazil or Hy Brazil was the name of a land across the unexplored Atlantic. Then, when Brazil was eventually discovered, it was given the name of the legend. But the name seemed to contain a message, as B-R-Z-L meant *iron* in Hebrew and also in Aramaic, the one-time general language of Mesopotamia and the Levant. And only much later did it become evident that Brazil possessed the largest iron ore deposits in the world.

ANTARCTICA

The rediscovery during the 20th century of a number of maps that had been copied and recopied from charts thousands of years old indicated that mariners of antiquity were aware that large parts of Antarctica were ice free at a time thousands of years before the present, when the poles were located in more equatorial regions. Flavio Barbieron, an Italian naval officer and researcher working on this theory of Atlantis in Antarctica, believes that artifacts, records, and ruins of an Atlantean civilization can be found under the ice; most probably in the section of Antarctica claimed by Argentina.

A SUNKEN CONTINENT IN THE PACIFIC OR INDIAN OCEANS

In various islands scattered through Micronesia there are a number of enormous stone ruins and earth pyramids whose purpose and

Remarkable coincidence between examples of the script of Easter Island and the cities of the Indus Valley, the two cultures being at the distance, one from the other, of half the circumference of the globe. Neither script has been deciphered.

whose builders have been forgotten. A ruined stone city on Ponape is built along stone canals and dikes that still cover eleven square miles on a series of islands, some of which are artificial. Legends of the Pacific Islands recount that their island groups were all that remained from the continent of Kalu'a, destroyed by explosions and tidal waves. A Hawaiian legend recounts: "Our motherland rests . . . at the bottom of the Royal Ocean."

On Easter Island 600 enormous carved stone statues, many mounted on platforms whose stonework resembles that of the Incas, suggest that the island is a relic of a much larger land area. Writings on sacred wooden tablets closely resemble the prehistoric writing of the Indus Valley cultures, half a world away. Many researchers believe that a continent or a number of island chains existed in the Pacific or in the Indian Ocean (lands variously called Mu or Lemuria) and think that the existence of these lands could have been the basis for the Atlantis legend or that they were coexistent in time with the Atlantic continent.

THE SAHARA DESERT

It has been ascertained that the Sahara was once part of the ocean, later a diminishing lake, and then, before becoming a desert, a verdant area suitable for human habitation. Sophisticated cave paintings in the Tassili Mountains of Algeria, thousands of years old, depict men and domestic and wild animals living in a land of trees, rivers, and lakes. Count Byron Kuhn de Prorok (*Mysterious Sahara*) has led expeditions to some of the most desolate sections of the Sahara in search of vestiges of Atlantis and the possible connection with the mysterious Tuareg tribes of the Sahara, which

Rock painting from the Tassili Mountains of Algeria indicating sophisticated painting techniques at a time that the present desert contained rivers and lakes. In a number of cases, crude figures have been drawn across the original figures, apparently at a time when the climate had changed, as the lake had dried up and the original culture had vanished.

possess a written language of great antiquity, distinct from their spoken language.

OTHER PARTS OF EUROPE

Sites in Europe suggested for Atlantis based on climate changes and the presence of stone ruins difficult to classify also give evidence of regional pride. Atlantis has been placed in Portugal, near Lisbon, on the southwest coast of France and England, on the Massif Central (central plateau) of France, in Sweden near Upsala, under the sea and coast of the Netherlands and Belgium, and in Mecklenburg, East Prussia, now in the Eastern Zone of Germany. The advanced but mysterious pre-Roman rulers of most of Italy, the Etruscans, have been suggested as Atlanteans, especially since Plato specifically mentioned their lands in Tyrrhenia as part of the Atlantean empire. Even the island of Spitzbergen, one of the last land masses before the North Pole, has been suggested as a northern Atlantis, perhaps inspired by the memory of Thule, the northern edge of the world.

AREAS IN ASIA

Several possible locations for Atlantis have been claimed in the USSR. One of them is the Caucasus Mountains, possibly because of the survival there of extremely ancient cultures and languages. Another is the Sea of Azov, which has shrunk considerably during the last 2000 years. Legends of great prehistoric cities in central Asia and northern Iran have motivated some theorists to suggest that Atlantis may have been located not in the Atlantic but on an island in the Theytis Ocean, which once covered large areas of central Asia. The island of Ceylon, with its enormous cities covered by the jungle and its traditions of having been cut off from the Indian mainland by a rising of the waters of the Indian Ocean, is considered still another possibility.

An overall opinion of the majority of investigators who have searched for the location of Atlantis, however, agrees with James Bramwell (*Lost Atlantis*), who wrote, "Either Atlantis was in the Atlantic Ocean or it was not Atlantis." Major Kurt Bilau, an officer in the German army during World War I and later an enthusiastic researcher of Atlantis, expressed this idea in inspiring terms in an article he wrote in 1923. Basing his opinion on the then recent findings by oceanic research ships in the Azores region of the Atlantic (especially the *Meteor* discoveries), he echoed the feelings of generations of believers in Atlantis before and after him:

Deep under the ocean's waters Atlantis is now reposing and only its highest summits are still visible in the shape of the Azores.. . . . The great island rose in steep cliffs from the sea. . . . Its cold and hot springs described by the ancient authors are still there as they flowed many millenniums ago. The mountain-lakes of Atlantis have been transformed now into submerged ones. . . . If we follow exactly Plato's indications and seek the site of Poseidonis among the half submerged summits of the Azores, we will find it to the south of the Dollabarata. There, upon an eminence, in the middle of a large and comparatively straight valley, well protected from the winds, stood its splendid capital, the 'city of the golden gates.' . . . It is strange that the scientists have sought Atlantis everywhere, but have given the least attention to this spot, which after all was clearly indicated by Plato.

In spite of, or because of, the continuing public interest in Atlantis, a number of books and studies on the negative side have sought to prove not where Atlantis was but rather that it was not or is not anywhere except in the minds of those who believe in it. Some scholars who totally reject the possibility of Atlantis have dedicated years of their lives in an attempt to prove that the study of Atlantis is a waste of time.

Among oceanographers and archaeologists in general it is the custom to regard any search for or reference to Atlantis with amusement and sometimes with considerable intolerance. N. Susemihl, a specialist in Platonic studies, who has been quoted by Nikolai Zhirov (*Atlantis:* 1964), expressed his attitude toward Atlantis and its adherents when he said, "The catalogue of statements about Atlantis is a fairly good aid for the study of human madness." In other words, if you do not agree with the established (and my) opinion, you are probably insane and perhaps dangerous. This type of response, useful in categorizing individuals who hold new or unusual opinions, has been applied in the past, with varying degrees of success, to innovators such as Galileo, Copernicus, and Columbus.

A major criticism of the Atlantis theory has been the diversity of the locations that have been proposed for it. But the very proliferation of these suggested sites, the majority of them near or under the sea, may also be considered as an indication of the common culture of a previous civilization, whose great stone remains on all continents (except Australia and Antarctica—and perhaps there too when further explorations are made) tend to resemble one another in construction and astronomical orientation.

An opinion expressed by Dr. Bruce Heezen, an outstanding oceanographer with the Lamont Geological Observatory of Columbia University, seems to introduce a more liberal tendency on the part of modern oceanographers regarding sunken lands in the ocean. Although still labeling Atlantis as fascinating fiction, he details the extent, depth, and dating of lost lands on the ocean's coasts:

Eleven thousand years ago the ocean level all around the world was perhaps three hundred feet lower than it is today.

The eastern coastline of our United States, for instance, was some one hundred miles farther out in the Atlantic Ocean in that bygone era.

Then, suddenly, about eleven thousand years ago, the Ice Age was over . . . billions of gallons of ice and snow poured into the sea. The result was a dramatic, sudden, and terrifying rising of the sea level all around the world—an inundation which we have verified by half a dozen different types of research available to us today. The rise undoubtedly caused the flooding of many low-level seaside communities where primitive man had chosen to build his early towns and cities.

Dr. Heezen, stressing the world impact of the great melting of the glaciers, added: ". . . every continent in this era felt the terrible impact of the ocean's rise."

But this theory, made by a respected member of the scientific establishment, does not contradict the possibility of Atlantis having existed. For if the rising of sea level was so sudden that it caused flooding and disappearance of towns and cities of coastal areas, would it not also have caused large islands to be swallowed by the ocean, leaving only their highest sections above sea level just as the legends tell?

While other parts of the world have experienced and continue to experience land and sea inversion, the Atlantic seafloor has consistently demonstrated an especially chaotic impermanence. The Atlantic has a tendency to raise small islands or to swallow them, as well as to raise or lower its depths, even in modern times, by thousands of feet. Several grinding tectonic plates, the floating islands on the sima crust of the Earth's surface, meet in the Atlantic in the vicinity of the Azores Islands. These clashing tectonic plates, the Eurasian, African, North American, and Caribbean, are responsible for the many volcanic eruptions and earthquakes that continue to occur throughout the Atlantic area. They may be connected with the disappearance of Atlantis or even be a continuing result of it.

6

THE RESTLESS OCEAN FLOOR

The Mid-Atlantic Ridge is the world's greatest mountain range although, being largely under water, the tremendous height of its mountains can be appreciated only on bathometric charts. It divides the Atlantic into east and west sections, each containing its own abyssal plain. One of the world's most active seismic areas, it has been characterized by earthquakes, seaquakes, and volcanic explosions throughout history and is still in a state of violent seismic activity.

The appearance and disappearance of islands in the Atlantic and the destructive earthquakes on its islands and coastal shores occasionally remind us, on a small scale, of the legendary destruction of Atlantis.

▲ In 1622 the city of Villa Franca, capital of the Azorian island of São Miguel, was buried by a sudden seismic convulsion, opening up great faults in the land and causing tidal waves in the ocean.

▲ The city of Port Royal, Jamaica, used as a rendezvous for buccaneers, fell into the sea without warning in 1692, complete with its pirates, ships, bawdy taverns, and booty.

▲ An earthquake which suddenly occurred in Lisbon in 1755 caused the death, within a few minutes, of 60,000 persons, many of whom had fled to safety from falling buildings to a large open stone quay which suddenly sank into the sea, taking them with it under water to a depth of 600 feet. The noise produced by this sudden earth and sea quake was said to be loud enough to be heard in Stockholm.

▲ In the middle of the 18th century a single earthquake, which extended from Iceland thousands of miles down to the Mid-Atlantic Ridge, resulted in the death of a fourth of Iceland's population.

▲ The island of Martinique suffered the explosion of Mt. Pélee in May 1902. The explosion, which blew out the side of the mountain, killed every individual in St. Pierre, the capital, except a convict and a madman in protective prison cells. A distinctive feature of the St. Pierre holocaust was a burning gaseous cloud—the *nuée ardente*—which rolled down from Mt. Pélee and killed all those—almost 30,000—who were not already dead.

▲ The destructive earthquake of Accra, Africa, in 1922 extended along fault lines laterally across the ocean all the way from the Puerto Rico Trench, one of the greatest depths of the ocean. Great earth shifts that take place under the ocean are not readily noticeable. The Grand Banks seaquake of 1929 caused a gigantic current thick with underwater mud and sand to flow down North Atlantic submarine canyons, cutting the northern series of transatlantic cables. When the cables were repaired, areas of the seafloor previously measured showed a rise of almost a mile since the last soundings were taken.

▲ A 1974 lava flow from a fissure in the earth in Heimaey, Iceland, completely buried the town with lava but fortunately at a tempo that enabled the townspeople, unlike those of Pompeii, to escape entombment.

▲ A number of islands have appeared, disappeared, and sometimes reappeared from the restless depths of the Atlantic. In 1808 a volcano on São Jorge in the Azores crested several thousand additional feet and in 1811 a large volcanic island appeared in the Azores which, after being given a name—Sambrina—and charted on maps, suddenly returned to the sea.

▲ In 1931 two islands suddenly rose from the sea bottom in the vicinity of the Fernando de Noronha group off the coast of Brazil. Great Britain, always interested in the acquisition of islands, lost no time in laying claim to them against claims by Brazil and several other countries. The problem was solved, however, when both islands unexpectedly sank beneath the waves.

▲ A new island, appropriately named for the Norse god of fire, Surtsey, emerged with flame and smoke from the sea bottom off the southwest coast of Iceland, shortly to be followed by two smaller islands in a three-year, more-or-less-continuous eruption starting in 1963. Other Atlantic islands, especially the Azores, Canaries, and Madeira, have witnessed a number of land-sea inversions for cen-

turies, with new islands appearing or disappearing or sections of existing islands dropping off into the sea.

If a great empire once extended over a large, now submerged area,
it would be logical to expect that some vestiges of it would remain
on the Atlantic floor and could be identified by exploring the bottom
in a deep-dive submersible. On the other hand, it would be even
more convincing if parts of the drowned lands could reappear at sea
level, as in the case of the surfacing islands, temporarily or per-
manently visible in the light of day.

A very curious example of this possibility occurred in March 1882.
Unlike many alleged sightings of Atlantean ruins before that time,
it was well reported in a ship's log and also in the press. It concerned
the encounter of a steamship with an uncharted island in heavily
traveled sea lanes and the unusual material that was found there by
the ship's captain and his crew.

The vessel was named the *S.S. Jesmond*, a British merchant ship
of 1495 tons bound for New Orleans with a cargo of dried fruits
from its last port of call in Messina, Sicily. The *Jesmond* was cap-
tained by David Robson, holder of master's certificate 27911 in the
Queen's Merchant Marine.

The *Jesmond* passed through the Straits of Gibraltar (the ancient
Pillars of Hercules) on March 1, 1882, and sailed into the open sea.
When the ship reached the position 31° 25′ N, 28° 40′ W, about 200
miles west of Madeira and about the same distance south of the
Azores, it was noted that the ocean had become unusually muddy
and that the vessel was passing through enormous shoals of dead
fish, as if some sudden disease or underwater explosion had killed
them by the millions. Just before evening on the first day of encountering the fish banks, Captain Robson noticed smoke on the
horizon which he presumed came from another ship.

On the following day the fish shoals were even thicker and the
smoke on the horizon seemed to be coming from mountains on an
island directly to the west, where, according to the charts, there was
no land for thousands of miles. As the *Jesmond* approached the
vicinity of the island, Captain Robson threw out an anchor at about
twelve miles offshore to find out whether or not this uncharted island
was surrounded by reefs. Even though the charts indicated an area
depth of several thousand fathoms, the anchor hit bottom at only
seven fathoms.

When Robson went ashore with a landing party they found themselves to be on a large island with no vegetation, no trees, no sandy
beaches, bare of all life as if it had just risen from the ocean. The
shore they landed on was covered with volcanic debris. As there
were no trees, the party could clearly see a plateau beginning several
miles away and smoking mountains beyond that.

The landing party rather gingerly headed toward the interior in
the direction of the mountains, but they found that progress was
interrupted by a series of deep chasms. To get to the interior would
have taken days. They returned to their landing point and examined
a broken cliff, part of which seemed to have been split into a mass
of loose gravel as if it had recently been subjected to great force.
One of the sailors found an unusual arrowhead in the broken rock,
a discovery that led the captain to send for picks and shovels from
the ship so that the crew could dig into the gravel. According to
what he told a reporter from the *Times Picayune* in New Orleans,
where he later docked, he and his crew uncovered "crumbling remains" of "massive walls." A variety of artifacts uncovered by digging near the walls for the better part of two days included "bronze
swords, rings, mallets, carvings of heads and figures of birds and
animals, and two vases or jars with fragments of bone, and one
cranium almost entire . . ." and "what appeared to be a mummy
enclosed in a stone case . . . encrusted with volcanic deposit so as
to be scarcely distinguished from the rock itself." At the end of the
following day, much of which was spent getting the rock sarcophagus
aboard the *Jesmond*, Robson, now worried about uncertain weather,
decided to abandon his exploration of the island and resume his
course.

Several reporters examined Captain Robson's unusual finds and
were informed by him that he planned to present the artifacts to
the British Museum. Unfortunately for Atlantean research, however, the log of the *Jesmond* was destroyed during the London blitz
of September 1940, along with the offices of the *Jesmond*'s owners,
Watts, Watts and Company, Threadneedle Street. There is apparently no record at the British Museum of their having received
Robson's unusual collection, although it is of course possible that
the artifacts are filed in the capacious attics and basements common
to all great museums. Nor was the island ever heard of again, existing
only in the sworn testimony of the captain and crew of the *Jesmond*.

There is, however, some corroboration of the incident: Captain

Robson was not alone in reporting the sighting of the mysterious island. Captain James Newdick of the steam schooner *Westbourne*, sailing from Marseilles to New York during the same period, reported on arrival in New York having sighted a large island at coordinates 25° 30′ N, 24° W. Newdick's report appeared in the *New York Post*, April 1, 1882. If the coordinates given by both captains were correct, the mystery island would have measured 20 × 30 miles in area. The volcanic activity that brought an island of this size to the surface would have killed, probably through heating the oceanic water, an enormous quantity of fish, just as Captain Robson reported.

The miles of dead fish, fanning out from the area first reported by Robson, were also commented on by a number of other ship captains and appeared in a variety of newspapers including *The New York Times*. One captain suggested that the kill could be explained by the wreck of a fishing vessel, however unlikely this explanation might be. For the quantity of dead fish, as estimated by the British Institute of Oceanography, covered 7500 square miles of the Atlantic and comprised at least half a million tons.

Crew members of various vessels that passed through the floating fish identified them as tilefish, cod, red snappers, shad, and many others. Some adventurous souls among the sailors sampled a number of the fish and suffered no ill effects. They stated that the fish were "hard and proved excellent food." One might speculate that these hordes of fish did not immediately rot since they had been "precooked" by the volcanic heat generated by the rising of the island from the ocean floor.

Since Captain Robson's brief viewing of allegedly Atlantean walls, recognizable features of buildings, walls, and roads have been reported with increasing frequency from various parts of the Atlantic. They have often been observed by pilots who have overflown them in their scheduled flights and have not had permission to depart from their flight plans to investigate further by circling in order to photograph chance sightings that in any case may have been illusory.

During World War II several pilots on military flights between Brazil and Senegal, formerly French West Africa, said they saw what looked like clusters of buildings or "cities" under the ocean surface near the St. Peter and St. Paul Rocks (1° N, 30° W). Other pilots and observers flying the same route have reported seeing what appeared to be underwater stone walls and ruins at approximately

The underwater stone construction east of Bimini has been called a road, wall, dock, or building. It is more than a thousand yards long and evidently continues on under the sand at each end. Two research ships and a diving craft are shown here investigating this artifact in one of the many expeditions that have taken place since Dr. Manson Valentine's initial discovery of it in 1969. *Jacques Mayol*

Underwater stone "terrace" on the sea bottom slightly east of the Bimini Road, showing close setting of flat stones partially revealed by the covering sand. *Jim Richardson with J. Manson Valentine*

Unidentified stone wall or raised road near Cay Sal extending out from shore almost a mile until it stops at 1600-foot-deep drop-off. A subsidiary construction turns off south-southeast of the main wall and continues on to small island. Underwater constructions in Bimini and other parts of the Bahamas were evidently built before the ocean level rose at the end of the Ice Age—12,000 years ago. *Bob Klein*

Semivertical view of underwater construction near Cay Sal. Flat stones on top of wall placed flush together have not been separated into lines by the tide, as has evidently happened in the Bimini area, possibly because of the more massive nature of the wall in this area. *Bob Klein*

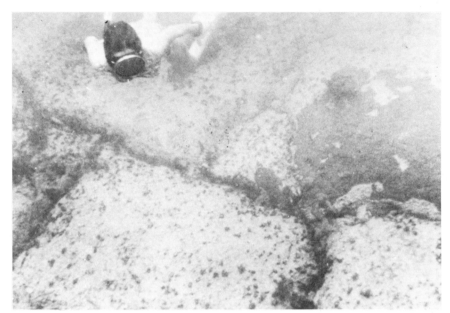

Underwater wall near Cay Sal showing striking similarity in the fitting of the stones to the wall of Sacsahuamán, Peru. *Herbert Sawinski*

Enormous walls at Sacsahuamán, Peru, showing very large cut stones closely fitted together inside as well as out. The careful fitting into angular cuts may have been a means of rendering the buildings resistant to earthquakes. *Herbert Sawinski*

Diver over top of raised road or wall in the Cay Sal Bank area. Side or road descending to true bottom can be seen to the right, going down an additional twenty feet. *John Sawinsky*

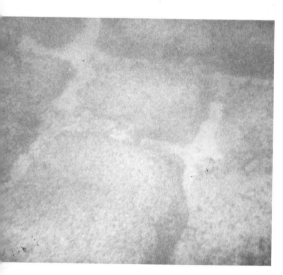

Aligned stone blocks at southeastern end of Cay Sal showing resemblance to similar construction at Bimini. *Lin Berlitz*

View in the Canary Islands showing a high snow-topped mountain (Teide) and, on the same island, lush semitropical vegetation, just as Plato described in Atlantis. On large fertile islands with an agreeable and invigorating climate of this type, it would be logical to assume the development of a maritime enterprise. *Spanish Tourist Office*

The hot springs mentioned in Plato's account still bubble and steam in the Atlantic islands, as here in the Vale da Furnas near São Miguel, Azores. Farther north, in Iceland, there is sufficient steam in subterranean springs to heat entire towns. *Photo courtesy Comissão Regional de Turismo— Azores Islands*

View of one of the "Seven Cities" lakes in the Azores. The surrounding terrain closely resembles the sea-bottom plateau surrounding the islands. According to tradition, cities and palaces of Atlantis lie under the bottom of these lakes. *Photo courtesy Comissão Regional de Turismo—Azores Islands*

Photograph of part of an apparent wall taken with automatic underwater camera by the *USSR Academician Petrovsky* expedition in the vicinity of the Ampere and Josephine Seamounts southwest of the Azores. These seamounts rise from a depth of 10,000 or more feet to a summit of several hundred feet below the surface. Round object at right is end of plumb line lowered from research ship.

The same wall from directly above showing cut stone blocks in position or scattered on both sides of the wall. This series of submarine photographs from the *Academician Petrovsky* may represent the first indications of buildings on the ocean floor in the very area Plato gave as the location of Atlantis.

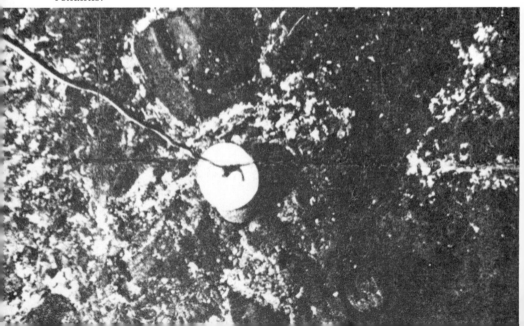

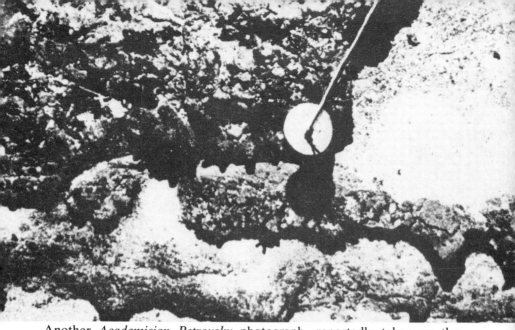

Another *Academician Petrovsky* photograph, reportedly taken on the fairly flat summit of the Ampere Seamount showing apparently artificial steps partially covered by lava. A leading Soviet scientist, Professor Aksyonov, has stated, "In my opinion these structures once stood on the surface."

Side view of underwater wall formed of huge cut stone blocks off the coast of Africa. The wall continues on for several miles under forty to fifty feet of water. *Bruno Rizatto*

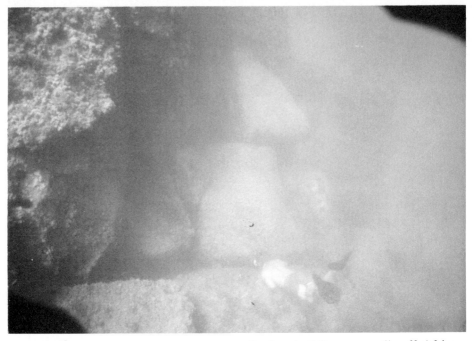

Sunken buildings or walls off African coast (Morocco) at depth of fifty to sixty feet, extending for several miles. Size of set stones are comparable to those of Sacsahuamán and Bimini. *Bruno Rizatto*

The Piri Re'is map, found in the former Turkish Sultan's palace, the Topkapi in Istanbul, in 1929, and thought to be a partial copy of a world map extant in the library at ancient Alexandria 2000 years ago. It indicates ancient knowledge of spherical trigonometry as applied to maps (not rediscovered in Europe until the reign of George III) and shows the coastline of the Antarctic continent (not discovered until 1838–1840) as it would be without the ice. *Library of Congress*

6° N, 20° W, near the Sierra Leone Rise. Although it would be easy to discount these claims by supposing that the pilots reported clouds or shadows on the ocean (it is relatively easy for imaginative individuals, pilots or otherwise, to visualize fantasies in the sea or sky), nevertheless it is also true that some of the subsurface islands in the Atlantic, especially the flat-topped seamounts that rise suddenly from the ocean floor, come fairly close to sea level in a number of places. At certain times of the day a special slant of the sun's rays in the afternoon and a low rate of diatoms in the sea could make parts of the ocean over such seamounts clear enough to catch a glimpse of former human settlements built on large seamounts when they were once islands.

In the western Atlantic, near the United States, pilots of both scheduled and charter flights have remarked on pyramidal formations, stepped terraces, and walls on the ocean floor between the Bahamas and Florida. A Pan American pilot has described seeing an archway in a submerged wall about sixty feet from the surface. Charter pilots have described underwater roads leading eastward out to sea from the coast of Yucatán, which they followed until the roads were lost in deep water, but which presumably continued to other destinations now beneath the sea.

An expanse of stone ruins, several acres in area and apparently white, as if they were marble, was reported off the northern coast of Cuba by the late Leicester Hemingway, former resident of Cuba and brother of the famous novelist, but these ruins are located well within Cuban waters and are therefore inaccessible to American divers.

A number of rather convincing photographs have been taken from the air of what appears to be underwater stonework on the Bahama Banks and off the Caribbean coast of Mexico, but no aerial photographs have yet been made available of sunken cities in the mid-Atlantic.

However, within the last several years a number of unusual photographs have been taken not from aircraft but from submarine cameras lowered from research ships. Pictures of apparently man-made ruins, photographed at much greater depths than ever before, have been obtained by oceanographers not engaged in looking for Atlantis but simply photographing the sea bottom in the general area of the legendary island continent. The vessels and the oceanographers were from the USSR, a nation far from Plato's Atlantic Sea.

7

THE MOUNTAIN PEAKS
OF ATLANTIS

It has sometimes been suggested that Atlantis did not sink into the
sea but was "drowned" by the ocean through the rising waters re-
leased by the sudden melting of the glacial ice. The distinction between these two dooms, relatively unimportant to the victims of the
disaster, would nevertheless imply that the present small islands
which exist where Atlantis was reputed to have been might contain,
in the seamounts, plateaus, and marine valleys surrounding them,
some underwater vestiges of buildings or walls indicating the one-
time presence of an advanced culture. Soviet underwater research
has recently provided a certain measure of corroboration of this
theory.

Russia, although not bordering on the Atlantic, has nevertheless
maintained a lively interest in that ocean and in the tradition of the
Lost Continent that perhaps gave the Atlantic its name. Russians,
perhaps through the often mystical aspect of the "Russian soul,"
have produced a number of important writers who have dealt with
the subject of Atlantis. These have included Dmitri Merezhkovski,
of Czarist times, who likened the doom of Atlantis to the future
doom of Europe; Nikolai Zhirov, whose book (*Atlantis*: 1964) extensively examines the historical references and geological material
available on Atlantis and its probable location in the Atlantic; and
V. Bryusov, an historian, who traces all ancient civilizations as descending from an "X" culture, or "a culture as yet unknown to
science," as the teacher and impulse of the beginnings of civilization—Atlantis.

Members of a Soviet deep-sea expedition carried out by the *Academician Petrovsky*, a Soviet research ship, were at first unaware

that certain of the many photographs of the seafloor obtained by their underwater cameras showed not only the bottom topography but also archaeological relics where legendary Atlantis was supposed to be located.

The aim and results of the expedition, which took place in the early part of 1974, were summarized by M. Barinov, and appeared in the Soviet publication *Znanie-Sila*, Number 8, in 1979, at the time that numerous articles about the find appeared in the world press.

The purpose of the expedition was to study the sandbanks in the shallow waters of the Mediterranean Sea and of the Atlantic Ocean not far from northwest Africa. On board the ship as part of the team were geologists and biologists. The origin, structure and population of the sandbanks, the peaks of underwater mountains and of the shallows comprised the main scientific interest of the specialists. In the team there was also a researcher from the USSR Institute of Oceanography, Vladimir Ivanovich Marakuyev, who was a specialist in underwater photography.

Whenever the research ship was within the desired coordinates for shots of the bottom,

. . . lighting equipment and special cameras were lowered to a depth of about three and a half meters above the bottom, after which the lights were switched on and a series of photographs were taken using a simple automatic device. Each series took about an hour to an hour and a half to complete. At the same time other members of the expedition carried out experiments and a series of tests with the aid of other apparatus. The water in the Atlantic near Gibraltar was exceptionally clear and the work of the expedition depended only on the weather. During the winter storms when the ship started to roll from side to side work had to be discontinued and sometimes shelter had to be sought.

In light of subsequent revelations it should be pointed out that the researchers and crew had other purposes in mind than searching for remains of Atlantis, although what they found may prove to be the first photographs ever taken of sunken ruins on the Lost Continent.

The *Academician Petrovsky* began its underwater camera survey of the Horseshoe archipelago about 300 miles west of Gibraltar in January 1974. A large number of photographs were taken of the bottom hundreds of feet under water in approximately the same area where Captain Robson's mysterious island appeared and then vanished. This underwater chain of islands has been described in *The Atlantic Floor*, by Heezen, Thorpe, Young:

> . . . an important group of underwater mountains arranged in a horseshoe. Some of them, such as the underwater mountians Ampere and Josephine, rise to a depth of less than 100 fathoms. . . . Photographs taken of the surface of these mountains show cliffs, traces of ripples and isolated living corals. The underwater mountains of the northern half of the Horseshoe, which have not yet been properly studied, stretch from west to east. The southern half of the group apparently resembles volcanic cones, while for the northern half tectonic changes played an important role.

A previous American expedition from the Lamont Geological Observatory had investigated this same area by taking cores, photographs, and dredging the bottom. Although certainly not the primary object of the oceanic research, no traces of ancient man were found, reminding one of an observation made by Dr. Maurice Ewing, who said he "spent thirteen years exploring the Mid-Atlantic Ridge [but] found no trace of sunken cities."

The Soviet expedition apparently had better luck. When the extensive series of photographs taken from the *Academician Petrovsky* were being developed, studied, and catalogued, it was noted by Marakuyev, who had been in charge of the photography, that the pictures taken on the summit of the Ampere Seamount, a submarine plateau which thrusts upward from a 10,000-foot depth to within 200 feet of the surface, showed a number of unexpected features. Marakuyev has expressed his initial reaction to the surprising objects that appeared on several of the photographs:

> While still on the expedition, when I had developed the photographs and made the first prints, I realized that I had never

seen anything like it before. The Institute of Oceanography of
the USSR has a huge archive of underwater photographs that
have been taken on countless expeditions over many years in
all parts of the world's oceans. We also have copies of many
thousands of photographs taken by our American colleagues.
Nowhere have I seen anything so close to traces of the life and
activity of man in places which could once have been dry land.

The following comments from the *Znanie-Sila* point out some
salient features of the underwater discoveries:

On the first photograph we can see this wall on the left side
of the photograph. Stone blocks on the upper edge of the wall
are clearly visible. . . . Taking into account the foreshortening
of the photograph and the height of the wall, it is curious to
examine more closely the strip of vertical masonry. Although
the lens was pointing almost vertically downwards, areas of
masonry can be seen quite clearly. One can count five such
areas, and if one takes into account the deformation of scale
caused by the nearness of the lens to the object, one may suggest
that the masonry blocks of the wall are up to 1.5 meters high
and a little longer in length.

On the second photograph we can see the same wall from
directly above. It crosses the picture diagonally. The control
disc is in the center. It is not difficult to calculate that the breadth
of the wall is about 75 centimeters. The masonry blocks are
clearly visible on both sides of the wall. Seaweed is visible on
all the photographs, thick, reddish brown in color. . . .

The third photograph is from another series taken at the
summit of the Ampere Seamount. An area over which lava has
flowed can be seen on it, and it appears to descend by three
steps. If one counts the upper and barely visible lower
edges . . . in all we can see five steps. They are broken down,
of course, and overgrown with glass-like sponges.

(The photographs mentioned in these excerpts can be seen in the
photo section following page 80.)

The article ends with a vigorous recommendation for the continuation of Soviet exploration for the Lost Continent.

... the science of oceanography has made gigantic strides in knowledge over the last 10 to 12 years; the techniques of research have received powerful aids. The chief of these are automated underwater devices which have considerable range of depth. These microsubmarines can descend several kilometers, move along horizontally, have powerful searchlights, mechanical "hands" to take samples of rock or any other objects from the seabed. Since the *Kurchatov* is one of two of our boats that have such underwater equipment on board, and is more or less a "permanent resident" in the Atlantic and almost every year passes the region of the Horseshoe, one can only repeat, what are we waiting for?

The Soviet discoveries at the Ampere Seamount, unpublicized for several years, received world-wide publicity in 1978 through an interview with Professor Andrei Aksyonov, deputy director of the Soviet Academy of Science's Institute of Oceanography. The interview took place in Moscow and was published in *The New York Times* on May 21, 1978.

Professor Aksyonov was quoted as wondering why the pictures did not come to his attention until 1977. "I don't know why it took him [Marakuyev] so long to get to them." He later observed, according to the *Times* reporter, that he was sorry he could not produce the pictures since "They belong to Marakuyev and he is very sick with a heart condition in a hospital," adding encouragingly, "I think they will be published in one of our scientific journals sometime soon."

Professor Aksyonov, while guarding a seeming neutrality on Atlantean identification of the ruins, further stated, "I believe that the objects in the pictures once stood on the surface."

In a later AP release from Moscow in April 1979, Alexander Nesterenko, director of the Fleet Department of the Institute of Oceanography, confirmed the report that a Russian research ship had taken photographs of "what might be ruins" but denied reports that another Soviet research ship, the *Vityaz*, was investigating the same site, stating that the *Vityaz* was "engaged on other business."

An indication of what the "other business" might be was touched upon by Egerton Sykes, a life-long student of the Atlantis mystery, in an interview with the author in November 1982.

Question: *Why do you think there have not been further declarations from the USSR about the Soviet discoveries on the Ampere Seamount?*

It must have been of considerable importance to them, as nothing more has been given out about it. They probably wish to conceal the real place where they made the pictures.

Where do you think that was?

I think they may have been made off the Azores, which is a more strategic location anyway. They [the Russians] are not looking for Atlantis but for places to park submarines under the sea in case of nuclear war. The ship that made the discovery was a highly qualified Soviet spy ship, as most of them are. I think it is possible that the photographs were taken off the Azores between Santa Maria and São Jorge, somewhere comparatively near the Formigas Rocks. The picture of a plumbline 200 feet down would be applicable there as well as on the Ampere Seamount. The Russians could not officially report having taken photographs there as they should not be there anyhow.

What is your opinion of the stones and platforms shown in the photographs?

They are very intriguing. The stone staircase that is distinctly visible was evidently cut into the cliff. There must be a lot of stairs below the point where the part shown in the photograph started. It was probably a flight of 100 steps or more up a rock face, dangerous to go up or down, like the steps on the Mayan or Aztec pyramids. One of the other photographs shows a leveled-off stone platform which may be a landing connected to another staircase, as in a step pyramid.

Do you know of any other recent finds in the Ampere area?

Not near Madeira, but I have seen photographs of sunken walls and pavements several miles out at sea from Cádiz, Spain. They are very well defined and should be of easy access, but unofficial exploration in this area tends to encounter Spanish naval units, which take a dim view of unauthorized undersea investigation of areas near the Spanish coast, especially near

Cádiz and the naval base at Rota. When diving near these installations you are apt to find yourself in a minefield.

An interesting example of how the United States Navy almost became involved in the search for Atlantis occurred in 1963. Charles Hapgood, professor of geology at the University of New Hampshire, has become internationally known for his convincing theories concerning the Piri Re'is map and other "portolano" charts (see photo section following page 80),which implied that ancient mariners had made fairly accurate maps of the Americas, the Atlantic Ocean, and Antarctica (without the ice) thousands of years before Columbus crossed the Atlantic.

During his long examination of the Piri Re'is map Hapgood had noted an unusual coincidence concerning an island in the Atlantic no longer indicated on modern maps and reports from military aircraft pilots about underwater cities. Hapgood, like many other scientists and World War II pilots, had heard reports that pilots flying across the ocean between Dakar, Senegal, and Recife, Brazil, had observed what looked like buildings under the ocean visible from the air in the late-afternoon sun when the water was still and clear. Because of their flight plan the pilots did not have time or permission to circle and research further, but the unofficial reports specified that these sightings took place near the St. Peter and St. Paul Rocks, a small rock outcropping about 700 miles east of Recife.

What especially intrigued Professor Hapgood was a detail on the Piri Re'is map. While other islands and coastlines seemed to be in place, a large island appeared precisely where the barely perceptible St. Peter and St. Paul Rocks are now located, as if another surviving part of Atlantis still remained above the surface at the time the original Piri Re'is map was made but had since continued its descent into the ocean, bearing its cities with it.

Hapgood decided to go to the top for help with his Atlantean research. In his as yet unpublished memoirs he tells how, in 1963, he approached the White House with the hope that he could "borrow an aircraft carrier to investigate the cities under the sea." He observed: "It was fortunate that I had had previous contacts with the White House when I did some errands for President Roosevelt during World War II. . . . It was no problem to find someone close to the Kennedys in Massachusetts who could arrange a meeting for me

Physiographic profile of the St. Peter and St. Paul Rocks, located between Brazil and Africa, considered by Professor Hapgood as remnants of a much larger island, possibly connected with other sunken islands that composed Atlantis.

with the President. . . . We had mutual friends in the Democratic Party in Boston."

Prior to such a meeting Hapgood made preparatory studies and plans for the exhibition. Planes would fly in widening concentric circles from the St. Peter and St. Paul Rocks and, if something was observed, the ocean bottom of the Atlantic area would be researched with the aid of electronic depth finders capable of functioning a mile down, underwater cameras and television, and the establishing of grid systems. Through government contacts he produced studies of possible anchorage for the carrier and for shifting it around the rocks according to the direction of the winds. The rocks themselves were not large enough for a land base and were also covered with guano from great flocks of birds (see above).

Professor Hapgood further suggested that the "Atlantean aspect" of the investigation be kept secret and that the search be reported as "just another oceanographic expedition to the Mid-Atlantic Ridge to study the flora and fauna of the deep sea."

By October 1963 he had succeeded in arranging an interview with

President Kennedy—but history intervened in the month of November.

More than one hundred years ago the question of using naval vessels to search for Atlantis was already being discussed. In the 1880s, perhaps as a result of Ignatius Donnelly's books on Atlantis, as well as those of other authors, there was a surge of public interest in Atlantis as well as in the possibility that it could now be located by extensive soundings and dredging operations. Donnelly, in the closing chapter of his *Atlantis*, sounded a clarion call for governmental research of the Atlantic floor:

> Nor is it impossible that the nations of the earth may yet employ their idle navies in bringing to the light of day some of the relics of this buried people. Portions of the island lie but a few hundred fathoms beneath the sea; and if expeditions have been sent out from time to time in the past, to resurrect from the depths of the ocean sunken treasure-ships . . . why should not an attempt be made to reach the buried wonders of Atlantis? A single engraved tablet dredged up from Plato's island would be worth more to science, would more strike the imagination of mankind, than all the gold of Peru, all the monuments of Egypt.

While this may seem wildly overexuberant, it is nevertheless interesting to note that a poll of British newspapermen taken at that period gave the finding of Atlantis a number-two rating in a possible world news break, of which the first place was reserved for the Second Coming of Christ. Donnelly's enthusiastic summons, however, found an adherent in the person of William Gladstone, the Prime Minister of Her Imperial Majesty Queen Victoria. Gladstone not only sent Donnelly a letter of appreciation but also requested that Parliament approve use of the Royal Navy in a series of investigations in search of Atlantis. His effort was unsuccessful, as Great Britain was concerned with a number of small wars and crises at the time and had plans for the Imperial Fleet to show the flag elsewhere than over the mid-Atlantic.

Donnelly may have previously aroused, with lesser immediate results, the interest of another statesman. As Lieutenant Governor of Illinois during the Civil War, Donnelly, a strong Union supporter, became friendly with Abraham Lincoln. During their friendship, and owing to their common interest in history and Lincoln's lively and inquisitive mind, Donnelly doubtless had occasion to discuss his consuming interest in Atlantis with the President and perhaps as well his concept of using naval vessels in a search for the Lost Continent. During the years of Donnelly's acquaintance with President Lincoln, however, all United States Navy ships were occupied with more pressing engagements than explorations. It is nevertheless interesting to consider what Donnelly might have accomplished had his project not been interrupted by assassination—as was Professor Hapgood's proposal almost one hundred years later.

In other countries where "Atlantean" organizations have flourished, especially in France, conflicts and contending theories under discussion have resulted in the use of tear gas and bombs to emphasize the opinions of conflicting theorists. In the late 1920s, after police intervention in "Atlantean riots," it was determined by police headquarters that such Atlantean meetings "constituted a danger to Paris," imperiling surface and subsurface structures such as cellars, sewers, and the Métro tunnels (which might, perhaps, be considered an archaeological field for future ages).

Oceanic searches for Atlantis have recently been carried out by a number of privately financed groups, as no governmental or scientific institutions could be expected to justify participation in the search for a legend, although scientific and naval expeditions from various governments have inadvertently uncovered pertinent evidence of sunken lands in the course of their exploration of the seafloor and the search for oil and mineral resources.

A recent example of an archaeological discovery by an independently financed expedition was made by a group of Spanish scuba divers along the underwater shelf off the Canary Islands. According to the tradition of the vanished original inhabitants, the Guanches, the shelf consists of the former mountain peaks of a submerged continent. In 1981 a private expedition organized by P. Cappellano found large stone slabs set on the sea bottom at a depth of about fifty feet covering what first appeared to be a 900-square-foot area. The stones were carefully set, and wide stone steps led down from the central pavement as if they were steps going down to a landing dock. Certain marks carved in the stones appeared to be symbols or signs that resemble "letters" carved on rocks on land in the Canary Islands. Further investigation will determine whether the signs are indigenous and resemble one another only, or if they contain signs or letters from the languages of other races that may have landed on the islands. These languages could include the Punic brought by the Carthaginian fleets, the archaic Greek of the Minoan seafarers, the ancient Libyan of North Africa, and even Tifinagh, the written script of the Tuareg tribes of Morocco and the Sahara.

Land investigation of the Canaries is being intermittently carried out by special expeditions from Spain with a view to ascertaining whether or not there exist undiscovered remains of the original Guanches culture (or even, as rumored, surviving Guanches) in villages or caves within the mountainous islands.

An undersea wall off the Moroccan coast, extending several miles in length, first discovered more than ten years ago by a diver while he was spearfishing, has since been further investigated and photographed. Some of the stones, either a fallen part of the wall or an auxiliary building, are comparable in size to the foundation stones used in the temple of Baalbek, Lebanon—the largest building stones known to have been quarried in ancient times.

The coastal shelves of Western Europe, northern Africa, and the Atlantic Islands are now being explored more frequently by scuba divers engaged in industrial search for oil or mineral deposits, or personal searches for treasure wrecks or ancient ruins. The recent finds of the last category suggest the eastern limits of a former Atlantic civilization.

The western limit of this submerged culture can be discerned in the relatively shallow depths of the Bermuda Banks and parts of the continental shelf of the Caribbean. Investigation has been considerably aided by the use of aircraft from which underwater ruins can be sighted, photographed, and then explored by divers. Some of the most provocative of these submerged remains of buildings, walls, roads, and giant stone circles lie in the area called the Bermuda Triangle.

8

UNDERWATER RUINS IN THE BERMUDA TRIANGLE

The section of the western Atlantic called the Bermuda Triangle contains a number of curious formations on parts of the shallow sea bottom of the Bermuda Banks. Since the end of World War II, some of these formations have been seen by pilots as they flew over the islands and surrounding waters on search missions for signs of ships or planes reported missing in the Bermuda Triangle. Some pilots, on regularly scheduled or charter flights, have remarked on what seemed to be walls or roads under water. Other pilots, flying at low altitudes, have suggested that some of these formations may be the tops of buildings sunken under the seafloor.

These supposed structures, located on the Bermuda Banks or off the continental shelf, have been ignored for centuries even though they must have sometimes been encountered by fishermen or divers. There are a number of reasons for their not having been known previously. In earlier days the crews of treasure ships and the pirates who customarily pursued them were uninterested in anything other than negotiable treasure. What seemed to be stone structures seen in later years by fishermen or oceanographers were thought to be natural formations or ballast from wrecks. The evidently artificial composition of such structures is not apparent from sea level, but is often quite clear from the air, where the straight lines and geometric angles on the bottom may be more clearly discerned. And, finally, there was no appreciable interest in man-made building artifacts in the western Atlantic as there was no reason to suspect that underwater cities could possibly be there. For if they were, they would have had to be built before 12,000 ± years B.P. (Before

Present), the approximate time when sea level rose to cover large sections of the coasts and islands of the ocean. This would be, in standard archaeological opinion, historically impossible—7000 years too early—for men to be building cities.

Not more than a quarter of a mile from the shores of Bimini a series of long stone walls, or roads as they are sometimes referred to, is presently easy to find and has been examined by divers and by archaeologists intent on defending or opposing the previously held concepts of history and the age of civilization. With continuing research and the widening scope of investigation, it is becoming increasingly difficult, however, to declare that these stone constructions are pieces of beach rock that accidentally and at random have built themselves into a wall.

Scores of other examples extend through the waters of the Bahama Banks; sometimes forming great stone circles, like Stonehenge in England, sometimes connecting existing islands by underwater walls or roads, sometimes consisting of circular walls built around freshwater springs far below the surface, often by a series of straight and intersecting lines along the bottom like the intersecting lines of the Nazca Valley in Peru, and often great rectangular forms traceable in distinct shapes by variations of bottom vegetation, the possible outline of a large building or platform which has subsided below the ocean floor.

These rather convincing indications of ancient constructions on the Bahama Banks have been investigated by a number of individuals, and especially by Dr. Manson Valentine, a paleontologist, geologist, and underwater archaeologist of Miami. Dr. Valentine has been studying the underwater area of the Bahama Banks for twenty-five years. In addition to his scientific background, and perhaps equally pertinent to his discoveries, he has been an active spelunker, an aircraft pilot, and a scuba as well as hard-hat diver.

Dr. Valentine became convinced of pre-cataclysmic (and pre-Flood) civilizations from his own investigations of caverns in Yucatán. These enormous caverns contain giant carved rocks in animal shapes that show signs of long immersion under water with oceanic fauna still adhering to them. This seemed to indicate conclusively that these caves, now well above sea level, had sunk below it and returned above it, in the periodic risings and sinkings of land areas throughout the Atlantic coastal area—and the world.

Dr. Valentine described his finds in the Bahama Banks:

The entire area of the Bahama Banks was above sea level during the last glaciation and became covered with the subsequent rise in sea level. I wanted to test the geological proposition which states: If the great submerged plateaus of the Bahamas were dry land in the relatively recent past, as seems certain, then their shallow waters might well yield signs of occupation by ancient man.

I started work in 1958, taking photographs from small planes. Since that time we have located well over thirty areas where there are probably man-made remains either on the sea bottom or below it. For example, between Diamond Point and Tongue of the Ocean there is a network of modular straight lines intersecting at right, obtuse, and acute angles. It resembles an architect's plan for a complex urban development with still more lines in the distance which I would call "ghost patterns" since they are the vague outlines of other structures too deeply buried to be traced in detail.

Where did you start your investigation?

Between Orange Key and Bimini. I saw a series of enormous rectangles along the sea bottom connected by straight lines.

Why did you believe they were ruins?

I considered them man-made as they were straight lines running along the sea bottom right to the drop-off of the continental shelf. What is down there below these lines influences the ecology of the surface algae and the result is a pattern. At Riding Rocks a vast expanse of shallow water is divided into squares. At Orange Key, south of Bimini, there is an absolutely straight rectangle the size of a football field. All the way to Bimini there is a succession of architectural patterns, square and rectangular, indicating the size and shape of what lies below. All this suggested to me the one-time presence of ancient peoples.

Have you seen other ancient patterns like this at sea or on land?

In the Nazca Desert of Peru I saw on land the same apparent proof of occupancy including geometrical figures of various shapes, some of them comparable to those on the Bahama Banks.

When did you first encounter the Bimini Road or Bimini Wall?

I found it when I was returning by boat from a diving trip at
Paradise Cay on Labor Day, 1968. I had been looking for a
seamount near Paradise Cay, an enormous one that comes from
a depth of about 3000 feet to fifty feet below the surface. I was
with divers Jacques Mayol, Chip Climo, and the famous Bimini
fisherman Bonefish Sam. On the way back I asked Bonefish to
take me to a place where I could observe fish and he said he
knew about a reef west of Bimini in front of North American
Rockwell Point. When we arrived there Chip went over the
side and I followed him.

When I saw a regular pattern of these enormous stones I was
so surprised that I lost my weight belt, which must still be there.
I could hardly believe it; it was like a dream. It occurred to me
that it might be the Sacbé—the ceremonial white road of the
Maya—as it resembled what I had seen in Yucatán. I followed
it for hundreds of yards to the big stones that go under the
sand. Then I knew we had something.

Did you connect it with the Edgar Cayce prophecy about Atlan-
tis?

I did not know about the prophecy at the time. But when I
learned later that, twenty-eight years before we found the wall,
he had said that Atlantis would rise again, adding ". . . expect
it in '68 or '69, not so far away." And then when I learned that
he had further said that it would be discovered near Bimini, I
must admit that I was amazed.

What do you think of the criticism from the scientific establish-
ment implying that the road is not man-made but simply beach
rock?

Believe me, these are not squares of beach rock arranged by
nature in neat rows to fool gullible underwater archaeologists.
Many of the stones are of flint-hard micrite, unlike soft beach
rock. The lines of closely fitted stones are straight, mutually
parallel, and terminate in cornerstones. The stone avenue does
not follow the curving beach rock-line, which follows the shape
of the island, but is straight. The long avenue contains enormous
flat stones propped up at their corners by pillar stones like the

dolmens of the coast of Western Europe. Perfect rectangles, right angles, and rectilinear configurations are unaccountable in a natural formation. One end of the complex swings into a beautifully curved corner before vanishing under the sand. No one has yet dug underneath it, so we don't know how far down the stones go.

What do you think the ruin is?

I think it is a ceremonial road leading to a special site. After the curve the stone breaks into three ranks from two. A part of the Mayan ceremonial road, the Sacbé, goes underwater in Yucatán and continues for more than a quarter of a mile off-shore before disappearing. As the Sacbé was a raised causeway, I think that excavations under the stones and alongside would reveal buildings. But most archaeologists seem inclined to be allergic to water—they consider that, since the shoreline has probably always been the same, why bother looking under water for archaeological remains of buildings and roads?

Don't you think this sentiment is changing?

Not entirely. I think the reason scientists hesitate to look into these ruins and other unexplained ones is that they are afraid something will turn up that will upset their neat explanations. This prejudice goes way back and has to do with anticataclysmic opinion. Such thinkers don't want to find anything that has to do with sudden change. They prefer to consider many ruins and statues as freaks of nature. Nevertheless, with new and unexpected finds, cracks are appearing here and there among the "scientoid" community. I have hope for the future.

What race do you think was responsible for building these roads or walls?

These are the people who made the big spheres of Central America, the stone heads of Tehuantepec, the huge platforms of Baalbek in Lebanon, Malta in the Mediterranean, Stonehenge in England, the walls of Sacsahuaman and Ollantaytambo in Peru, the standing stone avenues of Brittany, the colossal ruins of Tiahuanaco in Bolivia, and the statues of Easter Island—this was a prehistoric race that could transport and position cyclopean stones in ways that remain a mystery to us.

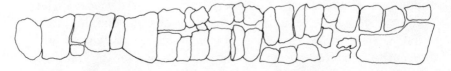

Line drawing of part of the Bimini Wall showing the close fitting of some of the large stone blocks. The separation in the middle of the drawing could have been the result of the wall tumbling on its side during a seismic shock.

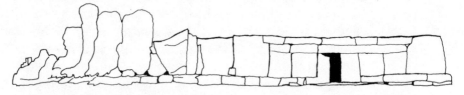

Drawing of prehistoric tomb or temple on Malta showing the use of carefully fitted stone blocks set without mortar. These constructions resemble other prehistoric structures in various parts of the world, such as those in Peru; Bolivia; southern Spain; Baalbek, Lebanon; and underwater ruins on both sides of the Atlantic.

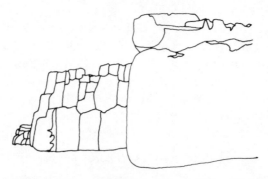

Drawing of colossal walls at Sacsahuamán, where individual stones weighing as much as 250 tons each are exactly fitted together, markedly resembling the prehistoric temples of Malta and the underwater walls in the Atlantic.

Dr. Valentine is referring here to places that he, in a long career as an explorer and archaeologist, has personally investigated. The drawings above show the resemblance between two of these still

standing ancient structures and the arrangements of the stones of
the Bimini Road or Wall. If the Bimini underwater construction is
a raised road, the supporting stones must still be under the sea
bottom, as would be the ceremonial center or centers the road was
leading to. If it is a wall, it must have fallen on its side, possibly
during a seismic upheaval.

Edgar Cayce, a modern clairvoyant whose startling prophecies,
many of which were exactly fulfilled, brought him world-wide renown, foretold in 1940 the finding of underwater ruins related to
the legendary Atlantis of Poseidon. His transcribed prophecy of
1940 read, "And Poseidia will be among the first portions of Atlantis
to rise again. Expect it in '68 or '69—not so far away." He added,
"A portion of the [Atlantean] temple may yet be discovered under
the slime of ages of seawater—near what is known as Bimini, off
the coast of Florida."

Under the impulse of this prophecy a number of pilots, including
Bob Brush, Trig Adams, Jim Richardson, and the French pilot and
undersea explorer Dimitri Rebikoff, began to closely observe the
Bimini Banks as they flew over them and, appropriately in 1969,
did report on an additional series of sightings off Andros, the Berry
Islands, and Bimini.

Two expeditions by boat to the Bimini site under the direction of
Dr. David Zink, historian, diver, and author (*The Stones of Atlantis*), remained anchored over the wall or road for months at a
time, long enough to examine the large stones and their surroundings
in detail. Zink is of the opinion that the stones do not represent
random beach rock, not only because of their composition but because a fracture in the limestone seafloor broke and changed the
position of the solid limestone in the vicinity and under the wall but
did not affect the alignment of the wall itself. A grooved building
block was brought up in the course of the expedition as well as a
"stylized head" estimated to weigh from 200 to 300 pounds—possibly the head of an animal—a giant feline, perhaps a jaguar.

Dr. Zink points out that the hard stones of the wall are distinct
from the ordinary beach rock, which "under certain conditions can
form rapidly, as evinced by beer bottles found cemented within."
Such beer bottles are of course considerably more modern than other
glass remains on the seafloor as, for example, the rum bottles found
in the sunken city of Port Royal, which in one short moment de-

scended with its rum-drinking inhabitants to its present site beneath the sea.

An expedition conducted in 1982 by Herbert Sawinski, an explorer, diver, and chairman of the Museum of Science and Archaeology in Fort Lauderdale, investigated another lesser-known section of the Bermuda Triangle: submerged banks with land outcroppings at various locations between 23° 50′ and 23° 30′ N and 80° 30′ to 79° 40′ W. Extensive stone pavements were located and photographed at a depth of twenty-five feet, as well as distinct walls with vestiges of a pavement running along the top. The main wall continues for a quarter of a mile out to sea, where it suddenly disappears into 2500 feet of water.

Part of this wall, or causeway, bifurcates near the shore and continues under water partially along the coastline of the present remains of what was once a larger island now under the ocean. At another point on this submarine plateau the divers followed a passageway under submerged rocks and discovered a sunken quarry, complete with shaped blocks of stone still inside it. Attempts to photograph the quarry failed because of heavy surface waves, low visibility, and strong underwater surges.

The entire underwater plateau on which these remains of buildings exist is about sixty miles on each side of a lopsided triangle between the Straits of Florida and the Santaren and Nicholas channels. It breaks the surface only around its edges, roughly establishing the boundaries of what was once a large island, one that could have supported many inhabitants. While there is no fresh water on the narrow land border, there are a number of freshwater springs in the ocean, just as there are in the Azores.

Within this area there are several unusual blue holes—not caves in underwater limestone cliffs, but circular holes half a mile in diameter, going straight down to depths of 1000 feet although the sea bottom surrounding the holes is only several fathoms deep. These holes in the ocean can be compared in shape to the *cenotes*, the large open wells at Chichén Itzá, into which Mayas used to throw jade, gold, and maidens as sacrifices to the gods.

It is in this very area that fishermen and pilots have given rise to a report of a large pyramid or pyramids off one of the Bahama Banks and rising from the ocean floor. A huge pyramid to the southwest of the Cay Sal Bank was reported in 1977 as having appeared in outline on the depth finder of a boat during a deep-sea fishing trip. Since then a number of soundings and dives, with as yet inconclusive results, have been made on the same or similar pyramidal formations located in deep water within the area. Eugene Shinn, a geologist with the United States Geological Survey, has been quoted in the press as declaring that a "pyramid" near Cay Sal is a natural formation, despite its pyramid-shaped profile. Some divers claim they have noted divisions or regular cracks along the side of an underwater pyramid that would be explainable if the pyramid were composed of large stone blocks. The matter has been further complicated by the probability that there is more than one pyramidal formation in the general area, just as there are a number—between fifty and sixty—of unexplained underwater stone walls, roads, and circles throughout the Caribbean and the Bahamas area of the western Atlantic.

An expedition in search of the alleged pyramid near Cay Sal was organized in 1978 by Ari Marshall, a Greek industrialist interested in the age-old legend of Atlantis. His expedition actually took closed-circuit television footage of a pyramidal mound off the Cay Sal Bank at a depth of over 750 feet.

Ari Marshall remembers some details:

> The first thing we noticed when we got near the area was that all the compasses were going berserk. We spent eight hours making tapes, starting at 700 feet to 1500 feet deep. We would go about a mile, then make a 90° turn and go back again. Finally I saw it coming up on the sonar screen. I told the captain to stop and then to proceed slowly. We were right over the pyramid. The top seemed to be about 150 feet from the surface, with the total depth about 650 feet. We lowered the camera and high intensity lights down the side of the mass and suddenly came to an opening. Light flashes or shining white objects were being swept into the opening by turbulence. They may have been gas or some sort of energy crystals. Further down, the same thing happened in reverse. They were coming out again at a lower level. It was surprising that the water in this deep area was green instead of black near the pyramid, even at night.

Divers were not sent down to the 350 feet and deeper level on this expedition. The resulting videotape turned out to be inconclusive because of the limited field of the video lens. While the "pyramid" seemed to show an inclined wall, it was not evident whether or not it was made of stone. But the unexpected photographing of the large holes in the side of the massive object through which glowing and apparently electrically charged particles were passing is a striking reminder of the many electronic anomalies often reported in the Bermuda Triangle.

There would of course be more than sufficient depth to contain a large pyramid in the deep ocean off the Cay Sal Bank and, considering the remains of stone pavements, walls, and roads already evident in various parts of the Bahamas area, the construction of pyramids or temple pyramids would be logical, just as it was in Yucatán, relatively nearby, and in Mesopotamia and Egypt.

An underwater pyramid would be difficult to chart, partially because of the changing bottom and partially because of the small area of the apex. US marine charts as well as the British Admiralty charts show what may be a seamount or a man-made pyramid at 23° 26′ N and 79° 43′ W off the bank in 250 fathoms of water, which suddenly rises to a shallow of forty-two feet. But another sudden rise appears only on the British Admiralty charts at 23° 34′ N and 80° W at a depth of 300 fathoms, which rises to thirty-eight feet. At a depth of 300 fathoms it is understandable that there could be large objects on the bottom that might have escaped previous notice unless they were being specifically searched for.

More exact measurements of the ocean floor will eventually establish whether these mounds are seamounts or man-made pyramids. Several years ago a US submarine suddenly struck an underwater hazard at a point near this pyramid area although there was no seamount or large wreck indicated on the charts. No damage was done, as the submarine was equipped for Arctic ice breaking and, after its encounter with what may have been a 12,000-year-old monument, it continued on its way.

Sightings of underwater pyramids have sometimes come from individuals who have flown over or otherwise visited certain areas of the Bermuda Triangle at the time of unusually turbulent sea action. Such turbulence may come from underwater surges, seaquakes, localized hurricanes (minicanes), scouring of the bottom cover by storm action, or tidal changes caused by seiche waves that may have originated far away and that suddenly draw water away from the land and then crest near the islands, or by other occurrences endemic to the Triangle that we do not yet understand.

One change in water level that uncovered a surprising view of the bottom was encountered by Ed Wilson (once a mayoral candidate for Orlando, Florida) on June 7, 1948. He was piloting an open Waco with a Continental engine, equipped for twelve-hour flights, engaged in shallow-bottom treasure hunting by air:

I was about 45 miles northeast of Miami and flying at about 250 feet above sea level when a hissing, smashing updraft hit me. It bounced the plane about 1000 feet upward. Now I have been in updrafts and downdrafts, but nothing like this. After I got back to more or less normal I noticed that the water had become bright and silvery. I noticed something big under the water and thought it was a wrecked ship. It was not far from the surface. Something was causing the water to rush past it at a fast rate. It curled around it and made a deep channel. The ocean seemed to be opening up. I was now flying low in a sort of trough in the water with both sides of it along the wingtips.

I suddenly realized that what I was looking at was not a ship at all, but seemed to be a huge building down in the water. The water seemed to get shallower around it. I could see a slanting side of a building that looked like a mountain. I was down at about fifty feet from the surface and could see it in the water. I circled around it for about a minute and a half. I could even see barnacles on it and water running past the top of it. At my point of angle and from my position I could clearly see it was a monstrous building. The sun was radiating in such a way that in its rays I could see this huge building clearly visible down under the water. I thought I saw other buildings around it but I could not see them well. The one I was looking at must have been 100 to 250 feet high according to the pattern I could get.

I started to time myself on the leg out to get readings of the location when out of this blue clear day another strange incident occurred: all my magnetics had gone to zero. Then a strange hue occurred all around me. At about 600 feet above water in the air that bright crimson hue simply baffled me.

That 240 H.P. Continental began to be the most crazily running engine I have ever had the experience to feel. It became motionless no matter what I did with the throttle and pumps. It glided and floated smoothly for at least two miles. Then the engine simply started itself. I could not dive because I was already on top of the water. Then I realized that some force was pulling toward a westerly direction.

Now, after all this I finally got back to the airport with my Bendix blasting hell out of everybody but not one single band would respond. After landing and getting inspection of Radio Communication and units every last unit was blown, shorted out by some high frequency electronic shock, or mysterious high voltage in the air. They said I might have run through a magnetic belt or something.

Over the past years I have been back many times, but I could never sight it again. A lot of damned Miamians made fun of my story. But I know I am right. You have hit with the sonar instruments the very object I talked about in exactly the same area.

A diving experience in Bahama waters, related by Dr. Ray Brown, a diver and lecturer of Mesa, Arizona, indicates how the sea bottom can change as a result of a violent storm. Within the Bermuda Triangle such a storm can sometimes uncover ruins for a short time only before they are buried again under the seafloor.

Dr. Brown, who was familiar with the Berry Islands of the Bahamas, where he had previously searched for Spanish treasure galleons, returned there in 1970. He detailed his experience in an interview with the author.

When we returned to where we had been before, looking for the sunken galleons, a violent squall came up. We had to hang on to mangroves on the island, it was so violent. Six- to eight-foot waves broke over us and we lost most of our equipment.

In the morning we saw that our compasses were spinning and our magnetometers were not giving readings. We took off northeast from the island. It was murky but suddenly we could see outlines of buildings under the water. It seemed to be a large exposed area of an underwater city. We were five divers and we all jumped in and dove down, looking for anything we could find.

As we swam on, the water became clearer. I was close to the bottom at 135 feet and was trying to keep up with the diver ahead of me. I turned to look toward the sun through the murky water and saw a pyramid shape shining like a mirror. About thirty-five to forty feet from the top was an opening. I was reluctant to go inside . . . but I swam in anyway. The opening was like a shaft debouching into an inner room. I saw something shining. It was a crystal, held by two metallic hands. I had on my gloves and I tried to loosen it. It became loose. As soon as I grabbed it I felt this was the time to get out and not come back.

I'm not the only person who has seen these ruins—others have seen them from the air and say they are five miles wide and more than that in length.

Reports from the other divers who were with Dr. Brown at the time are unavailable since three of them have died or disappeared in the Bermuda Triangle while diving. Dr. Brown still has the crystal, which he sometimes shows to lecture audiences. Inside the round crystal can be seen a series of pyramidal forms. When one holds the crystal, a throbbing sensation is felt in the hand of the holder, whether by autosuggestion or some quality inherent in the object.

Dr. Brown does not express an opinion as to the identity of the place that he visited except to say that it was an underwater pyramid surrounded by ruined buildings. He believes that the pyramid and the other buildings extended farther down under the seafloor, with only the upper portions visible. Brown does not reveal the coordinates of the pyramid, which, if located near the Berry Islands, is definitely not the one searched for by the Ari Marshall expedition. Divers and captains of small craft who have seen underwater ruins are understandably chary of facilitating directions to their finds. This applies equally to locations of treasure ships, where rival diving groups have engaged in underwater combat with one another in the best James Bond tradition.

If the pyramid has not sunk under the seafloor again, it should be able to be seen from the air under optimum visibility conditions, as the top would be about forty-five feet from the surface. While future divers could probably not count on retrieving crystals from interior passageways, the reward for finding such an architectural artifact as the pyramid should be sufficient.

Treasure divers represent a danger to archaeological sites and artifacts found under water just as generations of dry-land treasure hunters have disturbed buried remains of ancient cities by carrying off artifacts to sell to museums and private collectors. Suggestions have been made by treasure divers that some of the undersea ruins in the Triangle be dynamited to see what if anything is underneath.

For this reason divers and archaeological underwater explorers should exercise caution in their research, checking recovery of artifacts with the governments that control the local waters. Americans are cautioned to stay twenty-six miles away from the coast of Cuba despite the rumored sunken cities reputed to lie nearby under the sea, still unexplored because it never occurred to anyone until comparatively recently that perhaps an important section of the former civilized world, colonies or even part of ancient Atlantis, could be found under the western Atlantic and the Caribbean Sea.

It may be nothing more than a coincidence that the area of most of the underwater discoveries in the western Atlantic is within the Bermuda Triangle (a section of the Atlantic lying roughly between Bermuda, southern Florida, and a point past the Antilles at 60° W longitude), where hundreds of ships and planes, with their crews and passengers, have disappeared without a trace during the last fifty years and, before that, ever since the area was first traveled by ships in coastal trade or transatlantic travel. While the incidence of disappearance is relatively small compared with the number of daily flights over and boat trips across the Triangle, the question of what causes the disappearances and what happens to the victims is still unresolved.

In modern times, since the phenomenon has been more closely investigated, last messages from ships and planes as well as reports from craft that have encountered unusual conditions in this danger zone and succeeded in escaping have formed a clearer picture of what may have happened in a number of final disappearances and some survivals. Certain indications are common to both groups. They include compass spinning, sudden power failure, malfunction of navigational equipment, flight-indicator radar blackout, electronic drain, inability to control altitude of planes, light anomalies seen at night in the air and below the surface of the sea, the sudden appearance of enveloping, sometimes glowing fog over a small area at sea level or as a cloud in the sky (witnesses, sometimes hundreds at a time, have seen planes vanish into such a phenomenon—and not reappear), stress on the metal and wood construction of planes and ships, and strong magnetic pulls of planes and surface craft toward the sea and beneath it. These reported occurrences are apparently not related to sudden storms but seem to be connected with electromagnetic forces or stresses emanating from the sea itself. According to reports, these forces have even on occasion affected

Comparative elevations and chasms on the sea bottom in the western
part of the area unofficially but widely known as the Bermuda Triangle.
This area is characteristic for its unusual weather and sea phenomena;
the erratic behavior of compasses, directional and communications aids
on ships and planes passing through it; and above all for the mysterious
disappearance of air and surface craft and their passengers. Florida,
Cuba, and other large land masses are indicated in white, and smaller
islands in black. Other white areas contiguous to land were dry land
about 12,000 years ago. Vertical scale of underwater rises has been
emphasized for diagrammatic presentation. The sea bottom in the
Triangle runs a wide gamut of changes, from abyssal depths to extensive
shallow banks covering thousands of square miles, from underwater cave
systems to the weed-filled Sargasso, a "sea" in the middle of the ocean.

the minds of persons passing through the area, causing them to see visions or to change their actions, resulting in danger or death to themselves or others.

A recent theory suggests an unusual explanation for the disappearances of planes and ships in the Bermuda Triangle: sudden leaks or tears within the gas domes on the abyssal plains and continental shelves within the Triangle, where near-freezing sediments containing gas in the form of hydrate layers cause great clouds of hydrocarbon gas to pour out of the tear. When this gas comes to the surface it turns to bubbles and froth, lessening the concentration of the water and causing surface ships to subside into it and sink. Planes, if traveling at low altitudes, would encounter sudden gaseous whiteouts that interfere with the motor and the plane's operation and cause the pilot to lose his sense of orientation. This theory, encompassing as it does the mystery of disappearing ships and low-flying planes, also emphasizes the constant changes and stresses of the seafloor, which may have caused or been the result of the catastrophe that overwhelmed Atlantis. One might speculate that the reason for the disappearance of Atlantis may eventually be found in the abysses, trenches, and continental slopes of the ocean floor within the Bermuda Triangle.

It has been further theorized by some investigators that a tremendous magnetic bolide that hit the Earth in past millennia may still lie under the bottom of the Bermuda Triangle and be the cause of magnetic and communication aberrations. Egerton Sykes, the noted British Atlantologist, suggests that such a giant asteroid falling into the sea may be recognized in the records and legends of races on both sides of the Atlantic, especially by the Maya, the ones closest to it, who alluded to a like catastrophe in the *Popul Vuh.* Sykes observes: "You don't get this type of collision very frequently. But it has, nevertheless, often happened in the past. Perhaps the Bermuda Triangle should be called the Bermuda Crater. A massive meteor, driven ten or twelve miles into the surface of the Earth, might, over the years, be causing the aberrations."

There exist legends of extraordinary powers and magic (or technology) developed by former civilizations that ancient and primitive tribes, and a few modern historians, believe existed before history. The Hopi, Maya, and other Amerindian peoples tell of aerial warfare, the destruction of huge cities by explosions, sinking continents, and renewal of civilized life after catastrophes. Books of ancient India, transcribed from remembered legends handed down through thousands of years, describe rockets, and the destruction of whole armies in one brilliant cosmic flash, in terms which, after 1945, are perfectly comprehensible to the modern reader. In the psychic field Edgar Cayce, the "sleeping prophet," refers in his trance-readings to the use and misuse of great energy sources by the ancient Atlanteans. In the course of his readings of the past lives and experiences of subject individuals, Cayce told of the development, in Atlantis, of crystals as a source of power and destruction. He described in easily understandable, nonscientific language the workings of laser and maser—the enormous energy of disciplined light—many years before laser became an actuality or even an expressed theory.

From this background of historical legend and as yet unexplained psychic phenomena, a theory has been advanced which suggests that the unusual occurrences in the Bermuda Triangle may be caused by ancient power sources, preserved within pyramids or other constructions, which are still partially functioning with sufficient electromagnetic or other energy force spasmodically to interfere with ships and aircraft passing over their emplacements thousands of years later in time.

Controlled magnetic measurements over the area, and undersea explorations, especially of the depths off the Bahama Banks, could perhaps establish whether or not modern surface craft and aircraft are still being influenced by scientific artifacts of a lost prior civilization from a time when we believe that science as we know it was nonexistent.

But as our own scientific technology has developed, we have been able to examine unexplored parts of the Earth from space as well as from the air, to probe and chart the world's oceans and seas by improved deep-sea photography and sidescan sonar and DSRVs (deep submerged research vessels). Through a series of dating techniques, we can now determine with reasonable accuracy the age of artifacts as well as arrive at a better understanding of their probable use—often previously misunderstood.

As we stand on the edge of cosmic exploration, somewhat bemused by our own technological potential for self-destruction, we are also beginning to reassess the extent and development of a previous civilization on an earlier Earth, where the land and water area was considerably different from the one on which we now live.

9

UNEXPECTED DISCOVERIES FROM SPACE

It has sometimes been observed that the Great Wall of China would be the only man-made construction on Earth that would be visible from the moon. No one has yet tried to photograph this particular artifact from the moon, since temporary lunar visitors have been otherwise occupied. Nevertheless, other photographs of Earth taken from space at considerably closer distances by ERTS (Earth research technical satellites) may have picked up on film, completely by chance, ancient Earth constructions lost for thousands of years.

The ERTS satellites are launched by NASA and are designed to photograph for research purposes the topography, resources, agricultural potentials, and the water and forest cover of the planet. The information thus gathered is available to all nations. The different satellites have fixed orbits but wide photographic coverage, since the Earth revolves beneath them, constantly offering new areas to their fields of observation. The satellites have different bands that are used for the same shots, and when combined aid in the interpretation of the information received.

On their courses over the world's forests, deserts, and ice areas of difficult access, satellites, depending on absence of cloud cover, might obtain previously unsuspected indications of very ancient sites and artifacts; in fact, some may have already done so. Most ancient sites that have not yet been discovered would exist in a relatively undisturbed state only in the deep jungle, on or under the sea bottom, or under the polar ice. Otherwise, in all the thousands of intervening years, most of them would have been destroyed or incorporated into other structures built over them. Or they might be so big that they would be considered as natural mountains and recognized as constructions only when their orderly shape or alignation were seen from a point far enough away to have an effective perspective.

On December 30, 1975, *Landsat II*, an ERTS satellite, took in its normal course of activities a series of photographs at about 13° S latitude and 71° 30' W longitude, over the jungles of southeastern Peru, from a distance of 550 to 580 nautical miles in space. One of the photographs showed a series of eight unexplained "dots" that later appeared to be shaded protuberances, arranged in two rows going in straight lines, rows and objects equidistant from one another. When this curious arrangement was examined it was suggested, because of the shaded area of the geometrically regular rises, that they might not be rises but ponds—a river is shown nearby—but on infrared photographs they registered white, like mountains, an indication that they were made of stone. They were all well inside the jungle, miles from a nearby rock cliff marking the edge of the Andes plateau. Calculations made by the Institute of Andean Archaeology of Lima estimated from the *Landsat* photographs that each dot represented an object only slightly lower in height than the Great Pyramid of Gizeh, in Egypt.

Close investigation of this series of eight objects has been made by low-flying aircraft. It has been observed that they seem to be tree-covered pyramids and are not eight but twelve, as four additional smaller ones, also arranged in the two rows, did not show on the *Landsat* photographs. Several attempts have been made to get to the area by land, but these have been complicated by difficult jungle conditions that have resulted in the death and disappearance of some of the explorers. These hazards include poisonous snakes, insects, and distinctly unfriendly Indians who are apt to resist intruders with silent blowguns or long arrows and who believe that the area is a sacred city of the "old ones."

Several American explorers, including Herb Sawinski and Phillip Miller, both of Fort Lauderdale, Florida, have flown over the "pyramids" in small planes and taken photographs of them. Sawinski, who has overflown them at 200 feet altitude, remarks on their regular form or construction:

They look like structures covered with vegetation. They are symmetrically aligned in relation to each other. Several show a washout near the top, which would indicate that they were man-made or further built up by man. The difference in the color of the vegetation shows that they are made of different material than that of the surrounding basic jungle floor.

There are two other enormous rectangular formations now covered by trees and two semicircular ones, not so tall as the pyramids. They are to the south but are part of the complex. There are also high semicircular ridges at each end of the complex, which may turn out to be walls.

Question: Do you think that they are really pyramids?

They certainly look like it. We sent a request to the Environmental Institute of Michigan, and they suggested that the pyramids might be truncated ridges, like the Devil's Backbone in Colorado. But this would not explain the other structures. I think it is possible that the entire complex is the remains of an ancient city built by some race thousands of years before the Incas.

The possibility of the existence of stone pyramids large enough to be seen from space and located in a thick jungle area of eastern Peru recalls the insistent belief of Colonel P. H. Fawcett (which cost him his life) that great stone cities once existed in what is now the thickest jungle area of South America (*Lost Trails, Lost Cities*). In his opinion, these cities preceded the Incaic culture of the east coast, and their builders came originally from the east, refugees from lands that had sunk beneath the sea.

Fawcett, a colonel in the British army, who devoted years to exploration and boundary survey in the largely unexplored center of the South American jungle, believed that these great cities were thousands of years old and that the "connection of Atlantis with parts of what is now Brazil . . . affords explanations for many problems that otherwise are unsolved mysteries."

The presence of non–Indians in Central and South America had been established in earlier times by members of Spanish and Portuguese expeditions, who described encountering white tribes (one living in a city called Atlán) and also tribes of warlike blacks. In his own expeditions, Fawcett heard from a variety of tribes that white

Figure carved from volcanic stone un-earthed at Chinique, Guatemala, showing unusual physiognomy, bearded and quite different from Amerindian facial characteristics. Such finds, indicating visits in ancient times by Caucasian, Semitic, or Hamitic strangers, are not uncommon in Central and South America. *Herbert Sawinski*

Words, expressions, melodies, customs, and even games have traveled around the world since ancient times. The *parchese* of Persia and India somehow crossed the ocean before Columbus and was played by the Aztecs as *patolli*. The puffs coming out of the mouths of the players are invocations to the gods for success in the game. *Photo courtesy Timothy Kendall*

An ancient bust found in southeastern Spain, the Lady of Elche *(La Dama de Elche)* has long been considered the most outstanding example of prehistoric Spanish art. She is also thought by many to be a priestess of Atlantis, from the time of Atlantean contact with Spain. The peculiar headdress compared with that of a statue from ancient India points up an unexpected cultural connection. *Courtesy of the Hispanic Society of America and Eyra Marcano*

Unidentified cyclopean ruins near Niebla, Spain, which may have been part of the Kingdom of Tartessos, once located on the western coast of Spain and presumed to have been an Atlantean port on the Spanish mainland.

The three stones used in the foundation of the temple at Baalbek are reported to be the largest building blocks ever quarried and seem to be architecturally independent of the later Roman constructions above them. The casual use and setting of tremendous stones in very ancient times and in different parts of the world presents a yet unsolved mystery as to how they were quarried and how they were transported and set into place.
Tourist Bureau of Lebanon

Stonehenge is doubtlessly the most famous prehistoric monument in Europe. Partisans of various theories ascribe its construction to the ancient Druids, to the native Celts with help from Cretans, Egyptians, or Atlanteans. A Cretan double ax has been discerned on one of the pylons, but this may be the result of later visits. *Ivan Lee*

Stone fort on Aran Islands off the west coast of Ireland. The stonework and method of fitting the cut stones to last through the centuries resemble closely the buildings at Zimbabwe and Kuelap, almost as if they had been planned and constructed by the same unknown race. The forts in the Irish and Scottish islands were built, according to legend, for protection against the "people of the sea," referring to the sea on the west—the Atlantic Ocean.

High wall of Kuelap, Peru. It is not known what race raised this building complex, but its similarity to Zimbabwe, even to the ornamental top of the wall, is notable. *Herbert Sawinski*

Ancient walls of Zimbabwe, the mysterious ruin that has given its name to a new nation, perhaps the most sincere compliment ever paid to an archaeological monument. The high walls of this site and the apparent method of construction bear striking resemblance to other unidentified ruins on both sides of the Atlantic.

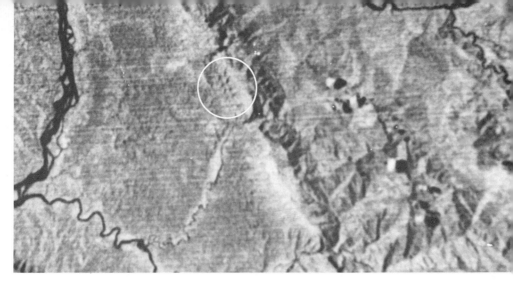

Landsat II satellite photograph taken from space at an altitude of over 500 miles, showing eight symmetrical structure-like objects on the edge of the Amazonian jungle. On subsequent closer inspection from light aircraft and helicopter, the mounds appeared to be a series of eight gigantic pyramids and four smaller ones, almost completely overgrown by the jungle. *NASA*

Closer view of pyramids from a helicopter. Several of them show "washouts"—a result of some trees failing to get a firm hold, a further indication of their artificial construction. Exploration of these pyramids is difficult because of the necessity of crossing through thick jungle from the Pini Pini River, part of the tributary system of the Amazon, and also because of the deterring presence of the Machiguenga tribal Indians, who consider themselves the traditional guardians of these "sacred places." *Jim Kinsrud*

Flat-top symmetrical formation 150 to 200 feet high in pyramid area taken from helicopter at approximately 400 feet altitude. Other circular and semicircular formations, covered by the jungle but thought to be massive constructions, are close by, suggesting a large city unconnected with previously known South American civilizations. *Jim Kinsrud*

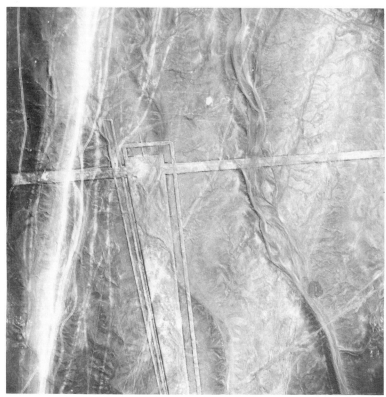

Rectangular lines at Nazca, some of which have been referred to as "landing fields" for prehistoric aircraft. *Foto Servicio Aerofotográfico Nacional del Perú*

Ridge of mountainous hill at Nazca, the top of which has evidently been sheared off to make an elongated platform several miles in length. Triangles, intricate designs, and unusual markings can be seen left of center on the photograph. *Foto Servicio Aerofotográfico Nacional del Perú*

men, many generations previously, had built great cities that still existed in the deep rain forests and that their high stone houses and stone streets were still illuminated at night by a steadily shining glow, the source of which was not known. Some Indians told him that there was great treasure in these far-off cities (a useful subterfuge sometimes employed by the Indians to persuade white men to leave the area for some other place, as distant as possible from the Indians' village).

Other Indians informed Fawcett that some of the ruined cities were still inhabited by a few descendants of the original builders and that certain savage Indian tribes formed an insulating protective barrier against intruders. Colonel Fawcett, searching for these mysterious cities for a number of years, occasionally met survivors of treasure-hunting expeditions whose companions had died or disappeared in the jungle. Fawcett himself vanished into the Amazonian jungle near the Xingú River in 1925.

His words before his fatal last expedition might serve as his epitaph:

Whether we get through, and emerge again, or leave our bones to rot in there, one thing is certain. The answer to the enigma of ancient South America—and perhaps to the prehistoric world— may be found when those old cities are opened up to scientific research. That the cities exist, I know.

If such cities exist in the Amazon Basin, they may eventually be found by satellite photography, although the South American rain forest is so thick that it is often referred to as "the green sea," and is frequently shielded from observation by the cloud cover standing over much of its area. New techniques of photography, however, pioneered in such disparate sites as over the planet Venus and Guatemala, may solve this problem.

A long-standing mystery of the pre–Columbian New World concerns the population density of the ancient Maya lands lying under the Central American jungle. It has previously been difficult to equate the enormous population that would have been necessary to construct the great temple cities of the Maya with their supposed method of agriculture; that is, to slash and burn the jungle foliage, plant and harvest a crop, and then move to another area, as is done by their descendants. Early reports of former very large concentrations of populations, as submitted after the Spanish conquest by the missionary priest Bartolomé de las Casas to the King of Spain in an effort to protect the Indians from genocide, were generally considered then and up to now to be extremely exaggerated.

When one flies over the Mayan lands, one normally sees only a canopy of trees. But recently a new type of radar—synthetic aperture radar—developed by NASA for use in penetrating the clouds of Venus during the *Pioneer* probe of Venus, and for other uses of a more military nature—was also employed over the jungles of Guatemala and Belize in 1977 during a geodetic survey. Continuing study of the photographs revealed the apparent presence of an extended system of canals under the forest cover. Follow-up verification by a land expedition under the direction of Dr. T. Culburt, of the University of Arizona, and Dr. E. Adams, of the University of Texas, has indicated that the Maya had an advanced system of irrigation and drainage, enabling them to grow continuing crops sufficient to feed millions of the inhabitants of their great cities and surrounding settlements.

Many of the world's early civilizations developed around river-connected irrigation systems from which grew the great ancient cities with walls, pyramids, and high temples built on stone or brick pyramids with stepped levels. These civilizations shared a common dedication to astronomy (a number of the towers and pyramid structures were used as observatories), and evolved a sophisticated knowledge of the stars, planets, and the measurement of time which in later centuries was lost.

As these cultures and their irrigation systems were destroyed by warfare and other disasters, most of them disappeared, although their vestiges are increasingly identifiable by aircraft observation over the desert, under the sea, and deep within the jungle.

A similar irrigation and pyramid culture seems to follow a fairly regular path around the world; from central Mexico and Yucatán to North Africa and Egypt, the Fertile Crescent of the Middle East, Iran, and the Indian subcontinent. They were generally located following a line along 30° N latitude, an area frequently called the "pyramid belt" of the Earth. This circling belt of pyramids, along which civilization, wherever it first appeared, seems to have moved east and west and only later to the north and south before resuming its path, "jumps" the Atlantic Ocean.

But in the past, perhaps it did not. One remembers that the continental island in the Atlantic, as described by Plato and others, was characterized by a huge circular irrigation system and great cities containing lofty towers from which the planets and stars could be observed. Furthermore, the supposed location of Atlantis, today theorized to be indicated by a huge underwater plateau and a series of submerged submarine ridges, is also traversed by north latitude 30°, running through its approximate center.

Extremely old Egyptian legends of extensive, well-watered lands, now desert, lying hundreds of miles west of the Nile and extending farther into the dry wastes of the Sudan and still farther to the west into Libya, received unusual confirmation from radar photographs taken recently by the space shuttle *Columbia*.

In November 1981 a radar scan was taken from the *Columbia* over the Sudan and southwest Egypt at an altitude of 125 miles and covering a width of over thirty miles. The scan was later enhanced by computer techniques and showed surprising results. While the ordinary photographs showed the normal desert, the enhanced radar ones showed the beds of buried rivers, some as large as the Nile but with indications of having flowed south and west. All these rivers showed traces of a number of tributaries and streams, which meant that thousands of years ago this extensive area would have supported forests and grazing lands for animals and, if man was present, crop-lands for organized agricultural and social development.

John McCauley, of the United States Geological Survey, after examining the radar photographs, suggested, "It is possible [the rivers] all joined up to one large basin of interior drainage as large as the Caspian Sea is now." In commenting on the use of the technique employed, he said, "We were able to look through and use radar as a time machine."

This discovery is yet another indication of the important land, sea, and climate changes that have occurred in comparatively recent millennia. It is estimated that the last time this area of the Sahara, including parts of Libya, Chad, the Sudan, Egypt, and most probably Tunisia and Algeria, enjoyed enough water and rainfall to support animal and human populations was about 10,000 years ago. This was coincidental with the period of very early Egyptian civilization which, according to Egyptian legends handed down by the Copts, was brought to Egypt by gods from the Western Lands.

Carved into the Tassili Mountains of Algeria, in what is now a completely arid landscape, there are representations of men and animals living in a pleasant country of forests, plains, and rivers. Many of these drawings are examples of an advanced and sophisticated art, often defaced or drawn over by later, more primitive artists, as if those who had originally made the pictures had departed.

These pictorial representations of how the desert once was were discovered by French military officers in the 20th century, but it was never understood how the land could have been so fertile and productive until the space shuttle *Columbia* rediscovered the ancient riverbeds, invisible to land or air observers.

But, underneath different parts of the Sahara, some of these underground rivers may still be flowing. There is even, among the Tuaregs, a specialized group of desert marabouts (Islamic holy men) called "the men of water wisdom," to whom has been handed down knowledge of the courses along which these hidden rivers still run. These water finders are reputed to be able to locate water in the most desolate parts of the desert, a talent inherited or developed from sources lost in remote antiquity.

The disappearance of the Sahara Desert rivers west of the Nile and the drying up of the Sahara area they once watered is a further indication of the world-wide climatic changes that occurred at the end of the last glacial period—which is also the time span applied by legend to the destruction of Atlantis.

An outstanding example of complicated constructions left by ancient builders whose reasons for making them has not been established exists in the Nazca Valley in Peru. Pilots engaged in determining water resources in Peru photographed mysterious lines drawn into the earth, crossing mountainous hills and continuing on the other side, and sometimes on the tops of mountains whose crests have been leveled off by artificial means, all in the Nazca Valley and surrounding mountains. Mixed in with a series of straight lines, parallelograms, rectangles, triangles, and enormous designs of animal figures hundreds of feet long, parts of these markings bear a startling resemblance to landing fields. The patterns of the geometric lines, animal figures, and "landing fields" are apparent only from the air. Their purpose is not known. Perhaps they were meant to plot the course of as yet unidentified stars or, as has been suggested, were meant as signals to be seen by former visitors from the skies. In any case they were unrecognized during the centuries that passed until new visitors from the sky—pilots flying on a hydrographic research project—observed them in the early thirties. Dr. Paul Kosak, an American archaeologist who first realized their true extent and import in 1930, later concluded that they may constitute "the largest astronomy book in the world." Dr. Maria Reiche, a German archaeological student who came to Peru in 1932, became so interested in the Nazca lines that, in 1946, she established her home close by, making the lines the subject of her constant study until her death in 1983. She considered them "the most important archaeological monument of Peru, and perhaps of the world." She noted their "great size, coupled with perfect proportion" and especially wondered how the ancient artisans were able to draw on the desert terrain the gigantic animal figures "with their beautifully laid out curves and well-balanced dimensions"—an incredibly difficult task to accomplish "unless the ancient Peruvians were able to fly." (The idea of ancient Peruvian aircraft has been advantageously used by the Peruvian national air carrier, AeroPeru, which has used in its advertising the motto—"Introducing AeroPeru, the world's newest—and perhaps oldest—airline.")

Photography from the skies has succeeded in finding an entire lost city in north Italy, concealed for centuries under water and mud. Spina was a large city of the mysterious Etruscans, the lords of most of Italy before the Romans overcame them. Their origin and early history is unknown and their language undeciphered. The section of Italy where they ruled was called Tyrrhenia, specifically mentioned by Plato in the *Critias* dialogue when he stated that "the island of Atlantis . . . [had] subjected the parts of Libya within the Columns of Hercules as far as Egypt and of Europe as far as Tyrrhenia."

Little is known about the Etruscans except from their tomb artifacts, which indicate that they seemed to enjoy a civilized and sophisticated daily life. The tombs were located by metal probes and, more recently, by altitude infrared photography, which clearly delineates the round circles of the subterranean tombs.

The city of Spina was considered for many centuries to be a legend, since no trace of it could be found. There were no remains on land or even under the coastal waters, as has been the case with many port cities in the Mediterranean. But high-altitude photography has revealed a series of patterns caused by different shadings in marsh grass indicating walls, streets, blocks of dwellings, large buildings, squares, and docks of which only shadowed outlines remain in what had become an extensive swamp into which the whole metropolitan complex had subsided into the mud and was forgotten by history.

There is one ancient artifact that certainly has not been forgotten, and has been searched for (and, according to many, visited) for many centuries. Its existence has been generally accepted up to the relative present, but for the last 150 years has been dismissed as fantasy by the scientific world.

But Noah's Ark is still being searched for by pilots, mountain climbers, explorers, and religious groups in "the mountains of Ararat" as mentioned in the Bible. Its existence, if it could be satisfactorily established, would indicate that a civilization before history was once a reality and that it was destroyed by a combination of disasters that caused tremendous floods throughout the world and whose tidal waves left at least one ship of refuge on a mountain 15,000 feet high; a mountain whose sides show evidence of wave action and sea deposits.

While it is true that every ancient race has its own version of such a disaster and its own particular name for a heroic Noah, its means of salvation, and site of debarkation, still, it has been the Ark on the mountains of Ararat that has captured popular imagination for thousands of years.

There have been alleged visits to and sightings of Noah's Ark through the centuries down through the two World Wars. Russian pilots in World War I claimed to have seen it in a mountain lake, which was later visited by an expedition whose records have been lost. During World War II, both Russian and American pilots claim to have seen and photographed the Ark, although no authenticated photograph is at present available.

According to rumors current among American pilots stationed in Turkey during the cold war, photographs of Noah's Ark were taken by U-2 pilots in the course of their high-flight reconnaissance missions over the USSR. But none of these, if they do exist, have been made public.

In 1974, however, an ERTS photograph, taken from about 500 nautical miles over Mount Ararat, showed an unusual object near the crest which, discussed in a United States Congressional session and entered into the Congressional Record, has already attained what one may qualify as lasting fame. Senator Frank Moss, then chairman of the Space Commission, in commenting on the object, observed that it was "about the right size and shape to be the Ark."

Among the recent searchers for Noah's Ark on Mount Ararat in eastern Turkey has been Colonel James Irwin, the astronaut of *Apollo 15* who drove the Lunar Rover land vehicle on its mission over the surface of the moon. It is interesting to speculate whether Colonel Irwin's interest in the survival of the Ark was awakened as he crossed over the Middle East in orbital flights over the Earth prior to his visit to the moon and perhaps wondered if the Ark really was still hidden high toward the peak of Great or Little Ararat far below.

In any case, his dedication to the Ark project is an interesting connection between very ancient history and the space age of today and tomorrow.

Continuing photography of Earth from space will doubtlessly reveal further unsuspected information about the past of civilization and of Earth itself. It may also accomplish a like result in photographing other planets from space, in our own system and ultimately in others. It may possibly have already done so, although most astronomers, understandably mindful of their professional reputations, prefer to consider certain curious formations on Mars, photographed by *Mariner 9*, to be simply rocks or cliffs on the planet's now arid surface, notwithstanding their peculiar resemblance to the way ancient ruins on Earth look from the sky, especially as seen by *Viking Orbiter I*. But there are exceptions. Antonio Ribera, a Spanish author and lecturer, calls attention to a well-defined photograph of the edge of the Coprates Depression on the surface of the moon:

> The disposition of apparent walls makes a series of rectangles which are not found in nature. We know from space photographs already taken that the surface of Mars was once traversed by rivers and tributary streams. Consequently, a depression into which the ancient rivers flowed was most probably a sea. The objects or buildings could be the remains of a former port on the now-dry ocean. In other places "farther inland" from this one-time seaport there appear to exist large four-sided pyramids typical of all ancient races who built for eternity.

Asked whether he thought that an earlier Earth could have been colonized from Mars as that planet began to dry up and lose its atmosphere, forcing its inhabitants to seek a more livable world, Dr. Ribera replied, "This of course we cannot presently know. I suggest however that it is an interesting possibility."

10

KNOWLEDGE FROM FORGOTTEN SOURCES

The round shape of the Earth, its movement, and its relation to the universe were known to the ancient world and, during the Dark Ages, had never been completely forgotten in Europe until the convincing proofs provided by Columbus and Magellan re-established this knowledge. The true nature of planets and stars, handed down from antiquity, was also known, although far from generally accepted, during the European Middle Ages, when individualistic speculation about these matters could terminate one's career either in the torture chamber or at the stake as a heretic, magician, or witch.

The scientific blackout was partially caused by the censorship imposed by new religions, but principally by the destruction of the great libraries of antiquity such as those of Alexandria, Pergamon, Carthage, Syracuse, Rome, and Athens by accidental fire or deliberate policy.

The Romans destroyed Carthage and with it all its books and records, and even sowed the site with salt. Most of the books of Rome later met the same fate at the hands of barbaric invaders, while private collections of books in the cities and countryside of most of the ancient world subsequently disappeared through the ravages of the Goths, Vandals, and Huns. Other attacks on surviving books were carried out by the adherents of new religions—Christianity and Islam—who were anxious to eradicate all accounts of life in the hedonistic pagan world.

The library of Alexandria, with its collection of several million rolls of books, was burned in Julius Caesar's time, restored, and finally systematically destroyed by Amru, the Moslem conqueror. After capturing Alexandria, Amru asked the Caliph for instructions about the disposition of the books. The Caliph answered: "The contents of these books are in conformity with the Koran or they are not. If they are, the Koran is sufficient without them; if they are not, they are pernicious. Let them, therefore, be destroyed." The books were thereupon burned to heat the city's 600 public baths.

Other ancient collections of books were burned, with more concern for the soul than for the pleasures of the mind, by Christian zealots down through the Middle Ages. Because of the shortage of writing materials, many surviving manuscripts were painted over and reused for copying religious texts, which generally ended up in monastery collections (an occurrence of interesting possibilities, considering the ribald nature of many classical works).

After the Spanish conquest of Yucatán, Bishop de Landa consigned at one stroke all written Mayan knowledge, with its possible reference to their origin and earlier civilizations, to bonfires, since the conquerors had decided that the New World religions, with their similarities to Christianity—with the exception of human sacrifice—were the work of the devil to confuse the faithful. Only four Mayan books still survive in European museums. An indication of the Mayan knowledge that may have been lost is given by the *Popul Vuh*, rewritten from memory after the conquest, which referred to their ancestors as: "The first race, capable of all knowledge [who] examined the four corners and round circles of the Earth, the horizon, and the four points of the firmament."

While more records have come down from the classical world than from the pre–Columbian one, it is still estimated that only 5 to 10 percent of written works or extracts from the pre–Christian Mediterranean civilizations have survived to this day. One wonders how many references to Atlantis would now be available had not the overwhelming majority of ancient books been destroyed.

Much information, however, has survived through ancient hieroglyphs written in tombs or on mummy cases and wrappings, and the cuneiform script of the Middle East, both of which were considered for almost 2000 years to be a form of decoration rather than writing. Since the cuneiform books of Mesopotamia were inscribed on clay, the fires that destroyed the cities and the people who wrote them often preserved the clay tablets by baking them to an even harder consistency. Nobody knows how many tens of thousands of these tablets have been built into the mud huts of the present dwellers in the area of these once tremendous cities which are now, except for giant mounds, under ground level.

The fall of Constantinople to the Moslem Turks in 1453 caused a dispersal of the holders of what ancient knowledge still survived and reawakened through Europe an interest in the culture and science of antiquity. The deciphering of Egyptian hieroglyphic writing in the 19th century as well as the cuneiform script of the Middle East has since made it possible to compare the knowledge and scientific attainments of the ancient world.

A curious contradiction became apparent—the mathematical and astronomical knowledge of the Greeks seemed to be developed from a much earlier source. Thales of Miletus (who invented a steam engine but did not popularize it) was convinced that the Milky Way was made up of stars, each one of which was a world containing a sun and planets, these worlds being situated in the immensity of space—a concept that came from Babylon. The use of *pi* by Euclid, the geometrical theorems of Pythagoras, the "golden section" and other mathematical verities that have so influenced the modern world may have been developed by Pythagoras during the period he spent in Babylon and Egypt, where this mathematical and astronomical knowledge had been available for thousands of years.

The Babylonian texts, generally expressed in astrological language, seem to indicate that the astronomers of thousands of years ago were cognizant of cosmic phenomena and theory that we have "discovered" only in the last 400 years and, in several cases, as recently as the last forty years. But a peculiar feature of ancient scientific knowledge is that the further it goes back in time, the more extensive it seems to be.

As the Greeks received their knowledge of astronomy from the Babylonians, the Babylonians themselves received theirs from the Sumerians, who preceded them. The Sumerians used the concept of zero, as did the ancient Hindus, and were able to make mathematical cosmic calculations of fifteen digits while younger races had difficulty counting in the thousands. Instead of the digital count based on ten fingers, the Babylonians used a system of counting by twelves and units of sixty, a system better suited to calculation since it divides into more factors. We still use this Sumero-Babylonian

The ancient Sumerians possessed surprising knowledge of the stars and planets, some of it so developed that it must have evolved after many centuries of controlled observation of the heavens. (The figure shown here is surrounded by twelve stars or planets, and has been thought by some students of Sumerian sacred and astronomical records to represent the Earth, sun, moon, and *nine* planets, one more planet than we presently recognize. According to Sumerian cosmology, this tenth "dark" planet could not be seen by observers on Earth because of its specialized orbit and was visible only at 3600-year intervals.)

system every time we mention dozens, inches, feet, seconds, minutes, hours, and the degrees in a circle.

Berossus, the Babylonian astronomer and historian, was familiar with the "Great Year," the grand count of the precession of the equinox, the total time for the passing of each of the zodiacal star signs through the skies of Earth—in other words the solar years elapsed before the Earth arrives back in the part of space that it was at the beginning of each zodiacal revolution—a total of 25,826.6 years. The Babylonian figure missed our modern approximation by only four-tenths of a year. The Sumerians, from whom the Babylonians inherited their civilization, were the first to name the figures of the zodiac (Greek for "animal circle"), which the Sumerians called "the shiny herd." The Sumero-Babylonian records also indicate a considerably wider understanding of the planets and stars than any succeeding culture has possessed up to the recent present.

Often unexpected cosmic knowledge is mixed in with the fabled doings of gods, demigods, and giants. A legend of the Amerindian Hopi tribe, for example, ascribes the ending of the Second World to the action of the twin guardians of the north and south axes of the world in abandoning their posts. The twins, Pöqanghoya and Palöngawhoya, the former guarding the north and the latter the south axis, were ordered by Sotuknang, nephew of the Creator, to leave their posts so that the Second World could be destroyed (its people had become evil) and a third one established. When the twins abandoned their posts, the Earth careened in space, changing the shape of the planet before a new axis and a new world were established. This legend of the guardians of the axes is imaginative and impressive, but through what ancient source of astronomical knowledge did a remote Amerindian tribe know that the Earth was round and turned on its axis?

A number of star features that could not be seen without the use of a telescope were given the same names in different languages in both the Old and New Worlds. Such was the Scorpion, a star cluster containing a comet, which reminded both the Babylonians and the Maya of Central America of a scorpion and was called by that name by both races. Greek astronomers adopted the observation of the Babylonians that Uranus regularly covered its moons, an occurrence also unable to be seen by the naked eye, and converted it to a legend that the god Uranus had the habit of alternately eating and later disgorging his children.

In mythology, Mars, the god of war, had two fierce horses, *Phobos* (fear) and *Deimos* (terror), to pull his chariot, the planet Mars, a legend possibly drawn from ancient knowledge that Mars had two moons. But in the centuries between ancient and modern civilization the moons of Mars were forgotten until Ashap Hall saw them by telescopic observation in 1877 and appropriately named them after the war god's two horses. But, strangely, Jonathan Swift, in 1726, in a guess or prophecy worthy of Jules Verne, stated in the fictional *Gulliver's Travels* that Mars had two moons and correctly gave their dimensions and distance from the planet—more than 150 years before their "official" discovery.

The ancient references, which are really astronomical data disguised as legends, to the two moons of Mars, the multiple moons of Jupiter, the five disappearing and reappearing moons of Uranus, the nine moons of Saturn, and even the horns of Venus, suggest that astronomers of former cultures were capable of using artificial sight amplification that was probably a form of telescope. But as far as we know, the first version of the modern telescope was not invented until 1609.

Ground-glass artifacts, however, found at different archaeological sites, seem to indicate that the ancients were able to manufacture an optical lens. In 1853 Sir David Brewster, a specialist in optics with the British Association for the Advancement of Science, produced a crystal that had been found in a buried "treasure house" in Nineveh. The audience, intrigued by this interesting jewel, was thrown into an uproar when Sir David insisted it was a "true optical lens" ground in antiquity. The "lens" was catalogued as a jewel and was put on exhibit at the British Museum with other Assyrian antiquities. Since then, however, other finds of lenses, brought up from under the sea off Esmeraldas, Ecuador, excavated at La Venta, Mexico, and jewel-like lenses found in tombs in Libya, in what was formerly part of the Roman empire, suggest that various ancient peoples used lenses for vision amplification. Some Roman accounts of the arena mention that certain aristocrats used colored jewel pendants to bring closer to them their view of the sanguinary Roman games. According to Plutarch, Archimedes, the inventor genius of ancient Syracuse, possessed instruments able to "manifest to the eye the largeness of the sun."

While most of the small artifacts of antiquity have disappeared, a number may be stored in museums throughout the world awaiting further study and classification of what they really were. A survey of some of these previously unidentified artifacts in museum exhibits stresses both the extreme age of civilized man and the scientific achievements of very early, even prehistoric, eras.

A re-examination of scratch carvings on mammoth bones and deer antlers of 15,000 to 35,000 years ago

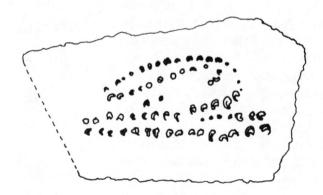

discovered in caves and later on exhibition in European museums, was undertaken by Alexander Marshak, of the Peabody Museum of Archaeology and Ethnology, who developed the theory that the markings on these bones, formerly thought to be incisions made to strengthen one's grip for throwing or wielding, were not only a predecessor but actually a form of prehistoric symbolic writing, for use as a lunar calendar. The symbols on the bones, some written so small that they have to be studied under magnification, appear to note phases of the moon, with the straight lines probably indicating days and recurring figures of women and animals within the calendar notations possibly referring to months, hunting seasons, and the menstrual cycles of women. In other words, the beginning of writing many thousands of years before writing of any kind was thought to exist.

Further development of such cave writing may have evolved into the pebble and stone notations found at Mas-d'Azil and other caverns in France, and in Spain and North Africa. (*References:* The Blanchard bone, Musée des Antiquités Nationales, St.-Germain-en-Laye, France; Mas-d'Azil pebbles, Musée de l'Homme, Paris)

An incised drawing of a wolf, pitted and partially surrounded by a series of carved dots, was found in Polesini, Italy, along with twelve

carved bones dating from the Ice Age.
At first considered to be a hunter's
charm or a cult object, the curious
arrangement of the dots has been interpreted by Ivan Lee, an archaeological investigator, as representing an
Ice Age directional star chart. He sug-

gests that some of the dots form a constellation resembling a wolf (a natural
shape for Ice Age hunters to imagine)
visible in the skies at that period. He
believes that the other dots can be
identified as parts of Scorpio, Libra,
and other summer constellations including Lyra, Sagitta, Serpens, and
Ophiuchus as they would have been
seen from northern Italy about 26,000
years ago. If this theory proves ten-
able, it would suggest that the constellation of the Wolf was not the fancy
of a single hunter but rather the result
of a close observation of the night sky
over a period of time by a prehistoric
culture. Perhaps it was this no longer
evident star pattern that inspired the
European tribes of the north to see
the vast shape of the mythological
"Fenris Wolf" in the night sky, the
wolf whose jaws were wide enough to
enable him to swallow the Earth.

An encrusted and fused metallic object containing wheels, found
by divers in 1900 on the sea bottom
near Antikythera in the Mediterranean Sea, was relegated to the Athens
Museum, where it was tentatively
qualified as a child's toy because of
the wheels. Upon re-examination and

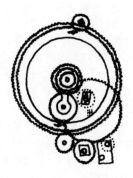

a series of chemical baths under the direction of Derek DeSolla Price, the author and archaeologist, the wheels proved to be gears, and the object, according to what could be read on the metal, turned out to be a "star computer" to shoot the sun, moon, and stars. The use of such a technical aid, the only one yet found, implies a much greater knowledge of navigation and archaeology among Cretan and early Greek sea captains than was previously suspected. They would have had the ability to sail by night out of sight of land and perhaps past the Pillars of Hercules to the far islands of the Atlantic Sea. (*Reference:* National Museum, Athens)

Dr. Wilhelm König, an Austrian archaeologist employed by the Iraq Museum, unearthed in 1936 a 2000-year-old vase, six inches high, which contained inside it a copper cylinder set in pitch, and inside that an iron rod secured with an asphalt plug. This object resembled others in the Berlin Museum, some larger with a repetition of the cylinder settings. There was no clue to their function except that they were "religious or cult objects," a useful designation, along with "toys," for unknown artifacts. It occurred to some investigators, including Dr. König, that these might be dry cell batteries which, understandably, were no longer in working condition after several thousand years. However, when they were exactly reconstructed and provided with a new

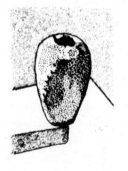

electrolyte, they worked! This ancient use of electricity may of course prove only that electric power was used for electroplating metals with gold and silver, as is still done in the bazaars of the Middle East. But it is also likely that it was used for the illumination of temples and palaces, although its use disappeared before the middle epoch of antiquity, that of the Greeks and Romans, who used oil for illumination. (*Reference:* Berlin and Iraq Museums)

When French archaeologists during the Napoleonic invasion of Egypt observed a wall carving in a temple at Dendera, they could not have realized that they were perhaps looking at a preview of something that would modify the whole world eighty years later—the electric light. On the walls of the temple at Dendera, now a national museum, there are incised figures on stone carrying what appear to be five-foot light bulbs, each one with an elongated "serpent" filament inside, held up by high-tension insulators and attached to braided cables which in turn are connected to a transformer. The overwhelming majority of Egyptologists interpret these apparent bulbs as "lotus offerings," "snake stones," or "cult offerings." The fact remains that the mystery of the illumination of the subterranean tomb and temple corridors of ancient Egypt has never been explained. How could the artisans carve tens of thousands of figures and color intricate

paintings far beneath the earth and leave no traces of torch smoke or oil smudge on the ceilings? The proposed theory of light reflection from the use of a series of mirrors would be too diminished for far underground illumination. The notation by the Swedish writer Ivan Troëng (*Kulturer Före Istiden*) may be hard to believe, although it has the advantage of being fairly obvious: "Pictures from Hall 5 of the Dendera temple show electric lamps held up by high-tension insulators." (*Reference:* Temple of Hathor at Dendera)

Strangely accurate maps were circulating around Europe at the time of Columbus, showing continents and shorelines that would not be discovered in some cases for hundreds of years. These were the Portolano maps, probably rescued from the ancient libraries and used for centuries as navigational tools by sea captains in great secrecy in order to protect their trade routes. But only in the last decades have these maps been recognized for what they were. At the time of their last copying they demonstrated a knowledge of the existence of, and even the coastlines of, "undiscovered" continents; continents that evidently were mapped by a past civilization but forgotten, except on the recopied maps, after something happened that considerably altered the face of the world. Investigations by Professor Charles Hapgood, of the University of New Hampshire, of the Piri Re'is map of the southern Atlantic and its shores (last copied in 1513) established that spheroid trigonometry was used to establish correct longitudinal coordinates, a process not rediscovered until the middle of the 18th century. The correct coastline of Antarctica was shown as it exists *under* the ice that now covers it. Another, the Oronteus Finaeus world map (1531), not only gives the most correct longitudinal coordinates but shows in the as yet undiscovered Antarctic continent rivers, valleys, and coastlines in their correct position under the glacial ice as well as the approximate location of the South Pole.

Further research by Professor Hapgood (*Maps of the Ancient Sea Kings*) revealed a treasury of ancient maps in the Library of Congress, many of which show an amazing knowledge of the Earth's true geography at a time when most people did not know that the world was round and when cartographers were apt to fill in blank spaces on maps with drawings of winged cherubs, monsters, or with the annotation "here be Dragons." The Buache map (1754) shows the Antarctic continent without ice, divided into two great islands, a fact not reestablished until 1958. The Hadji Ahmed map (1550) shows a more correct delineation of the west coast of North America and also a *land* connection between Siberia and Alaska, suggesting the extreme antiquity of the original map. The receding ice fields of northern Europe were evidently extant when the original Andrea Ben-

incasa map (1508) was made, as they
are clearly depicted thereon. The King
Jaime world map shows the Sahara,
not as a desert, but as a fertile land
of rivers, woods, and lakes, which it
once was—before the beginnings of
chronicled history (cf. Tassili rock
drawings, page 72). The Iehudi Ibn
Ben Zara map (1487) shows islands
above water in the Mediterranean that
are still in place but now under water,
while the Buache map (1737) of the
South Atlantic shows the Canary Islands in their correct positions and also
the correct outline of the underwater
plateau on which they are located, a
fact that can be explained only by ancient knowledge of their extended
shape *before* the glaciers melted and
the oceans rose. Several other Portolano maps show the legendary island of Antilia in the supposed vicinity
of Atlantis; perhaps, considering the
time that the maps were presumably
first made, effectively showing the
drowned remnant of the island continent whose sea kings charted the
world but whose knowledge of the
world's surface was lost for many centuries. (*Reference:* Ancient world maps
and ocean charts, Library of Congress)

An artifact found in a tomb in
Colombia and dated 1400 Before
Present was at first considered to be
a flying fish, moth, butterfly, or bird.
A number of individuals who examined the artifact, however, especially
pilots and others with a knowledge of
aviation, agreed with the late Ivan

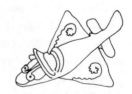

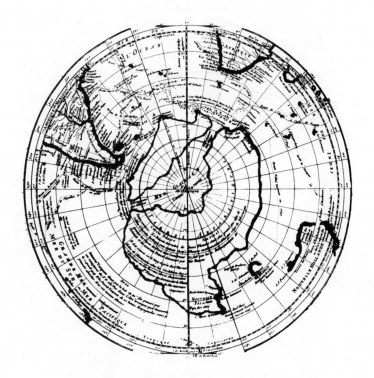

Buache map (1754) showing the sea division of Antarctica.

Sanderson, a distinguished zoologist,
that the object resembles not a bird
but a jet fighter plane with delta wings
and with a number of other features
not found in birds or insects, such as
ailerons, tail rudder, rectangular engine casing, and cockpit. If this artifact really represents a heavier-than-
air flying machine, we must consider
the implication that a prehistoric civilization on Earth, developing over a
period of thousands of years, could
have arrived at a point of experimenting with and constructing aircraft. If the civilization disappeared,
memories of such accomplishments
might be roughly copied in artifacts

and pictures by races in retrogression
after a world-wide catastrophe. (*Reference:* Museo de Oro, Bogotá, Colombia)

Within recent years a series of
strange-looking wooden birds thousands of years old found in Egyptian
tombs, and thought to be decorations,
models, or toys, have been re-examined by archaeologists at the Cairo
Museum, where they were stored, and
found to be working models of gliders. Dr. Khalil Messiha, who examined a number of these birds in 1969
together with his brother, a flight engineer, noted that their somewhat abnormal bird shape was perfect for
sustained flight—one does not have
to throw them; they fly away from the
hand with only a slight push. Messiha
pointed out that ordinary birds do not
have vertical tails and that the wings
of these unusual birds resemble those
of an aircraft, with correct dihedral
angle and depression in relation to the
fusilage. Whether or not the Egyptians of early history were trying to
keep alive or recapture former knowledge of aerodynamics, or were simply
experimenting, is not yet known. On
the right, the French Caravelle (top)
is compared with an Egyptian model
of what appears to be a flying machine
of more than 4000 years ago. (*Reference:* Cairo Museum)

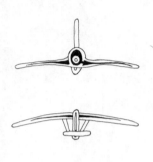

One remembers that Egyptian civilization seemed to *begin* at a
surprisingly high level, as though it had been brought to Egypt from
elsewhere, or, as told in Egyptian tradition, as though learning and
civilization had been carried to the Nile after the Flood by the god

Thoth, who came to Egypt "from the west." This suggestive reference to the colonists who settled Egypt from the west, bringing a ready-made civilization with them (possibly from Atlantis), is emphasized by a passage from Diodorus of Sicily, a first-century writer and historian: "The Egyptians were strangers, who, in remote times, settled on the banks of the Nile, bringing with them the civilization of their mother country, the art of writing, and a polished language. They had come from the direction of the setting sun and were the most ancient of men."

Diodorus' ancient comment on the appearance of an advanced, spontaneous civilization in Egypt received some recent confirmation 2000 years later from, among others, Professor W. B. Emery in his book *Archaic Egypt*. Noting that in the fourth millennium B.C. Egypt suddenly passed from the Neolithic Age into well-organized kingdoms, he writes, ". . . at the same time the art of writing appears, monumental architecture, and the arts and crafts, develop to an astounding degree . . . all the evidence [of] a well-organized and even luxurious civilization. All this achieved within a comparatively short period of time, for there appeared . . . no background to these fundamental developments in writing and literature."

Both the Egyptians and the Maya were sufficiently advanced scientifically to calculate the exact number of days in the solar year. The Egyptians even measured in stone: the sum of the four baselines of the Great Pyramid at Gizeh, measured in pyramid inches, gives a figure of 365,240, which needs only a decimal point to give a fairly accurate count of the days of the year. The ancient Mayan astronomers of the New World arrived at an even more exact figure— 365.2420 days to our current count of 365.2422.

There exists also an unusual correlation, reaching across the Atlantic Ocean and the Mediterranean Sea, between the Egyptian calendar and that of the Aztecs of central Mexico. The Aztecs, who inherited their civilization from their mysterious predecessors, the Toltecs, solved the question of leap year by dividing the months of the year into twenty-day periods, leaving five extra days to come at the end with still another day added every fifty-two years, celebrated with appropriate human sacrifices as a promise of life for the next fifty-two years. The Egyptians, who also knew the correct number of days, readjusted their own cycle every 1460 years. Both these races started their new cycles on our equivalent of February 26, which in Egypt occurred in the month of the god Thoth, the traditional inventor of writing and the bringer of civilization to Egypt.

The pyramid of Cheops or Khufu, the Egyptian name of the presumed builder, is reputed to constitute within its very shape and measurements a geophysical and astronomical marker. Although it is the custom among most archaeologists to discredit the so-called "pyramid cults" and the wide range of information often read into the dimensions of the Great Pyramid, it is nevertheless certain that its very construction, mystical or not, implies a scientific expertise not only in architecture but in geophysical information—perhaps a legacy from a superior civilization in the predawn of Egypt, before the numbered dynasties.

In the Middle Ages, the Arab conquerors of Egypt kept alive the pyramid mystique with tales of great treasure and magical artifacts within, causing the Caliph Al-Mamnun to order that Khufu's pyramid be broken into, revealing passageways but no treasure. It was during Napoleon's invasion of Egypt that some of the secrets of the Great Pyramid were "discovered," although they were always there for anyone to observe. This occurred when French army engineers, looking for a large object to use for triangulation of the Nile Delta, decided on the Great Pyramid. They found it was not only suitable for their purpose but also that it was aligned exactly with the cardinal points, that extensions of its diagonal baselines would correctly bisect the Nile Delta, that an east-west line through the center ran along the 30th parallel, and that the measurement of the pyramid itself seemed to coincide with the French meter, only then recently established as one ten-millionth of the polar axis of the Earth. It seemed to the French engineers that the pyramid had originally been planned to serve as a geophysical indicator, a concept reinforced by later discoveries. These include the 3.1416 value of *pi*, which is the base measure of the pyramid divided by twice its height, the Great Year of the zodiac, arrived at by adding the diagonals of the base and other measurements and calculations of weight and height, somewhat debatable, concerning the weight of the Earth, the number of days in the solar year (arrived by a change in decimal point of the total count of the pyramidal inches around the base), the distance of the Earth to the sun, and the land and sea division of the Earth. One salient feature is obvious: the long King's Passageway rising from the center of the pyramid diagonally toward an opening is fixed on the North Star (Polaris) in the Big Dipper, although at the approximate time the pyramid was built Polaris was in Draconis (the Dragon). Also, if a straight line is projected from the southern base through crossed diagonals at the center, it will miss the North Pole by only four miles, a deviation caused by the slight shifting of the Pole since the time the pyramid was built.

An Egyptian Copt historian, Masudi, writing during the Middle Ages, recounted a tradition that the Great Pyramid was built during the Reign of the Gods, *before* the Flood, to safeguard ancient knowledge. There is evidence that the Great Pyramid has experienced one or more floods, since shells and fossils from the sea have been found around its base, and indications of a salt deposit have been noted in the Queen's Chamber within the pyramid. Masudi wrote that the Great Pyramid was not a tomb, but a book in stone, a book that could be read when generations far in the future possessed enough scientific knowledge to understand its implications. Whether or not it is in effect a "book," its orientation, dimensions, and the relationships between them certainly speak volumes of the surprisingly advanced civilization of the Egyptians of the early historic dynasties—or previous to them.

What may be a remarkable coincidence of observation between the Sumerian watchers of the stars and that of the astronomers of today concerns certain sections of our galaxy where there are no visible stars. In modern theory these are the "black holes" of space, theoretically the core centers of exploded and collapsed stars, now of such density through their gravitational pull that they attract and "swallow" all other matter, even light, within their sphere of attraction. No light is emitted from these areas, but the pull on other bodies and sending of signals indicate that something solid exists within these spheres of darkness. Within recent years many astronomers have concluded that the best candidate for such a phenomenon may exist within the constellation Cygnus and have designated it as Cygnus X-1.

But what today's astronomers have only recently become aware of may have attracted the attention of the Sumero-Babylonian astronomers when the world was much younger. Six thousand years ago the Sumerians located the same area and named it "the abode of the demon bird of Marduk," or, alternately, the "open-jawed dragon," either of which would be an unsettling but aptly descriptive name for a growing black hole in space. Evidently some among the ancient astronomers shared the concern of their intellectual and spiritual descendants of thousands of years later about the black abysses in the galaxy.

There exist ancient records from India, written in Sanskrit, pertaining to theories about matter, time, and space that seem to be a preview of current theories about matter and the cosmos. The black holes in space, unlike the monsters of the Babylonians, are called "laya" centers in Sanskrit, and signify both the end and a new beginning of matter, in tune with some of today's most advanced theories.

The concept of relativity had apparently occurred to thinkers in ancient India many centuries ago. It is mentioned in the ancient *Surya Siddantha* that, since the Earth is a sphere, ". . . above and below is only relative. How can there be an upper or under side to it?"

One ancient Indian theory seems like a preview of a universal computer, the Akashic records, a cosmic memory bank supposed to store all the actions and memories contributed through the ages by human beings everywhere. It is further predicted that from these records spiritually programmed persons can obtain information about past events and past lives. While this possibility has probably not yet occurred to expert programmers of the modern computer industry, it is worthy of note that the concept of universal computerization somehow occurred to Hindu philosophers in the very distant past.

While the ancient Greeks surmised the existence of the *atom* (in Greek: "indivisible" or "cannot be cut"), the Indian philosophy went further, suggesting that the atom could be split—with the possible results that are now familiar to all of us. The Indian philosopher Aulukya discussed in his teaching the miniature solar system *within* the atom, molecular construction and transformation as well as the theory of relativity more than 2800 years before Einstein.

A reference to what appears to be the molecular composition of matter appears in Hindu-Buddhist texts pertaining to the attainment of Nirvana through the liberation of the soul from the Wheel of Rebirth. One of the Buddhist commentaries explains the composition of matter by comparing it to separate reeds, tied and held together in bundles, with the bundles then held together by other bonds, which, according to how they are combined, form all matter, animate and inanimate. Working in reverse toward the liberation of these bonds, the large bundles disassociate into smaller ones and the smaller ones then disassociate as well, indicating thereby the path of the liberation of the soul. Since this concept was written thousands of years before atoms and molecules and their bonds were known, it was not recognized for what it seems effectively to be: a simple and understandable concept of the atomic theory, perhaps inherited from the same scientific philosophers who so well described the real or imagined effects of a prehistoric atomic bomb. (See Chapter 13.)

The only figure given in any former culture that exceeds the currently accepted age of the universe as fifteen billion years is the one given by ancient Indian scientific philosophers as approximately two billion years. However, the "Year of Brahma" lasts 311 trillion years, representing the contraction and expansion of the entire cosmos. The theory of cosmic expansion and contraction is shared by many astronomers of today. The Hindu year-count refers not to the end of time but to a cycle, with each "cosmic breathing" starting another cycle of trillions of years in duration. The philosophers of early India, whatever the source of their cosmic calculations, bring us, again like Einstein, in touch with infinity itself and the curving circles of endless time.

An unusual example of the apparent survival of specialized astronomical knowledge in an unlikely place has been found to exist among the Dogons, a tribal people living in Mali, formerly a part of French Equatorial Africa (*The Sirius Mystery*: 1978, Robert Temple). This relatively primitive tribe has preserved over the centuries memories of a tribal connection with Sirius, the Dog Star, which they commemorate in special yearly festivals. This fact alone would not be unusual, as Sirius played an important part in the calendar of ancient Egypt, its dawn rising in July indicating the annual rising of the Nile and perhaps other African rivers. But what makes the Dogon preoccupation with Sirius unique is the fact that they have, from their legends, long been aware of another star—a dark companion of Sirius—invisible to the naked eye and referred to by most astronomers as Sirius-B. The Dogons inexplicably know that Sirius-B has an elliptical orbit of fifty years' duration and also claim that it is "the heaviest thing in the universe"—a logical description for a collapsed dwarf star, which it is. The Dogon legends share with modern astronomy the concept that the Milky Way is composed of far-off stars, that Saturn has rings, that Jupiter has four moons; and the Dogons possessed, before the moon landing, knowledge that the moon was arid and uninhabited.

The Dogons credit their astronomical knowledge to visitors from Sirius or the vicinity of Sirius, creatures who could live both on the land and in the water, and who, aeons ago, brought knowledge of civilization and the cosmos to Earth. They are still present on Sirius, to where the souls of the Dogon dead return. This awareness of invisible stars and planetary rings and moons by a primitive tribe has no easy explanation: one theory assumes that they received this information from Egypt (although the Egyptians were not aware of Sirius-B). Another theory supposes that the tribe was visited by a traveling French astronomer or student of astronomy anxious to share his theories (although this would not explain the extreme age of the legend or the passed-down tribal festivals concerning Sirius and the Dark Star). A third explanation suggests that the legend of "amphibious" visitors from the stars actually refers to space travelers who, after making unexpected contact with the ancestors of the Dogons, left them cosmic information, among other gifts, before re-embarking in their space vehicles on their return journey across the void.

Not only the Dogons believe in teachers from the stars. As we become more aware of the potentialities of space travel and the possibility of life on other planets, some theorists have assumed that unexplainable ancient knowledge or artifacts on this Earth have been brought here from somewhere else.

This theory, suggested by the world-wide interest in UFOs, suggests that the Earth, before the beginnings of recorded history, was visited by extraterrestrial explorers from close or distant star systems. These visitors, according to the theory of Erich von Däniken and others, made contact with the tribes of Earth and taught them the beginnings of civilization—an explanation presupposing, of course, that space travelers would have a benign interest in the welfare of dwellers on a minor planet, as Earth would seem to them. Nevertheless, the theory of ancient (and well disposed) astronauts effectively visiting the Earth and teaching the beginnings of civilization to our ancestors would, from an historical and archaeological viewpoint, tend to explain a number of unusual artifacts of great age and unidentified cultures and even some of the huge ruins still standing, whose original means of construction and planetary and cosmic alignment represent an enigma.

Ancient rock paintings in Australia, said to portray gods from "dream time" (the distant past), show them dressed in unusual garments resembling those now worn by astronauts. This is also true of the figures in the Tassili caves of North Africa, with further examples in the prehistoric caves of Europe and with other examples depicted in stone on Amerindian temples and pyramids. The prehistoric Dogu artifacts found in Japan depict individuals who also seem to be wearing space suits.

But a re-examination of ancient legend and literature contains some cryptic references that have been interpreted as contacts with members of a civilization from *the sea*, possessing a culture vastly superior to that held by the tribes visited by them. The bringer of civilization to Sumeria, Oannes, is portrayed as being half fish and half human, reminiscent of the amphibious star people who visited the Dogons. The saving avatars of Vishnu in Vedic literature also often have the shape of miraculous half animals, one of which is a fish. The mythical Quetzalcoatl, who brought civilization to Mexico and Central America, was referred to as the "Feathered Serpent" who came from the sea and returned to it. Other civilizing gods visited America from the sea; Kulkulkan and Itznama came to the Maya lands, as did Votan, who "passed by the islands of the Eastern Ocean," Bochica to Colombia, and to Peru, Viracocha, whose name means "Windy Sea."

Among references often quoted by supporters of the ancient astronaut theory there are several that have existed for thousands of years in the world's "most read" book—the Bible. They appear as two verses in Genesis, the first book of the Bible, and concern the very beginnings of mankind. They are:

> That the *sons of God* saw the daughters of men that they were fair; and they took them wives of all which they chose. (*Genesis 6:2*)

> There were giants in the earth in those days; and also after that, when the *sons of God* came in unto the daughters of men and they bare children to them, the same became mighty men which were of old, men of renown. (*Genesis 6:4*)

As this puzzling reference does not clearly state from where these "sons of God" (*Nefilim* in the original) came, the ancient astronaut theory assumes that they came from space, although the reference might be equally applied to a memory of people from another civilization on Earth existing from a time before the Flood, especially considering the reference to successful mating with "the daughters of men." The reference to the apparent visitors from heaven fathering offspring by mating with Earth women would imply that they were of the same species—a doubtful implication if they came from space but a logical one if they had arrived from another part of the planet. (Discoverers, explorers, and conquerors in Earth's past history have seldom overlooked the possibility of mating with females of the aboriginal populations they encountered.)

The many reports of strange visitors possessing cultural advances suggest that a superior civilization may have developed in another part of the world, and that when its representatives came to the less civilized parts of the world they were considered gods or demigods (and sometimes devils) by the people with whom they came in contact. This has happened in many still isolated parts of the modern world, where tribal populations are still living in jungles on what one might term a prehistoric level. This was the case during World War II, when tribesmen of New Guinea, brought into unexpected contact with Allied air-transport forces, considered the soldiers to be gods or magicians brought by celestial machines but were terrified only by the incredible animals that also came from the sky—army mules.

While not denying that the intermittent presence of unexplained objects in the skies of Earth may certainly have influenced the imagination of the world's dwellers for thousands of years (as still happens), the legends of primitive peoples could equally be interpreted as referring to a superior earthly culture. Civilizing colonists from a superior culture, arriving unexpectedly from the sea, would be remembered as gods by the local inhabitants and be so recorded in their legends. This was the case in the Americas, the Mediterranean, and parts of Europe. Presumably it was explorers or colonists from another civilization already existing on Earth who introduced cultural and architectural techniques, the connection of astronomy to agriculture, the measuring of cosmic time, record keeping, and writing to less developed coastal and island populations in areas of the world whose cultural similarities indicate a common source. When the contact was interrupted, perhaps because of a world-wide catastrophe, the surviving population would regress, perhaps for centuries, before regaining momentum, unless in the meantime it was absorbed by another race or culture. It is a striking fact that the earliest Egyptian, Sumerian, Chaldean, and ancient American eras seem to have been the most advanced, followed by deteriorating cultures in successive ages.

The concept of one or more prior civilizations—such as Atlantis—on Earth lends itself to the explanation of archaeological artifacts that otherwise seem to defy historical logic. These would include ruins of abandoned cities in South and Central America, the original foundations of great temples, such as Baalbek in Lebanon, and the unidentified ruins under the oceans and seas, many made of stones so huge that moving them into place would seem impossible for the supposedly primitive peoples of prehistoric times. It would also include the number of intriguing references preserved over the centuries by peoples whose remote ancestors possessed and used scientific and technical knowledge of which their descendants, in pictures, writing, or in retold legends, have kept alive only a memory.

One has but to consider the time span up to now of our own civilization, starting from herding and early agriculture perhaps 6000 to 7000 years ago and progressing, in accelerated fashion only in the last century, to air travel, space travel, and the thermonuclear bomb. It is beginning to become evident that part of humanity began to reach an increasing level of mental development from the use of fire at about 750,000 years Before Present and began to attain a level of organized culture between 100,000 and 75,000 years Before Present. During these thousands of years there was ample time for a civilization like Atlantis or others to develop, to decay, and to disappear through a series of natural or induced catastrophes. The theory of civilizations rising and declining like great moving wheels was succinctly expressed by Greek historians, who suggested that such cataclysmic ends of civilization occurred approximately once every 10,000 years. (If this supposition is valid, and we are now at the end of one of these 10,000-year periods, our prospects for the near future are not overly encouraging.)

A common objection to the theory of a prehistoric civilization is contained in the following question: If there were an extensive civilization of such great antiquity, why have no cultural artifacts been found? One answer would be that any artifacts remaining from a period so far back in time would no longer be easily recognizable or would have disappeared through disintegration or rust. But there may be certain few exceptions, found by chance, embedded within other strata; objects that have been reportedly discovered within the last 150 years, although there is no way of telling how many others have been found and simply discarded.

There exist some intriguing examples that suggest technical achievements by unknown civilizations of great age. In 1851 a silver chalice of intricate design was discovered embedded in a granitic rock split during blasting operations in Dorchester, Massachusetts. The time needed to have had the rock form around it would imply an age of hundreds of thousands or even millions of years. In 1844, workmen cutting rock in a stone quarry near the River Tweed, Scotland, found a worked gold thread within rock eight feet below ground level.

An iron screw contained within a split granite boulder was found by miners in a mine near Treasure City, Nevada, in 1869. Spanish invaders who penetrated an Andean mine during the conquest of Peru found that someone before their arrival (and the Amerindians were unfamiliar with either iron or steel) had used iron nails in a wall of a passageway in the mine. Modern copper miners near Lake Superior have broken into passageways constructed many centuries before them by miners belonging to no known culture.

In Coclé, Panama, a golden animal figure, excavated in the jungle, was found to contain a system of mechanical gears, a technique apparently forgotten or never known by the succeeding Amerindian tribal nations.

A stone geode, picked up in 1961 in the Coso Mountains of California and cut into by rock collectors, was found to contain a metal core wire surrounded by some ceramic material encased in a sleeve of now petrified wood. Since then the Coso geode, discovered in a more commercially aware age than some of the other artifacts listed above, has been offered for sale at $25,000, which, considering that the geode appears to contain a technical artifact tens or hundreds of thousands of years old, might be considered a relatively modest price.

Occasionally a surprising archaeological find out of historical continuity can be recognized as a capricious turn of chance. During the excavation of a Carthaginian tomb in North Africa, a coin was found that when cleaned was recognized as a one-kopek coin of Imperial Russia—certainly not current in ancient Carthage. Such intrusive events are usually attributed to rodents, which tend to collect shiny objects and store them in their underground burrows—with resultant consternation to future archaeologists.

But it would be more difficult to explain an incident that occurred during the excavation of a mastodon skeleton in Blue Lick Springs, Kentucky, as anything other than a striking relic of "the world before." The mastodon was excavated at a depth of twelve feet, and the digging continued three feet farther until it struck a set pavement of cut-stone tiles—the floor of a prehistoric building. There also exist records of large wooden constructions in unlikely places. A large ancient ship was found after an earthquake split open a mountain in Naples in the 16th century. An oceangoing galley of exotic design was cut into while digging within mines on the coast of Peru, and another very ancient one was found at the turn of the last century deep under the ice in Alaska.

The presence of man-made artifacts in mines and geological layers where their assumed age would not be compatible with that of recognized civilization would not negate the possibility that they were made by human beings and not by visitors from space. For if it is true that the world received a cosmic shock thousands of years ago, exploding its volcanoes, causing floods of molten rock, sinking great islands, and overwhelming continental coastlines with tidal waves while raising other coastlines and mountain ranges to new heights, it would be within reason for some surviving artifacts from a lost world to be found in unlikely places—within molten rock or buried in layers of solidified strata.

From 30,000 to 10,000 B.C a number of settlements appeared in Europe, generally referred to as belonging to the Cro-Magnon race, which demonstrated a striking cultural advantage above the level of the race then dwelling in Europe—the Neanderthal. But in the period 13,000 to 9000 B.C. the number of these settlements increased dramatically, almost as if there had been a sudden migration from another part of the world, a population shift of groups whose cave paintings and artifacts show a highly developed level of art and tribal organization.

During this period, and continuing down to almost the early Greek and Roman periods with the written history that has become our own, an intermittent artistic culture flourished in Western Europe. It has left us memorable examples painted or incised on the walls of caves and on rock faces as well as tools, receptacles, weapons, and small statues. Some are complicated and oddly sophisticated, as if transplanted cultural groups were trying to re-establish their culture and themselves in a savage world. A preoccupation with

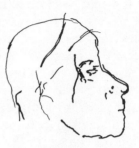

Figure 2

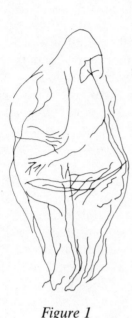

Figure 1

Figure 3

Cave picture of apparent prehistoric figures embracing, from the Grottes de Lamarche, France. Although most Ice Age representations concern animals, a number of drawings of people, some using curiously modern sketching techniques, have been found within the last several decades. After original copy from the Musée de l'Homme, Paris. *(Figure 1)*

A face from 25,000 years ago. Some of the Ice Age drawings show clean-shaven "cavemen," others with trimmed beards or mustaches, and men and women wearing apparently stitched garments, footwear, and head covering. To make such clothing, needles would have been necessary. Such needles, made of bone, some with small eyes for detailed sewing, have been found among prehistoric remains at Solutré, France, and elsewhere in Western Europe. *(Figure 2)*

Prehistoric cave drawing of lion's head from the Grottes de Lamarche, France, reinforced to show essential lines. Although many cave drawings are primitive, some "centers" of Aurignacian and Magdalenian art show a surprising sophistication, as if a higher culture had suddenly appeared or developed in primitive areas from 20,000 to 15,000 years ago. Courtesy of Musée de l'Homme, Paris. *(Figure 3)* drawing the great beasts of the northern forests is understandable, but it is the treatment of the animals that is often surprising. The paintings and bas-reliefs of wild bulls on the ceilings of the Altamira caves of Spain demonstrate a fusion of decorative art and a knowledge of the animal's muscles. The curious well-drawn but many-legged reindeer patently indicates the rapid motion of the animal, 18,000 years before Picasso's multilimbed figures. The impressionistic portraits of prehistoric individuals of 30,000 years ago at Lamarche, France, approach caricature but indicate at the same time that some of the supposedly savage cave people were clean shaven, or had trimmed hair and beards, and wore shaped clothing rather than bear skins. These Ice Age works of art may have been the coincidental flowering of a creative urge, but also in some cases may represent the final period of a more developed art brought into Europe from elsewhere.

The sites that were occupied by these cave artists seem to be concentrated along the Atlantic coasts of the various nations of Western Europe almost as if a wave of civilization and culture had broken over the European coast from the ocean at approximately the time of the legendary sinking of Atlantis. This suggests a common source, not from space colonists but from an advanced civilization of Earth—one of much greater age than any previously accepted by archaeologists.

A close examination of the world's earliest tribal legends indicates that in almost every case civilization was brought from the sea, usually by gods or demigods, for so would they seem to people of an undeveloped culture. That the bringers of civilization were sometimes thought to be amphibious creatures from the stars would seem simply to emphasize their unfamiliar technology or "magic." These civilizers presumably used their colonies more or less as their European descendants would do thousands of years later in various parts of the world. But when the island centers of population were destroyed, the colonies would start in again, this time on their own and evidently with a new calendar based on the way of counting they had been taught but starting from a different date.

It is interesting to note that various and unconnected calendars from different parts of the world, whether counting time by the solar, lunar, or zodiacal count, come close to agreeing on a new starting date, probably the date of the catastrophe—a date that also agrees with a geological estimate of the melting of the last glaciers.

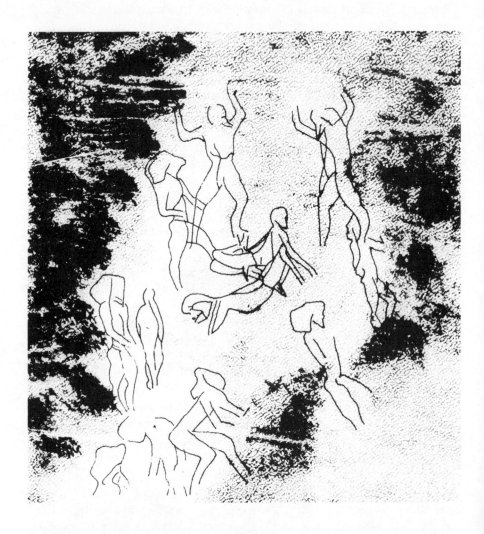

Copy of an unusual example of prehistoric art, 8000 to 9000 years old,
found in a cave on Monte Pellegrino, near Palermo, Sicily. It was
discovered after World War II when an explosion of munitions stored in
the cave knocked off covering encrustations of thousands of years to
reveal these incised drawings indicating an advanced cultural
development and sophisticated drawing and design. While art work in
the majority of prehistoric sites shows an understandable concern with
animals, other sites along the coast of southwestern Europe seem to
have been decorated by a culturally advanced race, apparently arriving
along the coasts of Europe from the Atlantic Ocean. (Compare to map
of intensive geographic distribution of prehistoric art on page 153.)

It is a convincing indication that a prehistoric world civilization was developed on Earth through the peoples of Earth, and that their earliest surviving records seem to refer to the end of this early civilization.

The Hindu, Egyptian, and Babylonian calendars start or commence a new cycle from a point of 11,500 to 11,000 B.C., fairly close to the figure given by Plato for the *end* of Atlantis, or 9500 years before *his* time. These dates also correspond closely to the melting of the last glaciers 1200 years ago as well as to the penetration of the warm waters of the Atlantic into the far northern Atlantic—as if a land barrier that formerly impeded a warm southern current from flowing so far north had been removed.

According to Egyptian historians, the legendary Reign of the Gods—those who ruled before the historical dynasties began—commenced 10,000 years ago. The period of the sophisticated rock painters of the once fertile northern Sahara has been estimated at 8000 to 7000 B.C., and it was about this time, according to tradition, that the god or teacher Thoth arrived in the Nile Delta, bringing to Egypt the knowledge of hieroglyphic writing, a product of an already developed civilization.

Major tectonic spasms were still continuing in the North Atlantic 10,000 to 9000 years ago, presumably destroying what land areas of Atlantis that still remained. It was after this that the Olmec/Maya calendar began about 8570 or 8500 B.C., the date rocket scientist Dr. Otto Muck ascribes to the destruction of Atlantis.

But there is more than the evidence of calendars, legends, and the uncertain memory of man. There still exist throughout the world puzzling buildings whose indications of extreme age or the fact that they are now under the sea place them within the time period of 8000 to 10,000 or more years ago. Buildings and a pyramid at Cuicuilco, south of Mexico City, have been found under a lava field resulting from a volcanic explosion of about 8000 years ago, thousands of years before the Aztecs appeared in Mexico.

The great stone ruins of Peru and Bolivia, still standing in South America, are so old that the recorders of the Inca empire had either forgotten who built them or had never known, since they were constructed centuries or millennia prior to the Inca empire. When the Spanish invaders asked about them, the Peruvians replied that they had been built by the gods, who caused the enormous rocks, weighing hundreds of tons each, to fly into position across mountain ranges, deep valleys, and rivers. Whether or not they were godlike, the builders were remarkable engineers, cutting and shaping enormous rocks into a series of angles (one cyclopean stone at Sacsahuamán has thirty-two different angles) so that they fitted with surfaces flush together with no space in between, not only on the outside, but on the inside as well. The technique and engineering ability implied in these constructions is out of historical sequence; in fact, with all our expertise, it would be almost impossible to accomplish today. It would certainly be considered impossible for prehistoric builders to have done so thousands of years ago were it not for the fact that the buildings are still there in the high Andes, a visible proof of their conquest of time. The ruins at Tiahuanaco have been dated by Poznansky (see Bibliography) as going back 10,000 to 12,000 years—perhaps before the Andes rose to their present height.

An unusual site in Yugoslavia, Lepinski Vir, has revealed that a small village culture of not more than 130 houses had constructed dwellings on poured-cement foundations incorporating indirect central heating at least 7000 years ago. The question arises whether a small settlement stumbled on cement making or whether survivors from an older culture remembered the process and used it in new surroundings—a possible explanation of the increasing number of finds throughout the world that indicate advanced techniques seemingly out of place in the historical time-continuum. In any case, it was not until 5000 years later that the process of pouring cement was used again, this time by the ancient Romans.

Stone buildings of great antiquity scattered throughout the world suggest a common culture of which only the great stones, a notably timeproof way of building, still remain. The megalithic culture of Malta, one of the oldest in the Mediterranean, is estimated to be more than 8000 years old. The circular walled settlements and tombs of the Canary Islands, which resemble the ruins of Malta so closely that they seem to have been constructed by the same architects, appear to be even older. Some of the other ancient ruins in Malta closely resemble the stone walls of ancient Peru and the walls and platforms on which the Easter Island figures were set.

The same type of corbeled arch was used by the Maya and the early Mycenaeans of Greece. The round stone towers of the Irish coast resemble the *nuraghi* towers of Sardinia and the circular *chullpa* towers of pre-Inca Peru. Great stone circles such as Stonehenge and the thirty-mile circumference of the Glastonbury circle in England are repeated in prehistoric sites along the coastal plains of Western Europe and in various parts of Indian America.

The meticulously fitted stone walls found in Zimbabwe, Africa, are remarkably similar to the walls of Kuelap in the jungle of eastern Peru (even to the design of the stone border along the top of the walls), and also to the stone forts of the Aran Islands off Ireland's west coast. These stone fortifications, similar in construction but separated by thousands of miles, are apparently of great age, but exactly how old is difficult to ascertain since stone cannot be dated in periods less than 50,000 years Before Present.

One might well imagine that there were a series of fortresses, later copied or repaired by the local inhabitants, originally built of time-resistant stone for the protection of colonizing forces, much as the Roman legions built their camps of wood and earthworks. While the Roman camps have vanished except for their names, which persist in the names of cities since built over their sites, these other much older and unattributed ruins still mark the building techniques of an earlier world.

In a number of cases later cultures have built over the giant monuments left by a previous civilization. Pyramids have been built over pyramids, new cities have completely covered older cities, new temples have been erected on the remains of older ones, often on gigantic foundations. This seems to have occurred at Baalbek, Lebanon, where a prehistoric foundation containing blocks weighing up to 2000 tons apiece was used as a base for a Greco-Roman temple to Jupiter. The original terrace foundation was of such size that Dr. Agrest, a Soviet scientist, and others have suggested that they were originally part of a landing and takeoff platform for extraterrestrial spacecraft. But it is perhaps more logical to ascribe the enormous size of such stones simply to the forgotten building techniques of very early peoples who had learned to move them with apparent ease and whose expertise in building can be recognized but not yet explained. Off the coast of Morocco similar single stones, each larger than two-story houses, have been discovered incorporated into a wall extending for nine miles under the sea.

The technical ability of prehistoric cultures to handle, cut, and set the enormous stones has often been ascribed to help from ancient astronauts, especially since some of the monumental constructions function or have functioned as observatories or cosmic calendars. But this does not necessarily mean that there was communication between the peoples of Earth and travelers from the stars, since examination of the heavens would be a natural development to establishing the passage of time, the change of seasons, and their related influence on agriculture. Moreover, the massive stone constructions that have lasted from prehistoric times show simply that the original builders were technically skillful and apparently had ways of handling, cutting, or perhaps fusing together huge stones according to methods still unknown to us.

The long ages of man before recorded history, and the common memory of humanity of a former world, suggest that man developed civilization here on this planet. This civilization spread from a center of world culture out to the islands, coasts, and up coastal rivers to the mainland of the world through contact by sea, radiating outward from an island continent in the Atlantic Ocean. About 12,000 years ago a catastrophe occurred that destroyed the cultural center and many of the most civilized points of the world—a memory kept alive in all races by legends of the Great Flood and by endings of the world by fire, earthquakes, and winds. Survivors of this catastrophe held on to some aspects of their former culture, modifying their calendars to indicate a new start for the world. The instinctive memory of the lost world and the golden age of mankind is one of the deepest and most general racial memories. It is only now, at the beginning of the Space Age, when we have at our disposal new methods of researching and studying the surface and subsurface of the earth and the ocean, that the ancient legend has become capable of being solved. Investigation of Atlantis is no longer limited to a study of legends, ancient writings, racial and linguistic coincidences, or continental distribution of animal life, but can now be based on close investigation of the lands beneath the Atlantic, where the vestiges of the lost eighth continent still lie under the accumulated debris of almost 12,000 years.

Map showing areas of cave paintings and prehistoric artifacts in Europe. Gray area is where they are most concentrated, suggesting that remnants of an advanced culture washed over the eastern shores of Europe from the sea.

11

THE GREAT ISLANDS UNDER THE SEA

Since the first photographs of the Earth were taken from the moon, we have become familiar with Earth as a water planet, a beautiful green-blue globe in the darkness of space. We are also familiar with the names of the world's oceans, seas, gulfs, bays, and large inland lakes. But it has been only within the last fifty years that we have been able really to ascertain the depths of our oceans and to form an idea of what the ocean floor looks like—which parts of it are mountains, flat plains, rising terraces, river canyons, or plateaus where precipices drop off into the abyss. It is only comparatively recently that man has been able to form an approximate idea of the geography of the ocean floor, of what is under the water that covers 71 percent of the planet. This area up to modern times was almost as unknown as the dark side of the moon. The increasing knowledge of the physical nature of the seafloor has, paradoxically, been perfected by research connected with warfare, as is the case with a number of other less commendable discoveries.

The first extensive soundings of the Atlantic were made by warships of the British, American, German, and French fleets in the latter half of the 19th century, using basically the same means of establishing depth as those used since ancient times. Throughout history captains of vessels were more interested in how shallow rather than how deep the waters were in order to prevent their ships from striking rocks on the sea bottom or being grounded on shoals. Until sonar was invented, depth was established by hurling loaded weights with measured lines, and later wire, off the bow of a ship under sail and then, when the ship caught up with the throw and the line was vertical, hauling it up to measure. This was repeated at intervals. If a vessel was stationary, a long line could be lowered to the bottom to establish an approximate depth. The composition of the bottom was ascertained by coating the underside of the lead weight with wax or grease so that when it made contact with material on the bottom it would stick to it and indicate that the bottom was composed of sand, mud, marl, shell, or other material. The accuracy of the measurements was limited, however, by the weather and the state of the sea at the time of the soundings.

Such age-tested methods, while successful for shorelines because of the frequency of the soundings, could give only an incomplete picture of the bottom of the open sea, although an improved lead-line method was still employed with the first naval research expeditions of the 19th century in the central Atlantic preparatory to the laying of the transatlantic cables.

At the time of the first large-scale controlled depth-finding operations in the deep Atlantic, a recurrent wave of interest in Atlantis arose in the western world. A number of people, apparently including some of the naval officers involved in the operations, were curious as to the possibility of there being a sunken continent in the center of the ocean more or less where Plato said it once existed. Although certainly the early scientifically controlled soundings over what we now call the Mid-Atlantic Ridge had nothing to do with the ancient legend, it still lingered as a memory in the consciousness of some of the participants and of those who read about the results.

Ignatius Donnelly, who might be called the Plato of modern Atlantology, interpreted the results of the soundings taken of the Mid-Atlantic Ridge in the 1870s as a proof that the site of Atlantis had been found. His words from his book *Atlantis* are like a clarion call to further exploration:

> Suppose we were to find in mid-Atlantic in front of the Mediterranean, in the neighborhood of the Azores, the remains of an immense island, sunk beneath the sea—one thousand miles in width, and two or three thousand miles long—would it not go far to confirm the statement of Plato that, "beyond the strait where you place the Pillars of Hercules, there was an island larger than Asia [Minor] and Libya combined." . . . And suppose we found that the Azores were the mountain peaks of this drowned island, and were torn and rent by tremendous volcanic convulsions; while around them, descending into the sea, were

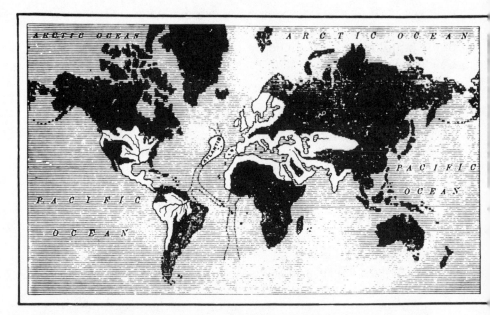

Ignatius Donnelly's suggested map of the general location of Atlantis and the lands that came under its influence or colonial rule. Donnelly places the central island near the Azores, along the Mid-Atlantic Ridge, and connects it by presumed former land bridges to the other continents. What we now know of the ocean bottom suggests other extensive island groups formerly above the surface, although not land bridges. All of the lands colored white retain pervasive legends concerning Atlantis, and many of them contain massive stone ruins constructed by as yet unidentified races.

found great strata of lava; and the whole face of the sunken land was covered for thousands of miles with volcanic debris, would we not be obliged to confess that these facts furnished strong corroborative proofs of the truth of Plato's statement, that "in one day and one fatal night there came mighty earthquakes and inundations . . . and Atlantis disappeared beneath the sea; and then that sea became inaccessible on account of the quantity of mud which the engulfed island left in its place."

And all these things recent investigation has proved conclusively. Deep-sea soundings have been made by ships of different nations; the United States ship *Dolphin*, the German frigate *Gazelle*, and theBritish ships *Hydra*, *Porcupine*, and *Challenger* have mapped out the bottom of the Atlantic, and the result is the revelation of a great elevation, reaching from a point on the coast of the British Islands southwardly to the coast of South America . . . thence southeastwardly to the coast of South Africa, and then southwardly to the coast of Africa, and then southwardly to Tristan d'Acunha. The submerged land . . . rises about 9000 feet from the great depths around it, and in the Azores, St. Paul's Rocks, Ascension, and Tristan d'Acunha it reaches the surface of the ocean.

Here then we have the backbone of the ancient continent which once occupied the . . . Atlantic Ocean. . . . The deepest parts of the ocean, 3500 fathoms deep, represent those portions which sunk first . . . the plains to the east and west of the central mountain range; some of the loftiest peaks of this range—the Azores, St. Paul's, Ascension, Tristan d'Acunha—are still above the ocean level, while the great body of Atlantis lies a few hundred fathoms beneath the sea. . . .

When the barriers of Atlantis sunk sufficiently to permit the natural expansion of the heated water of the tropics to the north, the ice and snow which covered Europe gradually disappeared; the Gulf Stream flowed around Atlantis, and it still retains the circular motion first imparted to it by the presence of that island.

The officers of the *Challenger* found the entire ridge of Atlantis covered with volcanic deposits; these are the subsided mud which, as Plato tells us, rendered the sea impassable after the destruction of the island.

The United States ship *Gettysburg* has also made some remarkable discoveries in a neighboring field. . . . The recently announced discovery by Commander Gorringe, of the United States sloop *Gettysburg*, of a bank of soundings bearing 85° W, and distant 130 miles from Cape St. Vincent, during the last voyage of the vessel across the Atlantic, taken in connection with previous soundings obtained in the same region of the North Atlantic, suggests the probable existence of a submarine ridge or plateau connecting the island of Madeira with the coast of Portugal, and the probable subaerial connection in prehistoric times of that island with the southwestern extremity of Europe. . . .

A member of the *Challenger* staff, soon after the termination of the expedition, gave it as his opinion that the great submarine plateau is the remains of "the lost Atlantis."

While one might criticize the overenthusiasm and certainty of his information with which Donnelly projected his theories—and oceanographers and geologists have been doing so with considerable gusto ever since 1882—it is nevertheless noteworthy that the ships he refers to made a good general outline of the ocean bottom before sonar was able to confirm their findings more exactly. Improved dredging operations during the present century have pulled up from the Atlantic seafloor a sampling of rocks which indicates that certain extensive portions of the bottom were above water until the end of the Ice Age, that great volcanic explosions occurred at the time that a continent or a group of large oceanic islands sank, and that several samples of rocks from the sunken land in the Aves Ridge of the Caribbean and in the eastern mid-Atlantic could be classified as being of continental origin because of the sial (continental) rock brought up from the depths.

An 1898 "Atlantean" discovery occurred by mistake. As the transatlantic cable was being laid, it suddenly snapped in two about 500 miles off the Azores. By a stroke of extreme good luck, dredging successfully retrieved the cable ends in a difficult maneuver, since the bottom seemed to be composed of valleys, cliffs, and sharp peaks. During the operation several rocks were brought up which became the subject of a controversy initiated by Pierre Termier, a prominent French Atlantologist. Termier contended that the rocks, a lava known as tachylite, would dissolve in seawater after 15,000 years and that their porous microcrystalline texture showed that they had solidified in the open air, probably from a once sea level volcano now under the ocean. While the area from which the rocks came is now known as Telegraph Bank in remembrance of the cable incident, the Atlantean aspect of the discovery is still being argued.

In recent years a number of rock samples collected by expeditions in the course of their normal research have added fuel to the Termier controversy. Dr. Maria Klenova, of the Soviet Academy of Science, after examination of rocks dredged up from a depth of 6600 feet on an expedition in the same general area north of the Azores, expressed her opinion that the rock had been formed at atmospheric pressure approximately 15,000 years ago.

Near the north coast of South America, granitic rocks were brought up by a Duke University expedition in 1969 by dredging along an underwater bridge running from Venezuela to the Virgin Islands. Dr. Bruce Heezen, a leading US oceanographer, assessed the find: "Up to now, geologists generally believed that light granitic or acid igneous rocks are confined to the continents and that the crust of the Earth beneath the sea is composed of heavier, dark-colored basaltic rock. . . . Thus, the occurrence of light-colored granitic rocks may support an old theory that a continent formerly existed in the region of the eastern Caribbean and that these rocks may represent the core of a subsided lost continent."

Increasingly exact information concerning the ocean floor could be expected to uncover vestiges and eventually even artifacts of the legendary sunken lands. It is in fact apparent that this has already occurred, although few marine scientists or oceanographers could be expected to complicate their reports with information that, if it concerned the one-time existence of Atlantis, would scarcely advance anyone's professional career. But information obtained from dredging, sonar, and taking of cores from the bottom is contributing to an overall picture of the location of the great sunken islands when they were still above sea level.

Sonar, the most important development for researching the topography of the ocean, was in use experimentally before World War II and was brought to a high degree of perfection during the period of naval action from the 1940s to the 1960s. It is now possible to sketch in considerable detail the bottom of the ocean: its mountains, rifts, plains, and rises are being defined with greater accuracy on marine charts as their depths from the surface are established at different points through repeated consecutive soundings.

Sonar is a sound wave bounced off the bottom and calculated for depth through time of return. It was used only sporadically for depth measurement until an operational mistake enhanced its effectiveness. This fortunate oversight occurred in 1944 on a naval vessel in the central Pacific under the overall command of Admiral Harry Hess. Sonar beamed at the bottom was checked every half hour or so as a general control for surface vessels except in emergencies such as the presence of submarines. The fact that a sonar technician forgot to turn off the sonar resulted for the first time in a running record of the bottom, a practice later adopted by hydrographic vessels researching a specific area. This record of the rises and falls of the bottom in a fairly straight line revealed the submarine presence

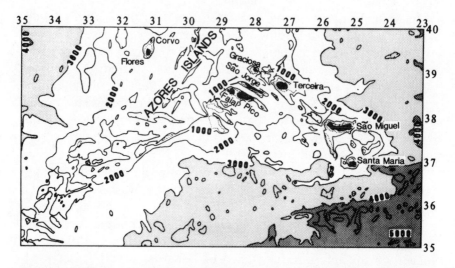

General depth levels on the Azores Plateau in meters. If the area down to the 3000 to 4000 meter level was once land (and cores and ash samples taken from the sea bottom suggest that this may have been formerly the case), a very large land area may be said to have existed in the mid-Atlantic within the memory of mankind.

of a series of flat-topped mountains never before noted as such, later referred to as guyots or seamounts. Many of these seamounts in the Atlantic lie fairly close to the surface, as though they had once been islands in an earlier and somewhat shallower ocean.

In recent years sonar has become so perfected that through side-scan sonar a wider spread of the sea bottom can be examined with the same sonar impulse. Another intriguing mystery has been clarified—that of the the DRL (deep-rising layer), which appeared on sonar as a false bottom that moved up and down according to the time of day. It was later established that this movable bottom was composed of a mass of squid feasting on plankton; the squid coming up at night to feed and descending back into the depths during the day. At present sonar can distinguish whales, schools of small fish, ships on the surface or lying on the bottom, or prowling submarines. Sonar can also pick out unusual formations on the bottom, sometimes man-made and, through sonar photography, depict their reflected form. Sonar photogaphy was employed on a search for the monster in Loch Ness in waters so murky that vision could not

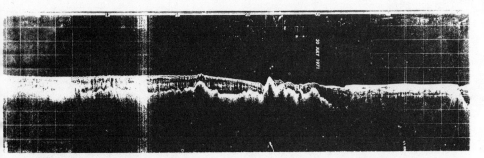

Side-scanning sonargraph of Atlantic Ocean bottom indicating ranges of hills and peaks on the Atlantic sea bottom near the Azores.

penetrate. Although the elusive monster was not captured on sonar, prehistoric stone ruins built at a time before the sea rose along with the water level of the entire planet were clearly indicated on the side-scan sonargraph.

Because of its obvious use in mapping the sea bottom, it is evident that high-technology sonar can be employed for locating the remains of man-made constructions such as cities, walls, or pyramids on the ocean floor without the use of cameras with artificial lighting.

Except for some privately financed expeditions prospecting for such remains in fairly shallow water, discoveries of architectural remains have been made by chance and generally have not been followed up. A notable case of this was pictures taken from a camera lowered from the *Anton Brunn* research vessel for the purpose of photographing bottom fish in the Nazca Trench off Peru in 1965. A chance photograph showed massive stone columns and walls on the mud bottom at a depth of one and a half miles. A further example was the experience of the French submersible *Archimède* which, in a dive off the continental shelf of the Bahamas, as it descended toward the sea bottom repeatedly bumped against a flight of giant cut-stone steps at a depth of about 1400 feet.

The great submerged islands of the Atlantic have been recognized by sonar soundings as consisting of a series of plateaus, often connected by underwater isthmuses and marked by present-day islands still above the level of the ocean. The sonar picture of the submerged islands as indicated on depth maps shows several great land masses and suggests the presence of large bays, numerous lakes, and river systems, indicated by underwater canyons.

In the western Atlantic, the Bahamas Islands group, if the sea level were dropped even a hundred meters, would form a single land mass as big as Florida. It would have a very large bay, the present one-mile-deep area between Andros and the Exuma chain called Tongue of the Ocean. It is on the present Bahama seafloor that more than fifty archaeological sites have been located as evidence of a stone-building culture far beyond the capabilities of the cannibal Carib Indians found there by the early explorers. Underwater limestone caves in the Bahamas—the famous Blue Holes—contain stalagmites and stalactites and usually connect through caves to deep water—a cogent proof that they were formed above sea level. An additional indication of cataclysmic events having occurred in the area is the position of some of these formations—not straight but tilted and broken, as though they had descended not gradually but precipitously into the sea.

An examination of the oceanic depth contours off Yucatán and the islands of the south Caribbean suggests that another extensive land area existed north of Venezuela and east of present Central America. It is from Yucatán and Belize that ancient Mayan roads continue out from the coast to destinations now under the sea. North of Venezuela an undersea wall extending for at least a hundred miles was judged not to be man-made because it was "too long." It was also in this general vicinity that a Duke University expedition found continental rock along the Aves Ridge.

The sunken islands or continent most closely identified with Atlantis include the Azores, the Canary Islands and Madeira, the Cape Verde Islands, and possibly the St. Peter and St. Paul Rocks and Bermuda. A number of seamounts both east and west of the Mid-Atlantic Ridge would have been small islands. All of these islands, when the now scientifically documented changes are taken into account, were double or triple their present size. This would explain Plato's description of the islands from which one might pass to "the whole of the opposite continent which surrounded the true ocean." (It was on the Ampere Seamount north of Madeira that a Russian expedition reported in 1977 that underwater photographs showed pictures of walls, pavements, and steps.)

It was in the vicinity of the Azores that the first modern searches for Atlantis were instituted and where rocks from the bottom gave evidence of great explosions and sudden sinkings, just as described in Plato's legend. A large continent island standing on a series of plateaus on which the present Azores and a number of seamounts rest (two of which were appropriately named Atlantis and Plato when being charted) extends into the central Atlantic from approximately north latitude 50° on a line between Newfoundland and northern France and then continues south through the Azores, turning southwest and passing through the Sargasso Sea down to north latitude 20° on a line between Yucatán and Mauritania, Africa. This underwater plateau is roughly comparable, in modern terms, to the size of France, Spain, Portugal and the British Isles together. Or, in Plato's terms (bearing in mind that when Plato said "Libya" he meant the coastal section of North Africa and when he said "Asia" he meant Asia Minor), "larger than Libya and Asia put together." The approximate dimensions of the island continent given by Plato, and supported thousands of years later by the finding of the great mountainous plateau along the Mid-Atlantic Ridge, would be of more than sufficient size to support the population, commerce, agriculture, navy and maritime culture detailed in the *Critias* and *Timaeus* dialogues.

Part of the Canary Islands complex was possibly a single land area attached to Africa as it is still connected with Africa's continental shelf. Atlantean dominion or culture could be expected to have spread to the continental shelves of the four continents bordering on the Atlantic, and it is precisely on these continental shelves of Spain, France, England, Africa, the West Indies, Central America, and northern South America that shallow and deep water architectural remains are being discovered with increasing frequency. Submerged shorelines and lowered sea-level terraces along the east and west coastlines of the North Atlantic attest to the extensive regions of the now drowned but probably once-inhabited lands.

Continental shelves are the undersea edges of continents, relatively shallow before they drop off into the oceanic abyss. An evident proof of the sinking of the continental shelves or the risings of the oceanic waters over them can be found in the undersea mapping of sediment-filled river canyons that flowed into the once more distant sea on both sides of the Atlantic. As they left the land and entered the ocean, some of these rivers continued their course along their ancient beds now under the sea. The upper reaches of the underwater Hudson Canyon, 100 miles long and several hundred feet deep, could not have been formed under water but was cut at a time when this present underwater extension of the Hudson was dry land. Other oceanic canyons include the Baltimore Canyon, probably cut by the Delaware River in ancient times, and the Norfolk Canyon, cut by the Susquehanna. On the other side of the Atlantic sonar soundings show that the same canyon-making pattern at the edge of the ocean basin was followed by the Loire, Rhône, and the Seine in France and the Tagus from Portugal, while on the west coast of Africa there are river canyons on the seabed although there are no longer feeding rivers flowing from the now-arid land.

The case of the submerged Rhine Valley is of special interest since it runs up the North Sea midway between south Norway and Scotland before it disappears, indicating that in fairly recent prehistoric times the intervening area was dry land. This theory has been reinforced by the recent finding of man-made artifacts on the bottom of the North Sea, with promise of more in the future as this oil-rich area is more extensively explored.

In the late 1920s the German scientist Alfred Wegener formulated a theory which had already occurred to a number of cartographers: that of continental drift. This theory presupposes that the continents evolved from one single land mass that drew apart, floating on the Earth's crust, to form the various continents. Wegener's theory had the advantage of being easy to demonstrate and understandable to anyone who had a world map since a number of the continental land masses apparently could be made to fit together like a gigantic jigsaw puzzle, were it not for the oceans that separate them. One can see how the shapes mesh, with Brazil fitting into the southwest coast of central Africa (even the types of rocks correspond), Egypt and the Sudan into Arabia, North Africa into Mediterranean Europe, Arabia into Iran, Madagascar into Mozambique, Greenland into west Norway, Florida into Africa near Liberia, Australia into Antarctica, and a number of other instances not always so evident, such as the west coast of Europe into North America. The continents are still moving at what might be called an unhurried pace—two centimeters a year. At this rate it will be millions of years before the west coast of North America catches up with Japan and China, toward which points it is now heading.

A by-product of this theory has been accepted as a proof by oceanographers and others that Atlantis never existed nor *could* have existed, as there would be no land mass left over for Atlantis

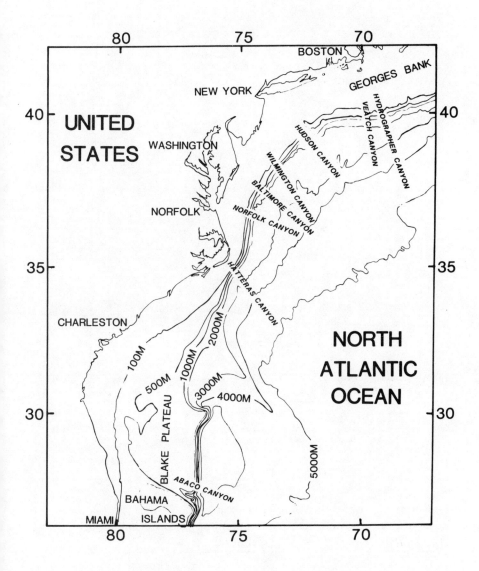

River canyons which prolong the course of existing rivers under the sea
are a strong indication that rivers from the American mainland (and also
from Western Europe) once entered the ocean at a point now far out at
sea at a time when large portions of the continental shelves were still
dry land.

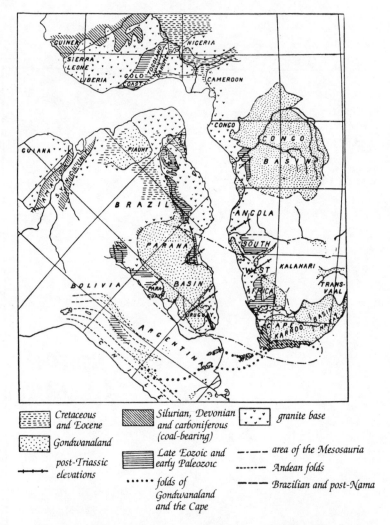

The east coast of South America fits fairly exactly into the southwestern coast of Africa, even to the continuation of subterranean deposits across the area where the continents seem to fit.

---

to fit into among the drifting continents. For all land areas fitted together—to the satisfaction of Wegener at least—almost without any missing pieces, *except* in the southern portion of the North Atlantic, where Atlantis reputedly was located. Here the "uplifted" plateau of the oceanic crust would form the fabled continent—a fertile, pleasant, subtropical land in the southern plains, with invigorating climatic changes in the northern mountains.

Wegener, a casualty of his own scientific research operations, died on an icecap in Greenland in 1930 and so did not live to see his theory of drifting continents incorporated into a more extensive one. The theory of moving tectonic plates, originated by Dr. Jason Morgan in 1968, describes more fully the motions of the separate sections of the Earth's crust. This generally accepted theory suggests that the crust of the Earth is divided between ten to twenty major tectonic plates with subdivisions, and that these plates and platelets cover all of the Earth's surface, dry land *and* beneath the sea. When the great plates, floating on the Earth's viscous mantle, grinding against each other on their plate boundaries or fault lines (e.g., the San Andreas Fault, an unwelcome reminder of doom to Californians), there occur earthquakes and volcanic explosions often of catastrophic dimensions. The crux of the tectonic-plate theory is that the movement of the plates is not only horizontal but also vertical, meaning that one plate can be pushed under another and, in the case of the oceanic plates, fed into the fiery interior mantle of the Earth, to eventually be spewed out again as lava from volcanic eruptions. The islands of Japan, among others, were formed by such a volcanic buildup and, like California, face the possibility of future subsidence.

The Mid-Atlantic Ridge marks the tectonic-plate boundaries—those of the North American, European, and African plates. It is also connected to the world's longest mountain range, 40,000 miles long and extending one and a half times around the world. It generally runs north to south in the mid-Atlantic and, after crossing between Africa and Antarctica, turns northeast and crosses the Indian Ocean. It is the world's longest and most active seismic area, especially active in the North Atlantic area, where a triple junction of tectonic plates occurs at the Azores and where volcanic explosions have rumbled and erupted for thousands of years.

Parts of this active triple junction, where tectonic plates are still pushing under, over, away from, or grinding alongside each other, have been reproduced by sidescan sonar at various depths, and contain intriguing details on depth profiles. Part of such a bathymetric profile is reproduced on page 171 and shows a section of the sea bottom 1000 to 24,000 feet deep southeast of the Azores in the vicinity of the islands of São Miguel and Santa Maria. Inspection of

Conceptual drawing of sea bottom near the Cape Verde Islands showing how steep underwater mountains, based on an undersea plateau, continue upward and, above the surface, form present islands.

this profile reveals what look like the remains of towers or pyramids on an otherwise sloping rise of an ancient plateau. While allowing for vertical exaggeration, which would make a towering structure wider at the base and more pyramidal in shape, it is thought-provoking to consider what these formations would reveal if submersibles could examine the seafloor at this plateau on the triple junction of the grinding continental plates.

The theory of tectonic plates makes the concept of Atlantis considerably more believable. The continental-drift theory deals with millions of years of leisurely separation of continents by horizontal drifting, while the tectonic-plate theory implies the probability of vertical movement, volcanic eruptions, and seismic convulsions and explains how great islands can be alternately thrown up or engulfed by the sea—a process still going on and which can be observed and measured. It also would tend to substantiate the comparatively recent age (1000 to 15,000 B.P.) of some of the lava flows found on the sea bottom of the Mid-Atlantic Ridge.

The late Dr. Maurice Ewing, one of America's most prominent marine geologists, and, incidentally, an outstanding critic of the concept of Atlantis, nevertheless arrived at the conclusion that lava had spread over parts of the Mid-Atlantic Ridge only recently in geological terms: "Either the land must have sunk two or three miles or the sea must have been two to three miles lower than now. Either conclusion is startling."

Examples of the composition of the seafloor are constantly being collected and assessed by coring accomplished by research ships. Some of the material found within these cores, which bring up a vertical sample of the ocean bottom of from ten to a hundred feet straight down, has revealed new information pertinent to sunken lands and their time—and speed—of sinking.

Considerable volcanic ash has appeared in cores and dredges taken from the Mid-Atlantic Ridge by the United States Geological Survey and by the oceanographic research institutions of the USA, England, the USSR, France, Germany, Canada, Denmark, and other nations. Under separate study many of these sediments and rocks have been dated radioactively and zoologically (the latter meaning the examination of insects and any molecules above and beneath the ash). Results indicate that the ash came from surface explosions of ten to fifty thousand years ago, well within the age span attributed to

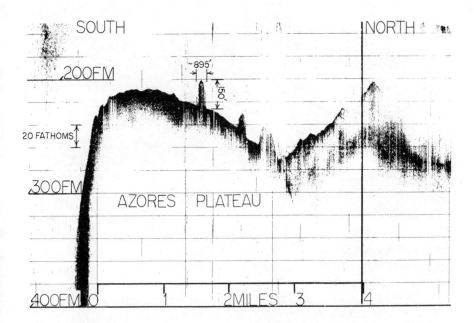

Bathymetric profile or echogram of portion of the undersea Azores Plateau. Protuberances on left, one of which almost reaches the 200-fathoms line, could indicate a mound, pyramid, or tower of man-made construction because of its regularity. According to speed or drift of sounding equipment, the highest of these structures would probably be more pyramidal than tower-like in shape.

Atlantis. Coral, hauled up by cable in small steel baskets from depths of over 3000 feet near the Great Meteor Seamount and other mid-Atlantic locations, indicates either a drop of thousands of feet, from close to sea level, where coral grows, or a great rise in the level of the sea, or perhaps both, since the time the coral was formed in shallow areas around former islands.

As a result of a Swedish deep-sea mid-Atlantic expedition in 1947–1948, Dr. R. Malaise announced in 1957 (an exemplary ten-year interval for checking!) that Dr. R. Kolbe had found numerous fresh-water diatoms (microscopic plankton) and remains of land-grown plants in cores taken from two miles down on the Mid-Atlantic Ridge; in other words, remains of animal and plant life that grew around ancient lakes when a great part of the ridge was dry land.

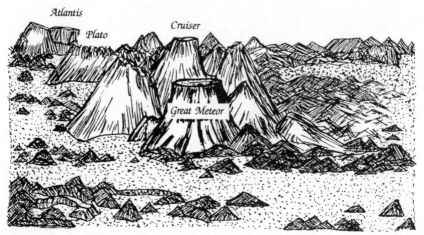

Comparison of height of underwater seamounts or guyots over their surroundings. Great Meteor and Cruiser rise to precipitous heights of 16,000 feet from the bottom and to within 1000 feet of the surface, and, like other seamounts, give indications that they were once above water. The Plato Seamount commemorates the name of Atlantis' ancient publicist, and a chain of seamounts appropriately named "Atlantis" exists to the northwest.

Dr. Malaise further stated that analysis of the find indicated that the last above-water period of the area was ten to twelve thousand years ago. This is a further corroboration of the dating of the most recent thick ash layers, which may have been produced by the volcanic eruption that occurred during the last days of Atlantis. The Swedish research ship *Albatross*, taking cores from a depth of two miles in the Romanche fracture zone in the vicinity of the St. Peter and St. Paul Rocks, brought up shallow-water microorganisms, preserved in bottom mud, along with twigs, plants, and tree bark, all of which had evidently descended rapidly into the depths at the same time.

It is through the progress of oceanographic geological research that the theory of the vertical movement of tectonic plates and its modification of the continental-drift theory has brought about a reassessment of the possibility that Atlantis once really existed as lands in the Atlantic Ocean. This is rather ironic, considering the long time and violent opposition of the geological and oceanographic establishment to any serious consideration of Atlantis. But the moving tectonic plates open the door to an explanation of how great islands could arise from or disappear into the sea as a result of catastrophic movements of the Earth's crust arising from the pressure against one another of these plates. (Perhaps, on some occasion, the pressure was further augmented by the collision of Earth with an asteroid, or an imbalance within the planet itself, or a modification of its axis of rotation.) The tectonic-plate theory brings Atlantis into a time frame of hundreds or even tens of thousands of years, instead of millions; in other words, within the experience and memory of the human race. It also appears possible that a number of species other than man remember Atlantis through evolutionary instinct. These species, by their sudden death during a global catastrophe, bear witness to an event that changed the climate and surface of the Earth.

12

EELS, SEALS, BIRDS, SHRIMPS, MASTODONS, AND TOXODONS

Supposing that the land mass of Atlantis were shaken by earthquakes as most of it descended into the sea, it would still have been possible for some forms of life to have survived on the tops of its mountains, which became small islands over the surface of the sea. This possibility would explain the survival on some of the isolated Atlantic islands of animals whose presence there would be difficult to otherwise explain unless they were brought there in ships from other continents.

The Canary Islands were not named for birds but for dogs (Latin: *canes*) observed in quantity by early European visitors. The dogs were native to the islands, as were the islanders themselves, who had not brought the dogs or other animals such as goats, sheep, and cattle to the islands by boat from Africa or Europe. In fact, the indigenous Canary Islanders did not use boats, so greatly did they fear the sea and remember the legend of their former homeland being swallowed by the ocean.

There is also the matter of a small crustacean and its connection with the legend of Atlantis. In Lanzarote, one of the Canaries, where there are ancient buildings and tombs of undetermined age and origin, there exists a small, blind species of shrimp whose sole habitat, as far as is known, is within one black tidewater pool under a cavern. This small shrimp, the *munidopsis polymorpha*, which has residual eyes but has lost its sight, is closely related to another local crustacean, the *munidopsis tridentata*, practically identical to the first except that, not being locked into the subterranean tidal pool, it is able to see. A theoretical explanation of the loss of sight by the *munidopsis polymorpha* is that it was trapped within the dark sub-terranean pool by a sudden seismic shift and, remaining in total darkness and not needing vision, lost it over the intervening centuries.

There were no people living on the Azores when the first recorded European navigators arrived, but there were so many land birds and rabbits evident that the explorers named the group of islands after hawks (*Açores*) and the individual islands after the land birds or animals found there. The present islands of São Miguel, Corvo, and Flores were recorded on the earliest maps as the Portuguese equivalent of Isle of Doves, Isle of Crows, and Isle of Rabbits. But there is no explanation for the presence of these mainland birds and animals on small islands a thousand miles from the nearest continent.

Two kinds of seals, the monk and the siren, are found off the coast of the Azores, although they both belong to a variety of seals that frequent continental coasts or inland seas: the monk seal the coastal waters of the Mediterranean and the Caribbean and the siren seal the coastal waters of west Africa and eastern South America.

As a supporting statement to the theory that such seals were among the birds and animals isolated on the ocean islands after the disappearance of their former habitat of continental proportion, there exists an unusual reference in classical literature about seals *and* Atlantis. Aelien, a classical writer of the third century A.D., made mention of the "rams of the sea" (seals) in his work entitled *The Nature of Animals*. He wrote: ". . . the male ram has around his forehead a white band. One would say it resembled the diadem of Lysimachus or Antigonus or some other Macedonian king. The inhabitants of the shores of the ocean tell that in former times the kings of Atlantis, descendants of Poseidon, wore on their heads, as a mark of power, the headband of the male rams, and that their wives, the queens, wore, as a sign of their power, headbands of the female rams."

This passing reference to the use of seal skin in Atlantis as a royal headpiece is an example of how a minor observation about dress, in this case, a style of head covering, can serve many centuries later as a substantiation of theories having to do with zoology, geology, oceanography, and the prehistory of the world.

Even such ephemeral species as butterflies have been suggested as a linkage between the existing continents on the western and eastern shores of the Atlantic and a former continent in the middle of the ocean. Among the species of butterflies extant in the Atlantic islands, two-thirds also exist in Europe and Africa and almost one-third in the Americas. Lewis Spence, the Scottish Atlantologist, has suggested that the *catopsilia* butterfly of the north coast of South America may genetically remember a land area in the ocean north-east of Guyana, since every year the male butterflies of this species undertake a fatal mass flight over the ocean until "in great coloured clouds they fly into the sea."

The instinctive urge of animals, birds, and insects to return to a remote homeland or breeding ground is termed *nostophilia* and may also explain a striking phenomenon reported by seamen and fishermen in an area south of the Azores as they observed flocks of migratory birds on their annual winter flight from Europe to South America. As the birds arrive within this area, the flocks begin to circle around over the open sea as if looking for a place to land, some of the tired birds falling into the ocean. After flying in great concentric circles and not finding land, the birds continue their flight and eventually repeat the same process when they return from South America.

This instinctive memory may also explain the mysterious mass suicide of the lemmings, small Norwegian rodents that periodically overbreed and exhaust their food supply. At this point some latent instinct impels them toward the shores of the Atlantic where, in great swarms, they enter the ocean and swim westward until they all drown. This instinct, which effectively serves as a form of population control, has also frequently been attributed by partisans of Atlantis to an instinctive memory of a land that once existed in the west, perhaps a common homeland shared with other small continental animals where food could be found by the starving lemming horde.

But perhaps the most striking example of instinctive memory is the case of the European and American eels, both of which species make a journey over thousands of miles of rivers, seas, and oceans, eventually to spawn in one of the most mysterious areas of the Atlantic Ocean—the Sargasso Sea—considered by some investigators to cover what was once the western part of the continent of Atlantis.

Aristotle, the Athenian philosopher, a pupil and later critic of Plato, was also an interested observer of natural phenomena. He made the first historical comment on the breeding habits of the

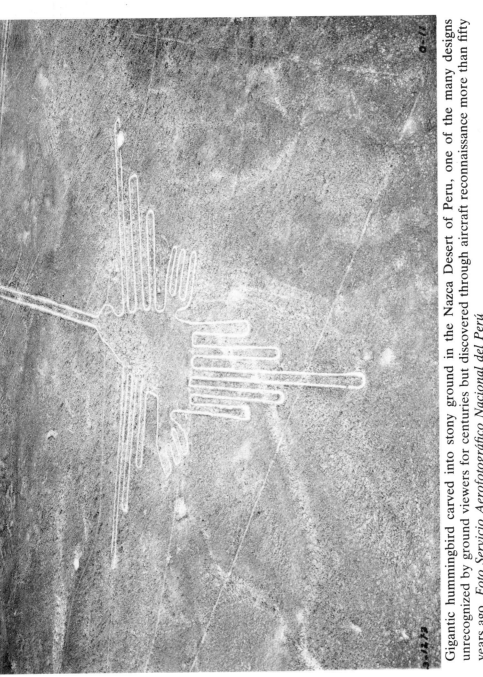

Gigantic hummingbird carved into stony ground in the Nazca Desert of Peru, one of the many designs unrecognized by ground viewers for centuries but discovered through aircraft reconnaissance more than fifty years ago. *Foto Servicio Aerofotográfico Nacional del Perú*

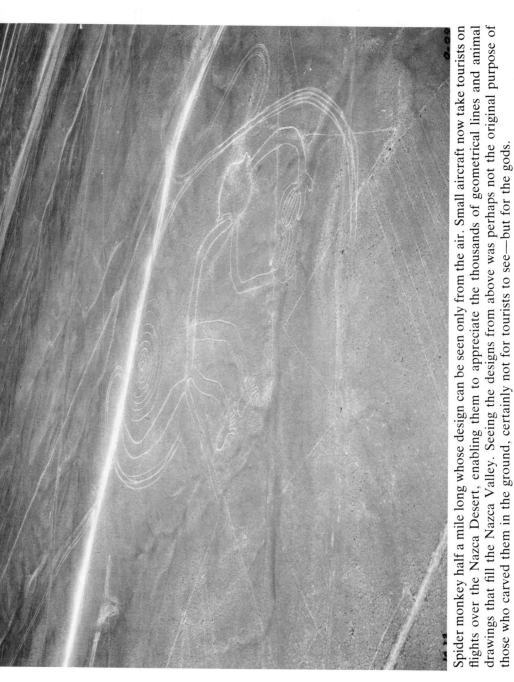

Spider monkey half a mile long whose design can be seen only from the air. Small aircraft now take tourists on flights over the Nazca Desert, enabling them to appreciate the thousands of geometrical lines and animal drawings that fill the Nazca Valley. Seeing the designs from above was perhaps not the original purpose of those who carved them in the ground, certainly not for tourists to see—but for the gods.

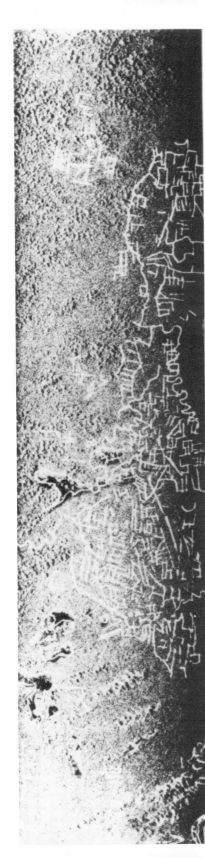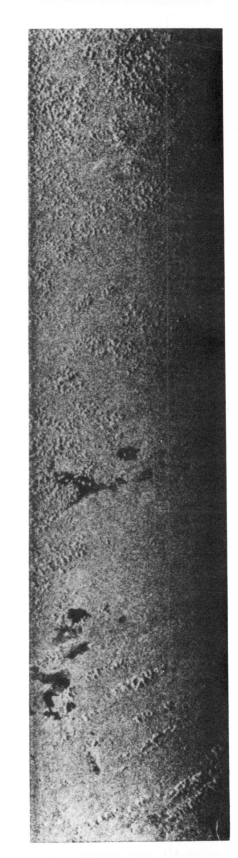

Comparison of radar imagery and regular aerial photograph taken over Guatemalan jungle. The lines in the radar imagery photograph prove to be irrigation canals dug by the ancient Maya. This tends to confirm the supposition that the Maya lands were once much more thickly populated than previously supposed. *NASA*

Advertisement for AeroPerú referring to the theory that the Nazca lines were landing strips and directional signs for prehistoric aircraft. Some modern investigators have constructed hot-air balloons from material thought to have been available at an early epoch and have wafted over the Nazca Valley as, perhaps, did the ancient Peruvians. *Photo courtesy AeroPerú*

Radar imagery photographs of the Sahara, taken from space by *Columbia* space shuttle, showing riverbeds and tributary rivers under the desert. The rivers corresponding to these underground riverbeds flowed through considerably different surroundings ten thousand years ago—fertile and wooded plains and lakes in what is now the arid desert. *NASA*

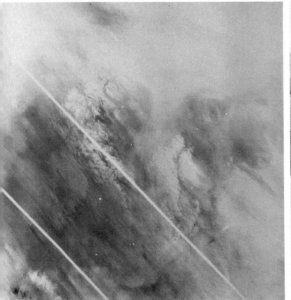

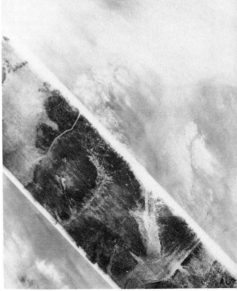

Many thousands of inscribed stones have been excavated and collected at Ica, Peru, some of which show recognizable representations of prehistoric animals. Although these stones have been labeled as modern deceptions by some archaeologists and journalists, there are records that a Spanish priest commented on them and sent some back to Spain in the early 1500s. *Photo courtesy of Hamilton Forman and the Instituto Nacional de la Cultura del Perú*

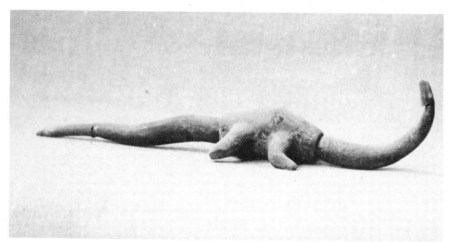

Clay statuette from Julsrud Collection of Acámbaro, Mexico, depicting what is apparently an allosaurus. If this and other statuettes of Jurassic animals are authentic, it could mean either that some prehistoric animals survived into the Ice Age or that their frozen preserved bodies had been found by men. *Courtesy Ivan Lee and the Julsrud Collection*

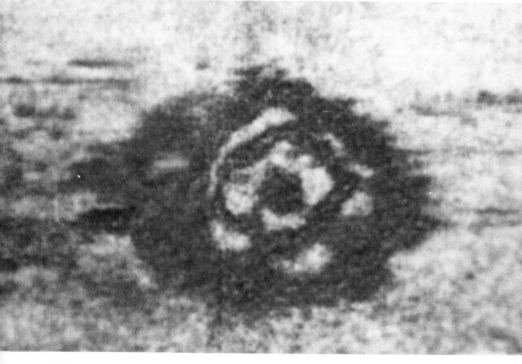

Side-scan sonar represents a valuable adjunct in underwater archaeological and geologic survey, enabling investigators to "see" objects under water and on the sea bottom through reflected sound. Martin Klein, who developed the Klein Side-Scan Sonar, encountered vestiges of ancient British stone circles on the bottom of Loch Ness in a search for the Loch Ness monster. The presence of stone ruins on the lake bottom are an additional indication of the lower water level during the Ice Age. *Martin Klein*

This round hole in the ocean plunges suddenly down from the shallow (three fathoms) Bahama Banks surrounding it to a depth which has not yet been firmly established. Depth recorders have not found bottom at 2800 feet. The diameter of the hole can be gauged by comparing it with the fifty-foot Carey Craft to the right of center. The cause of this and other round holes in the ocean has been variously ascribed to meteor or asteroid strikes or to leaching and subsequent tidal effects which may have started when this area was still above sea level. *Bob Klein*

Scar left by presumed asteroid strike at Manicouagan, Canada. Its diameter is seventy-five miles. A strike of this nature must have shaken the whole northern hemisphere. *NASA*

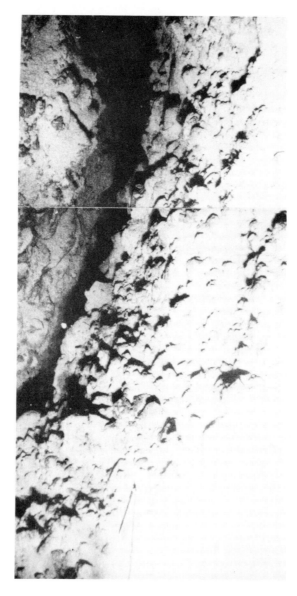

Fault in bottom of ocean floor near Mid-Atlantic Ridge, in the vicinity of the Azores, typical of constant activity between pushing, ascending, and descending tectonic plates. *NOAA*

European eel, which, every two years, disappeared from the lakes and ponds of Europe and swam down rivers into the sea. The young eels, born somewhere at sea, swam back up the rivers to the lakes, but their breeding grounds, somewhere at sea, remained unknown. It was not until the middle of the present century that the mystery of the breeding ground was solved. It is now known that the eels go to the Sargasso Sea, making their way under the ocean in a single enormous bank of eels in a journey that takes four months to complete. When they arrive at a point within the Sargasso, they spawn in underwater concentrations of seaweed, which protects the eggs, then die. The young eels return to Europe via the northern sweep of the Gulf Stream and the process repeats itself after another two years.

Aristotle would have been even more puzzled had he known about the eels from America, which accomplish a similar underwater pilgrimage to the Sargasso Sea but in inverse order to that of the European eels; from the west to the east, returning to America following the southern, west-directed sweep of the Gulf Stream (the same route followed by Columbus).

Although the mystery appears to be solved, the explanation is elusive. Possibly the genetic memory of eels on both sides of the Atlantic forces them to return to an ancestral breeding ground, a river or former waterway now covered by the sea, but whose residual vegetation, the seaweed of the Sargasso Sea, still affords the young eels the protection they need for survival.

It is also interesting to reflect that Aristotle, the skeptic who derided Plato's account of Atlantis, was the first to call attention to the mystery of the eel migration, which itself has become a thought-provoking suggestion concerning the one-time existence of a continental land mass now beneath the Atlantic Ocean.

During the last several thousand years, the finding of gigantic bones of dinosaurs in remote areas of the world has doubtlessly given rise to world-wide legends about dragons. Some cultures have tried to "pad out" the bones in an effort to portray how the monstrous animals looked when they were alive, and it is to these attempts that we probably owe the general concept of dragons as depicted on the walls of Babylon, in the old legends of Europe, and the art forms of China. Some western theologians of two centuries ago explained the giant dinosaur bones as having been created (and buried?) by God when He made the universe. The practical Chinese, however, for centuries have ground up the bones found in the Gobi Desert into dragon-bone pills, a reputedly effective remedy still being used for a multitude of ailments and for the reinforcement of virility. Some reptiles resembling small dragons are still alive. The Komodo dragons, or giant lizards of Indonesia, ten-foot-long saurians, can still be observed on their survival island of Komodo. The persistent native legends about the existence of these "dragons," at least, have proved to be an undeniable fact as observers who have been attacked and bitten by them can testify.

There exists a possibility that other isolated survivals of a few species of prehistoric animals continued to exist into the time frame of former civilizations on the planet; that is, before the end of the last Glacial Age, 12,000 years ago. On an example of ancient Scythian goldwork from southern Russia a struggle between hunters and animals shows men fighting what appears to be a clear portrayal of a saber-toothed tiger, suggesting that this animal survived to an age in which man was already sufficiently developed in the use of metals to cast this prehistoric tiger in gold as an adornment.

But it is in the Americas that the greatest survival mysteries occur. On ceramic pottery unearthed in the ruins of Tiahuanaco, Bolivia, and also on stonework there, an animal is shown that is easily recognizable as a paleontological reproduction of a toxodon, an animal resembling a hippopotamus, supposedly extinct for millions of years. The site of this unusual discovery is in itself extraordinary: Tiahuanaco, now 13,000 feet above sea level, gives indications of having been constructed at a time so long ago (estimated by the archaeologist Posnansky at 13,000 B.C.) that the climate as well as the *altitude* has since changed. It appears to have been a port, because of stone docks and quays, but the only nearby water is Lake Titicaca, several miles away. Tiahuanaco must at one time have supported a large population in order to have built the great city of which only ruins remain, but the area is too high and too barren to support such a culture. The remains of extensive terraced cornfields found under the permanent snow on the surrounding mountains are an indication that the climate was once considerably warmer and that agriculture once supported a large population. Saltwater ocean fossils are found on the land, in the mountains, and under Lake Titicaca. The probability of the whole area having risen from sea level is reinforced because of the great fault running through the Andes chain and the fact that the Andes are the most recent of the world's great mountains, the western part being about 30,000 years old.

The rising of the Andes may have been accelerated by the same enormous Earth change that resulted in the sinking of Atlantis and that caused parts of the South American coast to crest into the heights of the Andean plateau. The elevation of the Andes Mountains, from four miles below sea level at the Nazca-Milne Trench, then, within 125 miles, to a height of four miles above sea level in Peru and Bolivia, is one of the most precipitous elevations in the world's geology.

In widely separated areas of North and South America, construction of earth mounds and artificial shaping of hills and cliffs show familiarity on the part of the ancient artisans with animals supposedly extinct in the Americas for thousands, and in some cases, millions of years. A great mound in Wisconsin is shaped like the outline of an elephant or mastodon, perhaps meant to be recognizable only from the sky, like the animals of Nazca, Peru. Some pre-Incaic people carved the rock cliffs of the Marcahuasi Plateau of Peru into huge representations of lions, camels, and something resembling a stegosaurus.

In the vicinity of the villages of Ocucaje and Ica, in Peru, a collection of rounded stones totaling perhaps 16,000 and weighing from five pounds up to huge boulders of 800 pounds has been amassed by Dr. Javier Cabrera, who has about 11,000 of them in his crowded museum. What is unusual about these "stones of Ica" is that they are covered with incised drawings ostensibly made by carvers of past civilizations. The engraved drawings show people, extant and extinct animals, star maps, the star ring of the zodiac, and maps of unidentified land areas. The people are shown hunting or struggling with a variety of monsters that resemble brontosaurs, triceratops, stegosaurs, and pterodactyls, which properly belong to the Mesozoic Era. Even more surprisingly, human beings are portrayed as having domesticated animals that appear to be dinosaurs and are using them for transportation and warfare. People are shown using telescopes, looking at the stars, and performing surgery.

Understandably, these "picture stories" have been qualified as spurious by archaeologists, especially since their source has not been precisely pinpointed for them to be examined *in situ* and new stones keep appearing—the number is now approaching 50,000. In addi-

Recognizable prehistoric animals ridden by men as portrayed on incised prehistoric stones of Ica, Peru.

tion, one of the local villagers admits to having manufactured a number of like stones for sale to archaeologists, an example of business acumen on the part of the supposedly simple natives not limited to Peru. The Peruvian authorities eventually decided to classify the stones not as antiquities, which cannot be exported, but simply as artifacts to be labeled "made in Peru," as they all, the old and the new, undoubtedly were.

These undatable stones would be easy to dismiss as one more example of archaeological "plants" were it not for a report of their having been sent back to Spain by Spanish explorers in 1562—an indication that the stones are at least not of recent origin. That they are at least several centuries old is attested to by the oxidation produced by the aging of minerals covering the incisions of the drawings. Also, their very number, their size, and the time it would have taken to completely cover them with incised pictures would tend to indicate that a number of them are what they appear to be, however active the imaginations of the original carvers.

As far as the logistics of a modern family group carving the thousands of stones and then planting them to be discovered, it has been observed by Hamilton Forman, an amateur archaeologist who has researched the mystery of the Ica stones: "If one family did this they must have had an army of elves helping them."

Another unusual find of apparently ancient models of prehistoric animals and men was made near the town of Acámbaro, in the Mexican state of Guanajuato. This series of finds has been the subject of meticulous archaeological investigation which, however, has not yet identified or dated the culture to the satisfaction of the majority of archaeologists.

The figures were first found by Waldemar Julsrud, a Danish storekeeper living in Acámbaro. In 1925 Julsrud was on an inspection tour of his ranch, which he was making on horseback, accompanied by his foreman, when he noticed a small ceramic figure projecting from the side of a rut in the rain-washed road. The artifact was of a type quite unlike other Indian artifacts previously found in the area and, when he probed further, he began to uncover additional models of people and animals resembling those portrayed on the Ica stones, the giant saurians of the Jurassic period of millions of years ago.

Julsrud instructed his foreman, Tinajero, to look for further figures and subsequently paid him for such finds, apparently modestly, since Julsrud eventually was able to amass 33,000 of them.

The human figures and the animals were frequently portrayed together. Some of the dinosaur-like reptiles appear with women in nonviolent or nonhunting situations, as though they were domestic animals or pets. The human figures show details of dress somewhat resembling those of the ancient Middle East: laced sandals, chain mail, shields, and a variety of weapons.

Since the figurines are made of clay, containing bits of organic material inside them, some of the artifacts have been dated. According to carbon-14 tests, some of them were made in 5930 B.C., ± 170 years, while others appear to be of contemporaneous manufacture. This anomaly can doubtless be explained by the reward offered by Julsrud to the local Indians for additional artifacts, which encouraged them to make copies of the works of their presumed ancestors. Nevertheless, the verified ancient dates obtained from the Acámbaro figures would establish this Indian or pre-Indian culture as having existed thousands of years before any other accepted date of Amerindian civilization.

Other anachronistic drawings in out-of-the-way places cannot be dated. On a wall of the Havasupai Canyon in California, for example, some ancient artist has sketched a tyrannosaurus characteristically standing straight up with the additional support of its great tail, possibly a good guess on the part of the artist in an attempt to show how the great animal, whose bones were found nearby, would look if he were alive.

Ancient drawings or carvings of extinct animals, while they suggest through carbon-14 dating when possible that civilized or semicivilized man is considerably older than previously supposed, do not prove, of course, that human beings encountered surviving species of animals from the Jurassic period. It is nevertheless interesting to single out the example of the coelacanth, a fish with "legs," which has survived its supposed extinction twenty million years ago and is apparently still living in the Indian Ocean, where several examples have been caught within the past few years. Perhaps, like the coelacanth and the giant sloth of South America, other modified species from former periods have survived into the Pleistocene epoch, which ended, like fabled Atlantis, about 12,000 years ago.

But we do not need statuettes, drawings, or cave paintings to prove the presence and subsequent sudden deaths of a multitude of large animals in different parts of the world. The finding of their bones and quick-frozen bodies suggests a connection with a worldwide catastrophe both through the time of their death and the manner in which they died. This occurred in the case of the protoelephants that suddenly vanished in a variety of areas about 12,000 years ago as a result of sudden climatic changes or other disaster.

While Plato emphasized the presence of elephants in Atlantis, he did not specify the type—he may have been referring to the mastodon of the earlier Quaternary period, such as those whose remains have been found in North America, South America, and Europe. Mastodon bones, along with weapons of prehistoric man, have also been recovered from the bottom of the North Sea, now increasingly explored in the course of oil production operations.

Ancient Mexican representations carved on buildings and in picture manuscripts seem clearly to show elephant heads and not "macaws" as some researchers have suggested.

A more concrete example, the deposits of piled-up mastodon bones found near Bogotá, Colombia, indicate that these animals existed in ancient South America and died simultaneously as a result of some unusual occurrence. Colonel A. Bragine (*The Shadow of Atlantis*: 1940) suggests that the great herd was killed during a seismic convulsion that caused an enormous upthrust of their grazing ground.

In Siberia a number of dead mammoths, preserved for thousands of years in a quick-frozen condition, were evidently drowned at the same time in water and mud and so frozen that when thawed they have often served as food for dogs and native tribesmen. When examined by zoologists, their stomachs were found to contain food from plants no longer extant in Siberia. Professor Charles Hapgood has described one mammoth that suddenly perished while eating buttercups, which were still in his mouth. The age of the frozen Siberian mammoths and the Colombian mastodon bones have both been calculated as twelve to thirteen thousand years B.P.

Because of their size, protoelephant cadavers and bones have been found more frequently than those of other animals, just as the bones of dinosaurs, which died many millions of years previously, are still being excavated. In a number of places, however, massive conglomerations of other animals have been found crammed together into caves or earth pockets in Europe, covering with their skeletons the bone islands of the Arctic, or under the permafrost of Alaska and Canada where, as in Siberia, they drowned in mud and water and were frozen. Many of these myriad species are no longer extant in the areas where their skeletons or frozen bodies have been found: they include saber-toothed tigers, rhinoceros, lions, ostriches, auroch cattle, giant elk, and others, all evidently fleeing or trying to find refuge from earthquake, flood, or fire.

Frank Hoffer, in *Lost Americans*, gives a vivid picture of the effects of this world catastrophe as seen in Alaska: "The muck pits of Alaska are filled with evidence of universal death . . . a picture of quick extinction. . . . Mammoth and bison were torn and twisted as though by a cosmic hand in godly rage. In many places the Alaskan mud blanket is packed with animal bones and debris in trainload lots . . . mammoth, mastodon, bison, horses, wolves, bears, and lions. . . . A faunal population . . . in the middle of some catastrophe . . . was suddenly frozen in a grim charade."

So many animals died near the shores of the Arctic Ocean that the sea bottom in places is covered with their tusks and bones, and some islands, like the "islands of bones" and Llakov Island, off Siberia, are actually built of millions of skeletons, still preserved by the freezing weather.

Fish died too in the sudden tectonic changes. Near Santa Barbara, California, the United States Geological Survey has located a bed of now petrified fish on a former sea bottom where more than an estimated billion fish died suddenly within a four-mile area.

The tracing of death pits of large and small animals in different areas throughout the world indicates that the phenomenon was not a local but a general one. Something very sudden and deadly to the animal and human population of the Earth happened at the end of the Pleistocene Era about 12,000 years ago. It changed the climate and the land and water distribution over large sections of the world. While the story of the Great Flood is common to almost all the world's peoples, many tribal legends connect the Flood with earthquakes, fire from the skies, and the sinking of inhabited lands into the sea.

Many of the ancient tribes that witnessed the world catastrophe and the great tides which swept over the Earth saw the overwhelming doom as a flood. The waters that rose and suddenly covered large areas of the continents left, as they subsided, oceanic fauna, shells, and skeletons of small and large sea creatures scattered over mountain ranges such as the Andes, the Rocky Mountains, the Himalayas (where whale bones have been found), the Urals, and a spur of the Caucasus—the "Mountains of Ararat" (where parts of the world's most celebrated vessel are reputed still to exist).

Some of the chronicles of a world disaster that have come down to us from pre–Columbian America are notable especially because they describe violent seismic activity that occurred before a flood. The Book of Chilam Balaam, transcribed from memory of former records destroyed during the Conquest, relates:

> Ah Mucencab came forth and obscured the face of the Heavens . . . the Earth began to awaken. Nobody knew what was to come. Suddenly subterranean fires burst forth into the Sky, and fire rained down from above, and ashes descended, and rocks and trees were thrown down, and wood and stone smashed together.
> Then the Heavens were seized and split asunder. The face of the Heavens was buffeted to and fro and thrown on its

back . . . [the people] were all torn to pieces; their hearts failed them while they yet lived. Then they were buried in the sands, in the sea.

In one great sudden rush of water the Great Serpent was ravished from the Heavens. The Sky fell and the Earth sank, when the four gods, the Bacabs, arose who brought about the destruction of the world.

The *Popol Vuh*, another Mayan reconstituted manuscript, repeatedly mentions fire, as do many other Amerindian legends concerning a flood:

> Then the waters were agitated by the will of Hurakán, and a great inundation came upon the heads of these creatures. . . . They were engulfed, and a resinous thickness descended from heaven; . . . the face of the Earth was obscured, and a heavy darkening rain commenced—rain by day and rain by night. . . . There was heard a great noise above their heads, as if produced by fire. Then were men seen running, pushing each other, filled with despair; they wished to climb upon their houses, and the houses, tumbling down, fell to the ground; they wished to climb upon the trees, and the trees shook them off; they wished to enter into the caves, and the caves closed themselves before them. . . . Water and fire contributed to the universal ruin at the time of the last great cataclysm which preceded the fourth creation.

A curious European commentary emphasizing fire is contained in *Dera Linda Boek*, a Frisian chronicle from the Middle Ages, referring to the disappearance of Atland, an ancient land in the ocean:

> Atland, as the land was called by seafaring people, was swallowed by the waves together with its mountains and valleys, and everything else was covered by the sea. Many people were buried in the ground and others, who escaped, died in the water. The mountains breathed fire . . . the forests were burned to a cinder, and the wind bore the ash which covered the entire Earth. New rivers took shape and the sand in their mouths formed new islands. For three years the land groaned, and when

it recovered, its wounds could be seen. Many countries had disappeared and others had been rent asunder by the sea.

The theme of fire before the Flood runs through a number of other chronicles. It is notable that Plato himself makes reference to fire and earthquakes in the *Timaeus*: ". . . a great conflagration of things upon the Earth recurring at long intervals of time . . . [and] there occurred violent earthquakes and floods, and in a single day and night . . . the island of Atlantis . . . was sunk beneath the sea."

Perhaps the combination of fiery shocks from the sky, the resultant shaking of the Earth, and flooding from the sea was the sequence of events that occurred in the prehistoric world that perished. There are great scars still traceable on the surface of the Earth and the bottoms of its oceans that seem to witness a blow or a series of blows from the sky.

13

COMETS, ASTEROIDS, OR TERMINAL WARFARE

Fortunately for its inhabitants, the Earth is protected from most meteor strikes by its magnetic field, which deflects them, and by its ozone layer and its atmosphere, which tend to burn them up or considerably reduce their size. Otherwise the surface of the planet would be pockmarked with enormous meteor craters similar to the surface of the moon, in the words of Immanuel Velikovsky, "A great unmarked cemetery flying around Earth." Nevertheless, perhaps in times of magnetic shifts, periodic weakening of the magnetic field, or, simply dependent on the size and course of the invading cosmic object, a number of gigantic asteroids have struck the Earth, leaving great craters on its surface and perhaps vast declivities on the floors of its seas.

Some of these earth scars can still be seen: Meteor Crater in Arizona, the Curswell, Deep Bay, and Manicouagan craters in Canada, of which the last named is sixty-six kilometers from one edge to the other. An even larger one, measuring 125 kilometers in diameter, was identified in 1975 by the *Landsat* satellite in the Turtle Mountains between North Dakota and Manitoba. Craters exist throughout the world, including the Siljan in Sweden, the Ashanti in West Africa, the Araguainha in Brazil, and the Korla in Siberia, north of the Arctic Circle. What was once a huge meteor crater in Central Europe, the Ries Kessel, was hard to recognize since it was filled in with vegetation, woods, fields, and towns. In South Africa, the Vredefort Dome is also of so great a circumference that for a long time it was not recognized as having been caused by a giant asteroid. A cluster of possible meteor craters in Western Australia is now being studied in order to establish whether a metallic core, the remains of the original asteroid, can be detected buried under the earth near the crater. A dramatic explosion originating from space occurred in Siberia in 1908 and is known as the Tunguska meteorite or even as the Tunguska "event" since, although a forest was leveled by an explosion of cosmic dimensions and the area still shows considerable radioactivity, no obvious crater and no metallic core have been detected, which suggests an above-the-ground explosion.

Meteor strikes are thought to have taken place in various parts of the sea (a logical supposition since the sea covers 71 percent of the planet's area), sometimes leaving holes in the seafloor, opening up bays or lakes. It has been suggested that Hudson Bay, the Gulf of Saint Lawrence, Lake Baikal, the Aral Sea, and possibly the Gulf of Mexico were originally great craters, caused by asteroid collisions with Earth.

Some European meteorologists suggested, in the early part of the 20th century, that an enormous meteor struck the Earth thousands of years ago, smashing part of the Atlantean continent down into the ocean and leaving only the isolated islands that still exist in the Atlantic Ocean.

A recent exponent of this theory, the German rocket scientist Dr. Otto Muck (*Alles über Atlantis*: 1976), offers a detailed account as well as a suggested date when such a catastrophe may have happened. His theory is based on a huge meteor having struck the part of Atlantis situated in the western Atlantic. This asteroid, referred to in meteorology as the Carolina Meteorite, was accompanied by a vast number of smaller meteorites that formed the numerous craters or bays which are a feature of the American coast and have been identified in the tens of thousands. Muck thought that the main bolide struck the island continent of Atlantis, crushing part of it under the sea and causing volcanic explosions, tidal waves, and changes in the ocean floor—an understandable result of the cosmic shock that a large asteroid (which, if it were ten kilometers in diameter, would weigh 200,000 megatons) exploding on contact with the Earth would cause. Dr. Muck, whose practical experience during World War II gave him considerable insight into the effects of explosives, estimated that the resultant explosion would be equivalent to 30,000 H-bombs—a hypothetical number still somewhat in excess of the quantity of bombs held by the opposing nations of the present time, ready and able to send them east or west across the Atlantic, along the route of the ancient asteroid.

Dr. Muck has proposed that one of the first dates of the unusually exact Mayan calendar commemorated the destruction of Atlantis at the translated equivalent date of 8498 B.C. By a series of calculations he has also established the date of the end of Atlantis according to our present Gregorian calendar as occurring on June 5 at 1 o'clock in the afternoon, local or Central Atlantic (or Atlantis) time. This fatal date coincided with the opposition of the sun, Venus, the moon, and Earth, which prepared the way, through a series of interlocking poles, for the hypothetical "asteroid A" to crash (in Muck's words) "into one of the thinnest and most sensitive regions of the Earth's crust." It fell on a fracture zone dotted with volcanoes, the zone that we call the Mid-Atlantic Ridge. The multiple impact, according to his theory, was the cause of the "crater field of Carolina, two deep sea holes in the southwest North Atlantic and the shallower trough in the eastern Caribbean."

The force of the collision activated earthquakes and volcanic explosions throughout the world and caused huge tidal waves to break over the land and leave to all mankind the unforgettable memory of the Great Flood.

Part of the area predicted by Muck for the asteroid to strike lies within the Bermuda Triangle. This area is often considered, like Atlantis, to be simply a legend, although the continuing number of ship and plane disappearances within its tenuous boundaries, as well as frequent manifestations of other unusual phenomena, keep it vividly alive in the consciousness of those who fly or sail through it. It is worthy of note that if a large asteroid, like the one Muck suspects of sinking Atlantis, did effectively lie under the bottom of a declivity that it had caused in the western Sargasso Sea, the periodic magnetic force from this metallic mass might be responsible for some of the unusual events that have happened there. This might explain the interference with radio signals, spinning compasses, and the malfunction of navigational equipment so often noticed by crew members on air or surface craft crossing the area. The unusual whiteouts, magnetic fogs, and the luminous or shining waters off the Bahamas may also be the result of a sunken planetoid accompanied by a vast number of meteorites.

More than a hundred thousand meteor-type holes in the land and sea, concentrated along the Georgia and Carolina coasts, but extending hundreds of miles farther north and south, exist as a possible indication that part of a great meteor swarm once struck the area with cosmic force.

One of the mysteries of the Bermuda Triangle is that compass, communication, and instrument malfunction do not always occur in the same specific area. Muck's theory of multiple visitation of asteroids, buried beneath the ocean floor, could explain how magnetic equipment on vessels passing over the metallic cores in a variety of different areas is affected.

Although comets have been observed, described, and feared since remote antiquity, the concept of meteorites falling from the sky came rather late to general scientific acceptance. Even a brilliant scientist like Cuvier had stated, in an outstanding example of dogmatic certainty, that stones ". . . cannot fall from the sky because there are no stones in the sky."

It was not until a meteor shower fell over Paris in 1803 that convincing firsthand evidence was supplied to scientific observers. Before the "proof" of meteors it was easier for astronomers and astrologers to theorize that comets, passing by Earth in their sometimes erratic fashion, occasionally came too close to Earth, showering it with debris from the comet's tail. Others supposed that a comet had simply collided head-on with Earth with near-fatal results for the planet. This was first expressed by Count Carli and by Joseph de la Lande several hundred years ago in an effort to explain what had happened to Atlantis. The theory was reiterated by a number of other Atlantologists, including Ignatius Donnelly, whose second book about Atlantis, *Ragnarök* (an ancient Scandinavian reference to "The Judgment of the Gods") examined the memories and legends of all races concerning a time of darkness and destruction when, according to his theory, the Earth passed through the tail of a great comet, presumably a too-close visitation of Halley's Comet. Donnelly explained the layers of till found in various parts of the Earth as having come from the fatal comet, with other changes occurring at the same time, drowning or burying the pre-Flood civilizations. It now appears, however, that the cores of comets, unlike meteors, are more like gigantic snowballs than solid masses, a supposition that may be verified during the next visit of Halley's Comet in 1986, when it is scheduled to be observed by US spacecraft.

The theory that the Earth suffered a cataclysm as a result of being struck by a planetoid is supported by the many meteor craters presently evident on this planet. There is also the presence of the asteroid belt between Mars and Jupiter, where a vast number of asteroids, estimated at more than 50,000, of varying sizes and various orbits, are known to exist. Some of these asteroids have eccentric orbits that occasionally bring them dangerously close to Earth. It is therefore conceivable that under conditions of planetary and solar alignment a large asteroid could approach close enough to the Earth to fall into its gravitational or magnetic field. This almost happened in 1936, when the large asteroid Adonis came within 186,000 miles of Earth, and again in 1968, when the asteroid Icarus came uncomfortably close to this planet. Asteroids, while not presenting the dramatic effect of the comets, which have terrified the populations of the Earth on many occasions in the past, nevertheless represent a tangible danger to this planet and its inhabitants.

The asteroid belt and its circling planetoids and meteors represent not only a danger but a singular mystery. A mathematical formula determining the progressive distances of planets and their orbits from the sun outward in our solar system was clarified by the German astronomer Johann Bode in the 18th century and since then has been further corroborated by the discovery of several "new" planets at the outer fringes of our solar systems; planets that were unknown at the time Bode worked out his theory and effectively predicted their discovery. However, according to Bode's Law, as the theory is now called, there should be a planet between Mars and Jupiter, where now there is only a circling mass of asteroids and meteors, many of which have developed unusual orbits. Several possibilities have been suggested to explain the disappearance or the dissolution of the planet that, logically, should be coursing along the asteroid-belt orbit:

    1. The planet that was once there was struck by another planet or planetoid, which smashed it into pieces, most of which still follow its former orbit,

    2. The planet blew up for reasons unknown, leaving only its debris still in orbit,

    3. The missing planet, unlike the other eight, never formed into a planetary mass in the first place.

It is interesting that Bode himself opted for the second explanation, with its inferences of cosmic destruction.

A revolutionary scientific concept tying in legends and traditions of catastrophe from various parts of the Earth to a series of cosmic clashes between comets and planets within our own solar system was developed by Immanuel Velikovsky and expressed in *Worlds in Collision* (1950) and several subsequent books. Velikovsky, an eminent scholar, linguist, and astronomer, caused an uproar in the scientific world when he exposed his theory and reinforced it with ancient traditions and written materials collected from all parts of the world. He connected references to various disasters that had fallen upon the world and a number of incidents recorded in ancient history and the Bible with the appearance of Venus which, in his opinion, invaded our planetary system as a comet and caused a series of collisions and near collisions that changed ancient history. Throughout ancient records Venus, apparently a late member of the solar system, was spoken of as a star having horns or a beard, which could be interpreted as a reference to the trailing ends of a comet. Then this new arrival entered into close electromagnetic contact with Earth, causing a modification of the Earth's orbit and a series of world-wide phenomena and providing an explanation for a number of incidents in Biblical history: for example, the parting of the Red Sea, the stopping of the sun in the heavens, the destruction of the Assyrian army of Sennacherib, the turning of water into blood, and the manna from heaven. After its close contact with Earth, Venus struck Mars and as a result changed Mars' orbit to a circular one. Venus itself then began to function as a planet.

The most ancient available records of Mesopotamia, Central America, and a number of other parts of the world do not include Venus within the original planetary count, although, within the approximate time limit described by Velikovsky, they not only include it but seem to hold the wandering comet-planet in special awe, often to be propitiated with human sacrifices to placate the menacing "star" in the hope of preventing it from striking Earth again. During the time of the invasion of our solar system by Venus, tremendous geological and climatic changes took place on and under the surface of the globe, as the Earth was shaken on its axis, the sun seemed to change its position, the seasons became confused, the count of the days in the year increased by five, and extensive periods of darkness enveloped the Earth. Tidal waves washed over islands and continents, leaving among the peoples of the Earth the world-wide tradition of the Flood. Fissures opened in the tectonic plates, resulting in envelopment of considerable land areas by the sea.

Upon publication of *Worlds in Collision* and the following *Ages in Chaos*, Velikovsky's theories were derided and attacked forcefully by the scientific establishment. One exasperated scientist even called *Worlds in Collision* "the worst book printed since the invention of movable type." There were, however, several exceptions, including Einstein, who, as one might expect, maintained an open and inquisitive mind about events in the world of science.

Nevertheless, some of Dr. Velikovsky's revolutionary astronomical theories were confirmed when space exploration was further developed. His accurate predictions about Venus were especially striking. Contrary to the opinion of other astronomers, and, at a time when there was no effective way of establishing Venus' temperature, he predicted that when it was ascertained it would be in the vicinity of 800° Fahrenheit—which it was. The *Mariner 10* probe indicated that Venus still showed the remains of a cometlike tail. Venus, upon closer investigation, also showed its difference from other planets by rotating in the contrary direction, just as Velikovsky said it would. Argon and neon gases have been detected on Mars, as he predicted, and his description of what the pockmarked and cratered surface would be like was also verified by the first Mars photographs taken by *Mariner 9*.

It is easy and comforting to consider the Earth's later development as a somewhat leisurely one. One age passes into another, the glaciers gradually melt, the great saurians conveniently disappear (with a few exceptions, such as crocodiles) before the emergence of man. Man, too, gradually evolves from man-ape to cave dweller to agricultural town dweller. During the Tertiary and Quatenary eras the Earth settles down into a tame planet with only sporadic explosions from its molten interior and occasional slight changes on its surface. This has long been the point of view of the gradualist school of science, but planetary development is not necessarily like that, any more than is life itself, nor do cosmic developments take place in a gradual and orderly way. Professor D. Nalivkin, of the Soviet Academy of Science, has commented (*Geological Catastrophes*: 1958): "Observations of catastrophic phenomena are limited by the time span of no longer than 4000–6000 years. For geological processes this is a short period and it is quite possible that some of the most terrible catastrophes have not been recorded in the chronicles of mankind. . . . We must not fit into modern standards all that has happened on the Earth throughout . . . its existence."

But the understandable system of gradualism and its implications that nothing in the way of a cosmic disaster has happened to Earth within the last 50,000 years other than on a gradual, scarcely noticeable scale would of course nullify the concept of the destruction of Atlantis, whether by a meteor strike to Earth, changes of Earth's axis through contact with comets or other planets, sudden climate changes, melting of the glaciers, or other world-wide catastrophes. In any case there still exists widespread confidence that science stands ready to reverse the destructive exploitation of the planet and to confront anything in the way of extraordinary danger to the Earth.

Almost anything. For within the last forty years it has been this same scientific expertise that has unleashed a rising cloudlike specter that represents a terror to the consciousness of mankind and a destroyer of its innate optimism. For the first time we have perfected an effective way of destroying the planet.

There have been past destructions of large sections of the Earth's population, although the devastation was not total. The Mongol invasion of central Asia destroyed millions of lives in a localized area, and the captains of Genghis Khan once suggested to him that the whole Chinese nation be destroyed so that the Mongols would have uninterrupted pastureland for their horses. (He was dissuaded from this plan by a Chinese adviser, Yeh Liu-chutsai, who pragmatically convinced him that the Chinese would be more valuable alive, to build war machines.) The great population massacres of history notwithstanding, it is only in our own day that a situation has developed in which the decision or whim of one man could begin a process of wiping out humanity and conceivably blowing the planet apart.

It has sometimes occurred to students of what we might call the Atlantean concept of prehistory that certain weapons, or means of harnessing natural forces as weapons, may have been developed during the dim lost ages of mankind for use in warfare. This would account for the curious legendary descriptions, handed down through time, that man himself caused the destruction and desolation of large settled areas of the Earth, accompanied by explosions, floods, and darkness. Evidence for this theory has come mostly from legends and traditions, and while it seems at times to be a vivid and imaginative record of past events, it occasionally changes, especially in some of the records of India and even Indian America, into a startlingly exact prophecy projected from the past but applicable to the present.

Many of the surprising inventions of the ancient world were made by astrologers or magicians who today would be correctly labeled research and development scientists for warfare. A number of scarcely credible reports have come down to us even from classical times. Archimedes, a scientist enlisted in the defense of Syracuse against the Romans, is reported to have concentrated magnified sunrays against Roman ships and set them afire. Hannibal is said to have used an explosive compound to explode rocks and bring down cliffs on his Roman opponents. The fall of the walls of Jericho could be explained by the setting of land mines in passageways dug under the walls while the attention of the besieged was occupied by the procession of Hebrews circling the walls and blowing their trumpets. Byzantium, the surviving eastern part of the Roman empire, maintained itself for an additional thousand years principally through the offensive use of "Greek fire"—an inextinguishable fire thrown on enemy ships in grenades or bombs and which resisted water and even burned on water. While no one knows the physical cause of the destruction of Sodom and Gomorrah, the blast from the sky is reminiscent of the atomic blasts of recent years, and also recalls unusual details, as in the case of Lot's wife, of the danger of even looking toward the explosion. In China, gunpowder was developed at a very early period. In addition to its use in firecrackers for celebrations and to frighten dragons and evil spirits, it served as an offensive weapon in the form of rockets. During Alexander the Great's invasion of ancient India, more than 2000 years ago, his army encountered rockets, fired at his warriors from the walls of Indian cities and referred to by his scribes as "thunder and lightning."

It is unusual that a number of nations and tribes preserved legends of a highly advanced type of warfare which, at the time that the legends were formalized, could hardly have been known. This, for example, has been the case with the small and very ancient Hopi tribe of Arizona, whose legendary tribal tales tell of catastrophes that have previously destroyed the world. What is especially unusual about the traditions of this small tribe is that they dwell on a number of destructive potentialities demonstrating an awareness of military and social developments anachronistic to the time frame when the legends were first told.

These periodic destructions have occurred because the Earth's inhabitants failed to carry out the plan of the Creator; sometimes because of the wars they made on each other; sometimes because they neglected the rituals necessary to keep the world and the universe at peace; and sometimes because they became too materialistic and acquisitive. According to the retelling of Hopi legends by Frank Waters, in collaboration with White Bear (*Book of the Hopi*: 1968), when they had acquired what they wanted, "they wanted more still and wars began again." The peoples of the Earth created "big cities, nations, civilizations," and invented aircraft—*patuwvotas*—which they used to attack and destroy one another's cities. The warfare in this previous world ceased only when continents sank and the land and sea changed places, leaving the "third world" (the one before the present) lying on the sea bottom, "with all the proud cities, the flying *patuwvotas*, and the worldly treasures corrupted with evil." There occurs an odd reminder of Atlantis in Hopi tradition when the tribe is exhorted by Sotuknang, nephew of the Creator, to look backward toward the islands of the sea when they arrived at their present world: "Look back! These are the footprints of your journey—the tops of the mountains of the third world."

The Hopis believe that the "fourth world," the present one, has also been "betrayed by the frailty of mankind" and will soon end, destroyed by great explosions of cosmic force—a phenomenon easily understandable to the Hopi of today, living as they do fairly close to Alamogordo and the White Sands Proving Grounds in New Mexico.

It is in the books of ancient India, however, that we find allusions to aspects of prehistoric warfare that eerily parallel those of today as well as those of the foreseeable future (vide C. Berlitz: *Mysteries From Forgotten Worlds*). There are two possible explanations for this: either some scientifically minded Indians of six to eight thousand years ago let their fancies roam at will and imagined bombs of sufficient force to destroy most of the world, or perhaps the whole concept was inherited from an earlier civilization that had reached a stage of development propitious to experimenting with or using the destructive power of the atom.

In any case, passages from traditional Indian literature, such as the *Vedas*, the *Puranas*, the *Ramayana*, the *Mahavira*, and especially the *Mahabharata*, contain repeated references expressed in the poetic language of their era not only to aircraft—*vimanas*—rockets, and space travel, but also specific allusions to what is easily recognizable as combat aircraft, air bombing, radar and other forms of aircraft detection, artillery, rocket launching, explosive bullets, detonation of mines, and bombs of cosmic destruction comparable in effect to the atom bombs of the present world. In other sections of Indian scientific and philosophical literature there are mentions attesting to the awareness of molecules and atoms of different elements, a concept that might eventually lead to the use of the power of the atom in warfare, just as it has in our day within a relatively short period of time. From the time that the atomic theory was generally accepted by modern scientists to the construction of the atom bomb was only 130 to 135 years, while a previous world civilization, whose time span is as yet unknown, would presumably have had as much or more time for such development.

Hindus who had access to and could read the ancient classics either took for granted that their ancestors were able to produce the incredible weapons attributed to them or simply interpreted the references to the all-powerful might of the gods, to whom, naturally, all things were possible. But what seems impossible to the modern reader is that the detailed description of the effect of these weapons of many thousands of years ago closely parallels that of our modern refinements of warfare.

When the *Mahabharata* was to be translated in the last half of the 19th century into modern languages (into English by Protap Chandra Roy and into German by Max Müller), the fanciful descriptions of ancient warfare were generally ignored, except in the case of artillery—familiar to everyone—and aircraft, then considered to be lighter than air. V. R. Ramachandra Dikshitar, in his book on early Indian warfare (*War in Ancient India*: 1944), comments on the *decline* of artillery in medieval times, inferring that it was more used and more destructive in the distant past. He also defends the detailed references to heavier-than-air aircraft in ancient land and naval warfare, referring to "the vast literature of the *Puranas* showing how well and wonderfully the ancient Indians conquered the air." Since Dikshitar was writing during the period of World War I he, like a number of Indian officers and British officers in the Indian service, was aware that many of the "imaginary" weapons of Indian antiquity had made an appearance (or reappearance) in both world wars. Dikshitar wrote, during World War I, that the *mohanastra* or "arrow of unconsciousness" was generally considered "a creature of legend until we heard the other day of bombs discharging poisonous gasses."

The atom bombs of World War II, surprising as they were to the Japanese, were no great surprise to students of the *Mahabharata*, already familiar with the description of a fantastic bomb referred to as "the iron thunderbolt," capable of killing hundreds of thousands of people with one explosion or, as expressed in the *Ramayana*, "so powerful it could destroy the Earth." Even the size of the iron thunderbolt was roughly comparable in length—"three cubits plus six feet"—to the first atom bombs. According to the description in the *Mahabharata* its burst was as bright as the flare from ten thousand suns. The cloud of smoke rising after its first explosion formed into expanding round circles like the opening of giant parasols. Further less poetic accounts mention hair and nails falling out from surviving victims, contamination of foodstuffs from the blast, and the necessity for soldiers in the affected area to wash themselves and all their equipment in available streams or rivers.

A strangely modern injunction in the *Atharva Veda* cautioned opposing forces that the use of such a weapon was permissible only when the enemy "used it first," a moral choice still under debate perhaps 8000 years after it was first considered. There is even a mention in the *Mausala Parva* implying that on one occasion this weapon "capable of reducing the Earth to ashes" had been destroyed by royal command and the resultant powder had been "cast into the sea," another timely suggestion from the distant past of Earth.

Whether this legendary weapon was ever used, or was destroyed, or forgotten except in Indian literature, there exist certain burned sections on our planet that may be the result of meteor strikes or even the scars of thermonuclear warfare. One of these was found in Iraq in 1947 in the course of an archaeological probe dug vertically which penetrated a number of cultural levels containing recognizable artifacts of Babylon and Sumeria and eventually passed through a fourteen-foot level of clay, indicating deposits following a severe and prolonged flood. Past the flood level a stratum was eventually reached that proved to be fused glass—almost exactly similar to the desert floor at Alamogordo, New Mexico, scarred and fused after the first A-bomb test.

An unusual find of a number of skeletons on the street levels of the prehistoric Indian cities of Mohenjo-daro and Harappa indicated by their scattered positions and attitudes that they were trying to escape from something as, for example, the iron bolt or other weapons described in the ancient legends. Upon examination the skeletons were found to be highly radioactive.

The concept of the Earth, in its past history, having been damaged by nuclear warfare violent enough to have modified the climate, melted the glaciers, or affected its movement on its axis and caused, in the words of the legends, "land and water to have changed their places," would seem to belong to the domain of science fiction. But the boundary between science fiction and scientific fact has become increasingly tenuous, almost as though the former were an introduction to the latter. One notable example was a comic strip—Buck Rogers—prior to World War II, dealing repeatedly with atom bombs and their use against Space Invaders. The producers of the comic strip were persuaded by government intervention to drop mention of atomic bombs owing to the generally unknown fact that the real A-bomb was then being developed.

Ancient nuclear warfare is simply one of the various possibilities that may have caused the disappearance of former cultures on the planet. There is no proof that it took place; only certain writings that remained incomprehensible for so many centuries until mankind arrived at the point of atomic development that his remote ancestors had reached, at least in imagination, thousands of years before. Nor is there any proof that a nearby planet once exploded or that one of its many pieces may have collided with Earth. But the large asteroids that still pursue a planetary orbit between Mars and Jupiter may in themselves constitute a visible proof of a planet that was destroyed.

But it is the advance of scientific progress in the last hundred years, the discoveries concerning inner space in the last fifty, and the pushoff from Earth to the rest of the cosmos in the last twenty-five that have shaken and changed our concept of time, space, energy, and matter. We are confronted, as were the civilizations before us, with new mysteries and seemingly unbelievable information. And it is the expertise of modern science itself that has brought back the Age of Wonder.

14

THE BRIDGE THROUGH TIME

The word "Atlantis" has long served as a password to dreams. It recalls dimly perceived memories of a verdant lost continent in the sea, once the seat of a mighty empire in the Atlantic that sent its fleets to explore and colonize an earlier world, thousands of years before the time that we consider world history "officially" began.

To a person standing on the cliffs or beaches surrounding the Atlantic, it is easy to imagine a vision, partly hidden by clouds on the horizon, of golden-roofed cities in a fertile land bounded by high mountains. It is even easier on days of fog, when the drifting Atlantic mists seem to part for a moment, revealing formations suggesting towers, or the ghosts of towers, that once rose over the now-sunken lands of the Atlantic. One feels that if the sea would recede from the coast, dripping stone ruins would again be exposed to the light of day. Seneca, the Roman playwright and tutor to Nero, felt this 2000 years ago when he wrote: "When the ocean will relax its hold . . . and the sea will reveal new continents. . . ."

Legends of lost lands and cities off various coasts form a great circle around the shores of the North Atlantic: the bells of legendary sunken cathedrals off Brittany still sound to those who listen for them; the names of the lost lands of Ys off Brittany, and Lyonesse off the southwestern coast of England remind one, in the concept of James Bramwell (*Lost Atlantis*: 1938) of the sounds of the receding hiss of waves after breaking on the shore; the memory of King Arthur's last voyage to Avalon is revived with the setting sun over the Atlantic; the Irish, looking over the Western Ocean, remember the golden towers and castles of Tir-nan-n'oge. And, as we fly or sometimes sail across the Atlantic, we often wonder whether there really does exist a sunken continent miles below us, inaccessible and lost in time but one that we seem instinctively to remember.

But on a more realistic plane, more than memories suggest and point to lost lands under the sea, since vestiges of sunken civilizations have been found offshore at different places along the Atlantic coast and adjacent seas. The stone roads of Yucatán and the avenues of stone dolmens and menhirs of Brittany, both of which lead to the edge of the sea and then continue down under it, and the underwater stone roads or walls of Bimini, cut-stone flights of steps and roads on undersea plateaus in the Caribbean and on the Atlantic seamounts all seem to point to more extensive ruins farther out in the ocean.

On one unusual occasion, in the early 1970s, the ocean off Brittany actually did recede far from the shore during an exceptional neap tide. As this occurrence had been meteorologically predicted, the area was crowded with observers who hoped to see whether the ocean would reveal ruined cities, which, according to legends (and fishermen), existed on the bottom. Unfortunately, what looked like piles of dripping stone ruins were so far from shore that they could not be visited before the swift return of the tide.

The southwestern coast of Spain is legendarily and even historically close to a vanished civilization, that of Tartessos. Investigations now being carried out by Spanish and other divers may eventually prove that Tartessos was not an outpost of eastern civilization in the west but, on the contrary, an outpost or colony of Atlantis itself, from which Atlantean influence extended eastward into the Mediterranean.

The Mediterranean contains a variety of sites that lie in relatively deep water—at a depth of two to three hundred feet or even more. The immersion of these prehistoric sites is not a result of gradual sinking such as has happened to the ports of classical times like Carthage; Tyre; Leptis Magna; Baiae, the Roman pleasure city near Naples; and Kenchreai, the port of Corinth. These other sites indicate that they belong to an era so much further back in time that it cannot presently be calculated.

Out in the Mediterranean in front of Marseilles the passages of an underwater cliff have revealed a series of mine shafts and smelting facilities presumably established at a period when humanity was at the so-called "cave man" level. Jim Thorne, a diver and archaeologist, upon making a deep dive to the bottom in the vicinity of the

Aegean island of Melos, found that he was not on the real sea bottom but was standing among the columns of an ancient acropolis from whose center other roads led still farther downward into the blackness below. Captain Jacques Cousteau tells of having discovered a road along the sea bottom of the Mediterranean which he followed until his air supply got low. There was no indication of where the road started or where it led to, as has been the case of other apparent roads under the seas and oceans, including a long and wide one in the Atlantic off the coast of Georgia.

There is increasing evidence that the Mediterranean was a much smaller inland sea in the Holocene Era and supported a civilized population on what is now sea bottom, and that the Atlantic Ocean broke through the Straits of Gibraltar, flooding and filling the Mediterranean Basin about eleven or twelve thousand years ago.

As the ancient legends relate, land and sea have frequently changed places. We know that there are remains of sea life in the desert, whale skeletons near the summits of high mountains, and that the ruins of great cities lie under the sea. The outlines of these cities are not always evident and, like the wrecks of ancient ships, are recognizable only with difficulty under the coral growing over them. Their very existence is opposed by a number of scientists of different disciplines who should welcome instead of denigrate underwater discoveries the import of which has become evident over the last twenty years.

One can of course sympathize with the scientific recalcitrance to any mention of the possibility of Atlantis having existed and to the reluctance of the establishment to bring it out of the domain of dragons, gnomes, and ghosts. It is burdensome to be forced to rewrite history and change the theories previously held about the origin of civilization. However, the re-examination of scientific knowledge has been modified within the last hundred years—so why not history?

The underwater discoveries and the first steps to the filling in of the blank spots in history are beginning to extend our time boundaries backward to an earlier world, one with which we perhaps still feel a strong emotional connection. There still exists, despite the thousands of intervening years, a bridge between our present world and the lost one. It can be followed outward from the coastlines of the Atlantic by air observation and underwater exploration, first in the shallow coastal waters, then from the edges of the Atlantic islands and seamounts, and eventually from deep-water submergibles capable of diving to the several-thousand-foot-deep level where remains of the eighth continent still lie.

It is probable that conclusive proofs of Atlantis will be found or have already been found by explorers who were not looking for it, such as the personnel of atomic submarines cruising their way along the sea bottom while searching for and plotting the course of other atomic submarines during the cold war, or by commercial deep-sea probes for oil, gas, or minerals.

Other connecting links with the history before history may one day be found among the thousands of ancient documents, incised in baked clay, carved in stone, painted on wood, or written on papyrus, thousands of which have not yet been translated. They exist in the British and Vatican museums, and in museums in the United States, Russia, France, and Germany, as well as in a number of smaller museums and private collections. The search for Atlantis and its records may lead through the strangely cut passages under the Andes, to the lost cities of the Amazonian jungle, to the records of monasteries in the Himalayas, to the suddenly destroyed cities of the Indus, to the sophisticated cave paintings of Europe and North Africa, and to discoveries under the sands of Egypt and the Middle East and the ice of Antarctica.

But besides all the knowledge and records that were lost or that have remained hidden, the tradition of ancient scientific knowledge inherited from an earlier world was preserved by certain groups in Europe during the Middle Ages. It was generally camouflaged as magic or astrology and practiced by astrologists as individuals and also by secret groups or brotherhoods, as too evident an interest in astrology could often result in the practitioner being burned at the stake.

This tradition, handed down and recopied, as were the ancient world maps because of their usefulness, was responsible, when it became respectable again during the late Renaissance, for the later development of the Atomic Age. The theory of the component parts of matter was known and frequently the subject of comment in ancient Greece and India and doubtlessly in other places as yet unknown to us. Medieval astrologers and magicians (the scientists of the Dark Ages) isolated a number of the elements that later furnished the basis for Mendeleyev's (and others') arrangement of the Table of Atomic Weights—certainly among the most critical discoveries of science. Often astrologers and magicians employed their effects in the isolation of atomic substances for the purpose of transmitting base metals into gold for the enrichment of their patrons or themselves. While their motives were avowedly avaricious, it should be observed that the labors of the alchemists and others were far less dangerous to the world at large than the experiments successfully undertaken with the atom in 1945 by their scientific descendants.

Legends of space travel and cosmic exploration appear to have been current in the most remote periods of recorded civilization. There are references to space flights, space vehicles, and fairly accurate descriptions of how the Earth would look from space, again having to do with gods and supernatural heroes. It would of course be natural for primitive peoples to imagine flights through the air, although a number of details of the legends are curiously similar to the theories and actualities of our present Space Age.

Some of the ancient references that seem to concern modern warfare, particularly those from the Indian classics, such as the atom bomb called "the iron bolt" in the *Mahabharata*, which "bursts with the force of ten thousand suns," and an apparently chemical warfare weapon called "the arrow of unconsciousness" are familiar to us. Descriptions in Indian writings of powered aircraft, air attacks on cities, detection of enemy aircraft on screens, as well as how to avoid detection of one's own aircraft, would be almost unbelievable if they had not been written many centuries before their modern counterparts came into effective existence.

References to cosmic exploration are no less surprising—and equally familiar. Although the accounts deal with the actions of gods and supernatural heroes, they describe rockets and space flights in some detail.

In Chaldean mythology it is told that Etana, a Sumerian king who was taken up into the cosmos, told on his return of how the Earth looked from space. As he ascended, the Earth seemed to rush away from him below. First the mountains became small hills, and the sea looked like water in a big tub. Then the land became like a furrow in a field and the wide sea seemed only the width of a breadbasket. Finally the land and sea "ceased to be" as the Earth became no larger than the other stars.

Manned space rockets are discussed in some detail in the Indian

Samarangana Sutradhara, even to their means of propulsion. It is specified that a jet mercury engine was necessary to release the power latent in mercury, which "set the driving whirlwind in motion," causing the *vimana* "to rise like a pearl in the sky" accompanied by the "roaring of a lion"—an aptly put description of a rocket takeoff. Oddly enough, the account also observes that "one can build one," specifying "four mercury containers heated by controlled fire from iron containers with properly welded joints . . ." and furnishes other pertinent information, as though the construction of *vimanas* were a common occurrence in prehistory.

We cannot know whether or not ancient writers had a basis for these unusual accounts or simply let their fertile and perhaps enhanced imaginations run riot. Nevertheless, in the course of time, all of these activities have become true and must be considered simply as steps in the development of technology. Perhaps any race, given sufficient time and impulse would, within eight to ten thousand years, travel as far into progress and danger as we have, until it came to a choice of deciding its own eventual destiny—a choice that confronts all humanity today.

Humanity may have passed this way before through the employment of other forces inherent in the Earth itself. It may have been precisely the use and eventual misuse (according to almost all ancient legends) of these forces that produced a cataclysm that wiped out a world civilization, leaving its bemused survivors, our remote ancestors, to resume an upward climb, with frequent regressions, over the past six to ten thousand years.

The path through time back to Atlantis is becoming clearer. It is marked by the great stone ruins scattered around the world, as yet unexplained but which perhaps were markers of the seasons, time, and the signal lights of space—the sun, moon, and stars. The mystical elements of these ruins have come down to us through the earliest legends of man and through his religions, which constitute his oldest history.

It has been suggested that the vast prehistoric ruins in various parts of the world had a special purpose other than serving as temples, tombs, fortresses, or primitive observatories. Of course we are apt to classify all relics of antiquity in terms with which we are familiar from our own history, without considering that over a period of many thousands of years a civilization before ours would have developed differently and used for its own purposes sources of power dissimilar to ours. A facile and often used means of demolishing the idea of a presumed Atlantean civilization is to point out the lack of "civilized" artifacts dating from a prehistoric period. But if such tools or mechanisms were made of iron, steel, or wood, they would have long since disappeared. Of building materials only stone would have lasted through the intervening ages. Giant earth mounds and long walls, although they would have lost considerable height, would be discernible in some areas by contrast and are still being discovered from the air by the contrasting traces they have left in the terrain. Some investigators of the past have proposed that the enigmatic cyclopean monuments, earth mounds, and a system of barely discernible roads and paths may hold a key to the secret of a power source common to an earlier world civilization; a power source whose use has not yet been rediscovered.

We know that the Earth is a gigantic magnet charged with electromagnetic force. Several British writers have theorized that many of the prehistoric remains of buildings, walls, and roads in the British Isles were once part of a planned enormous "instrument" extending over other parts of the world as well as Great Britain. This explanation has been most clearly expressed by John Michell (*The View Over Atlantis*), who refers to this "instrument" as a means of marking and channeling lines of magnetic force throughout the globe. He thinks that the cyclopean ruins in different parts of the world may have belonged to the same world culture and that the purpose of the peoples who built them was not only to mark the force lines of the world's magnetism but to use them; in effect to control the magnetic field of Earth. He writes: ". . . the Earth's natural magnetism [was] known to prehistory [and] furnished energy to which their whole civilization was tuned."

His close examination of Britain in particular, based partially on observations of others over a period of hundreds of years, revealed a network of former straight roads and paths that seem to connect no known cities. This system of establishing straight lines by paths, great stones, mounds, and modified mountains he called "ley" lines, since the word "ley" appears on so many of the indicated paths. That surviving paths and great circular earth markings, whatever their use, still exist can be ascertained by helicopter flights over parts of western England and Ireland, northwestern France, and the many areas throughout the prehistoric world, which we now see as much larger than suspected, with the key section of the network still lying beneath the sea.

If these lines of magnetic force run over the whole surface of the Earth (a not illogical assumption, since the Earth itself is a huge magnet), it is not surprising that the Chinese have been cognizant of this phenomenon since their earliest records. The Chinese called these force lines "dragon paths," and until the recent past, observed a system of geomancy for establishing the location of houses, temples, cities, and even the gates in city walls, with particular reference to these lines of force or power. Chinese tradition not only considered that these lines and centers of force extended over the whole Earth, but also included them within the human body, as though the living Earth and the living body of man operated in relation to the same forces. (This concept of special force lines within the body is the basis for acupuncture, one of the few traditional beliefs still encouraged by the present rulers of China, principally because it seems to work.)

The theory of a former identification and control of the Earth's magnetic forces might be the reason for the varied and unusual locations of prehistoric markers in widely separated parts of the world. It would tend to explain the cyclopean complexes of Avebury, Glastonbury, and Stonehenge in Britain, the carefully marked lines that lead to nowhere, the great stones of France, and the mounds of Central Europe, the predynastic straight roads of Persia, the raised highways of Yucatán now under the sea, the straight-line pre-Inca roads of the western coast of South America, and the straight-line dragon paths throughout China. It might also have a bearing on the myriad lines in the Nazca Valley of Peru, formerly called "Incan roads" and later "landing fields," as well as the same kind of lines in the Atacama Desert of Chile and the Mojave Desert of California.

It would have to do with the man-made modification of large hills, even mountains, as in the artificially modified mountains of the Marcahuasi plateau of Peru, the apparently artificial hills and cliffs of the valley of the Amazon, Brazil, and Tepoztlán, Mexico. At Quito, Ecuador, what had previously been considered to be a natural mountain (El Panecillo) proved to be an artificial one, constructed among other, natural, mountains for reasons unknown. On a number of small islands in the Pacific there exist enormous statues and cyclopean ruins, and mountains that have been cut down to the shapes of step pyramids. To develop the marker theory even further, one might suggest that the world-encircling pyramid belt itself consists of the remains of ancient markers or copies made by subsequent peoples who had forgotten the purpose for which they were built.

Perhaps the moving of the tremendous stones of prehistory, so long an archaeological puzzle, was accomplished by the use of this magnetic energy, by contrasting positive and negative poles to lift enormous rocks over extensive areas and across deep valleys and by tapping and channeling the energy of the Earth itself to shape the contours of mountains. Eventually magnetic and perhaps the connected gravitational forces could be channeled and used for a variety of purposes—construction, transportation, and, as is apt to happen in the development of a power force, destruction.

The destruction of Earth recounted in the old legends of the world may have been a direct result of focusing and harnessing the magnetic energy of the Earth, almost as though the Earth itself, like a vast sentient entity, had shaken off the man-made forces that were channeling and restraining its natural ones. Something similar to this rejection has occurred in modern times when earthquakes have persistently struck areas where atomic wastes have been buried or when underground nuclear explosions seem to have triggered almost simultaneous earthquakes hundreds of miles distant.

In modern times the idea of a usable electromagnetic grid spread over the surface of the Earth has been considered not only by science fiction writers but also by some scientists. Nikola Tesla, the genius who invented alternating current and who gave his name to the tesla coil, may have been following a similar line of investigation in his experiments with electricity without wires and the relationship between harmonic sound and power. In the course of his experiments with electronics and harmonics in his Manhattan laboratory, Tesla attracted such violent lightning and thunder storms in his immediate vicinity that local residents demanded that the police stop these unsettling experiments. On another occasion harmonic vibrations that he had apparently engendered shook the whole neighborhood like an earthquake. (This same eminent researcher once stated that the attainment of a proper harmonic frequency could destroy the Earth.)

One is reminded of certain legends which recount that in the distant past the axis of the Earth had changed, with a resulting series of world catastrophes.

A New Zealand pilot and author, Bruce Crathie (*Harmonics 33*), has worked out a magnetic grid that he believes once extended over the Earth but that was broken during a polar shift. (This recalls, among other legends, the Hopi account of the Twins, each a respective guardian of the north and south axis of the Earth, who, when ordered to abandon their posts, brought the Second World to an end.) Crathie is of the opinion that the grid has since been recognized, is presently being repaired, and that the passage of alleged unidentified flying craft along its lines is an indication of its renewed use.

In a world in which science, as it advances, is constantly changing its concepts of space, matter, force, and even time, we should not deny the possibility that at some time in the past discoveries were made that will be made again in the future. As Einstein observed, time may be curved, and the events in time and time itself may come together again—a seeming impossibility, although no more illogical or unexplainable than time itself. In our own day we may be witnessing the completion of this cosmic circle.

The legend of Atlantis, now becoming a recognizable reality, is of importance to our modern world. Less than half a century ago it would have seemed incredible that mankind would be able effectively to destroy the human race and perhaps the planet itself. Nevertheless, this is the immediate possibility that we face from moment to moment. The possibility that a general catastrophe occurred thousands of years in the past through thermonuclear explosion or other discovery and eventual misuse of the forces latent in the Earth is supported by myths and legends from all over the world and also by geophysical evidence from the land and, notably, from the sea.

It is on the mountains, tablelands, and in the valleys and abysses of the ocean that the great centers of Atlantean civilization await discovery. One might hope that in the process of modern exploitation of the seafloor for military and commercial purposes by surface research vessels, deep-diving DSRVs, and atomic submarines, the various competing nations may experience a growing memory of the destroyed world of Atlantis, as well as a consciousness that we are all in a way connected with one another in a common descent from this former culture. Increasing knowledge of the reality and the fate of Atlantis, even if it means reassessing the beginnings of history, may have the effect of bringing the peoples of the world together spiritually, because of our common cultural roots in the civilization of the Eighth Continent, and intellectually, as it becomes more evident year by year and almost week by week that if the world does not soon attain a reasonable unity, it will destroy itself. Perhaps the memory and knowledge of an earlier world, as we learn more about it and what happened to it, can contribute to the preservation of the present world—a final contribution to its descendants from the ancient Empire of the Sea.

BIBLIOGRAPHY

Alfonso, Eduardo. *La Atlántida Americana*: Madrid, 1957.

Alvarez y López, José. *Realidad de la Atlántida*: La Plata, 1960.

Babcock, William H. *Legendary Island of the Atlantic*: New York, 1924.

de la Bara, Luis León. *El Misterio de la Atlántida*: Mexico City, l946.

Bellamy, Hans S. *The Atlantis Myth*: London, 1948.

Bergier, Jacques, and Louis Pauwels. *Le matin des magiciens*: Paris, 1960.

Berlioux, Étienne-Felix. *Les Atlantes*: Paris, 1883.

Berlitz, Charles. *The Mystery of Atlantis*: New York, 1969.

———— *Mysteries From Forgotten Worlds*: New York, 1972.

Bessmertny, Alexander. *L'Atlantide*: Paris, 1941.

Bory de St. Vincent. *Essai sur les îles fortunées et l'antique Atlantide*: Paris, 1803.

Bramwell, James. *Lost Atlantis*: London, 1938.

Bryusov, Vladimir. *The Teachers' Teacher*: Moscow, 1938.

Casgha, Jean-Yves. *Les archives secrètes de l'Atlantide*: Monaco, 1980.

Cayce, Edgar Evans. *Edgar Cayce on Atlantis*: New York, 1968.

Cazeau, Charles, and Stuart Scott. *Exploring the Unknown*: New York, 1980.

Charroux, Robert. *Histoire inconnue des hommes depuis cent mil ans*: Paris, 1963.

Châtelain, Maurice. *La fin du monde*: Monaco, 1982.

Chevalier, Raymond. *L'avion à la découverte du passé*: Paris, 1964.

Crathie, Bruce. *Harmonics 33*: Wellington, New Zealand, 1968.

von Däniken, Erich. *Chariots of the Gods?*: New York, 1969.

Dikshitar, V. R. Ramachandra. *War in Ancient India*: Madras, 1944.

Donnelly, Ignatius. *Atlantis: Myths of the Antediluvian World*: Chicago, 1882.

—— *Ragnarök: The Age of Fire and Gravel*: Chicago, 1887.

Doreste, Tomás. *La Atlántida*: Mexico City, 1976.

Fawcett, Col. P. H., and Brian Fawcett. *Lost Trails, Lost Cities*: New York, 1953.

Galanopoulos, A. G., and Edward Bacon. *Atlantis, the Truth Behind the Legend*: New York, 1969.

Gallencamp, Charles. *Maya*: New York, 1979.

Hadingham, Evan. *Secrets of the Ice Age*: New York, 1979.

Hapgood, Charles H. *Maps of the Ancient Sea Kings*: London, 1979.

Heezen, B. C., M. Tharp, and M. Ewing. *The North Atlantic*: Washington, D.C., 1959.

Hoffer, Frank. *Lost Americans*: New York, 1961.

Kjellson, H. *Forntidens Teknik*: Stockholm, 1956.

Leonard, R. Cedric. *Quest for Atlantis*: New York, 1979.

Lissner, Ivar. *Rätselhafte Kulturen*: Germany, 1961.

Luce, J. V. *The End of Atlantis*: London, 1969.

Marshak, Alexander. *The Roots of Civilization*: New York, 1972.

Mavor, James W. *Voyage to Atlantis*: New York, 1969.

Michanowsky, George. *The Once and Future Star*: New York, 1977.

Michell, John. *The View Over Atlantis*: London, 1969.

de Prorock, Count Byron Kuhn. *Mysterious Sahara*: London, 1930.

Poznansky, Arthur. *Tiahuanaco—The Citadel of American Man*: New York, 1945.

—— *El Pasado Prehistórico del Gran Perú*: La Paz, 1940.

Sanderson, Ivan. *Investigating the Unexplained*: Englewood Cliffs, 1972.

Soule, Gardner. *Men Who Dared the Sea*: New York, 1976.

Spence, Lewis. *The History of Atlantis*: New York, 1968.

Temple, Robert. *The Sirius Mystery*: New York, 1978.

Thomas, Gordon, and Max Witts. *The Day the World Ended*: New York, 1976.

Troëng, Ivan. *Kulturer Före Istiden*: Stockholm, 1964.

Valentine, J. Manson. *Underwater Archaeology in the Bahamas*: Explorers Journal, New York, 1976.

Velikovsky, Immanuel. *Worlds in Collision*: New York, 1950.

Wauchope, Robert. *Lost Tribes and Sunken Continents*: London, 1962.

Wellard, James. *Lost Worlds of Africa*: New York, 1967.

Zhirov, Alexei. *Atlantis:* Moscow, 1964.

Zink, David. *The Stones of Atlantis*: Englewood Cliffs, 1978.

INDEX

Mid-Atlantic Ridge

Flores

Atlantis

Great Meteor

...acture Zone